MW00613812

Woman Much Missed

Woman Much Missed

Thomas Hardy, Emma Hardy,
and Poetry

MARK FORD

OXFORD
UNIVERSITY PRESS

Great Clarendon Street, Oxford, OX2 6DP,
United Kingdom

Oxford University Press is a department of the University of Oxford.
It furthers the University's objective of excellence in research, scholarship,
and education by publishing worldwide. Oxford is a registered trade mark of
Oxford University Press in the UK and in certain other countries

Published in the United States of America by Oxford University Press
198 Madison Avenue, New York, NY 10016, United States of America

British Library Cataloguing in Publication Data

Data available

Library of Congress Control Number: 2023933407

ISBN 978–0–19–288680–4

DOI: 10.1093/oso/9780192886804.001.0001

Printed and bound in the UK by
Clays Ltd, Elcograf S.p.A.

                    Next
A dwelling appears by a slow sweet stream
Where two sit happy and half in the dark:
They read, helped out by a frail-wick'd gleam,
        Some rhythmic text…

                        ('The Interloper', CP 488)

        'Morning, noon, and night,
Mid those funereal shades that seem
The uncanny scenery of a dream,
Figures dance to a mind with sight,
And music and laughter like floods of light
        Make all the precincts gleam.

        'It is a poet's bower,
Through which there pass, in fleet arrays,
Long teams of all the years and days,
Of joys and sorrows, of earth and heaven,
That meet mankind in its ages seven,
        An aion in an hour.'

                        ('The House of Silence', CP 474)

Contents

Note on Texts	ix
Abbreviations	xi
Preface	xiii
Prologue: She Opened the Door	1

WHAT POETRY MEANT TO HARDY

1. Votary of the Muse	21
2. The Other Side of Common Emotions	45

LYONNESSE

3. Emma's Devon and Cornwall	67
4. Courtship	93

THE RIFT

5. A Preface without Any Book	123
6. Divisions Dire and Wry	148

AFTERWARDS

7. Dear Ghost	177
8. Two Bright-Souled Women	203

Acknowledgements	229
Selected Bibliography	231
Index	239

Note on Texts

All quotations from Hardy's poetry are taken from *Thomas Hardy: The Complete Poems*, edited by James Gibson and published by Palgrave Macmillan.

What was effectively Hardy's autobiography was initially issued by Macmillan in two instalments, *The Early Life of Thomas Hardy, 1840–1891* (1928) and *The Later Years of Thomas Hardy, 1892–1928* (1930), under the name of his second wife, Florence Hardy. It was subsequently published in a single volume as *The Life of Thomas Hardy*. It emerged in due course, however, that, although the text was written in the third person, Hardy was himself responsible for all but the book's last chapters. An edition of the original typescript that Florence prepared from Hardy's longhand manuscript and from original sources such as letters and journal entries was published by Michael Millgate in 1984 under the title *The Life and Work of Thomas Hardy*. The textual apparatus in this edition includes the alterations that Florence made to the typescript after Hardy's death. It is from Millgate's edition, its title shortened to the *Life*, that quotations are taken in this book.

Abbreviations

The following abbreviations are used to indicate the sources of quotations from primary texts (see Selected Bibliography for full publication details):

CL   *The Collected Letters of Thomas Hardy*, 8 volumes (eds. Richard Little Purdy, Michael Millgate, and Keith Wilson)

CP   *Thomas Hardy: The Complete Poems* (ed. James Gibson)

CPVE   *Thomas Hardy: The Complete Poems*, Variorum Edition (ed. James Gibson)

DR   *Desperate Remedies* (ed. Patricia Ingham (OUP))

EHD   *Emma Hardy Diaries* (ed. Richard H. Taylor)

FTQC   *The Famous Tragedy of the Queen of Cornwall*

JO   *Jude the Obscure* (ed. Patricia Ingham (OUP))

L   *The Life and Work of Thomas Hardy* (ed. Michael Millgate)

LEFH   *Letters of Emma and Florence Hardy* (ed. Michael Millgate)

LLI   *Life's Little Ironies* (ed. Alan Manford (OUP))

PBE   *A Pair of Blue Eyes* (ed. Alan Manford (OUP))

PM   *Thomas Hardy's 'Poetical Matter' Notebook* (eds. Pamela Dalziel and Michael Millgate)

PN   *The Personal Notebooks of Thomas Hardy* (ed. Richard H. Taylor)

PRE   *Poems and Religious Effusions* by Emma Hardy

PW   *Thomas Hardy's Personal Writings* (ed. Harold Orel)

SR   *Some Recollections* by Emma Hardy (eds. Evelyn Hardy and Robert Gittings)

SS   *Thomas Hardy's 'Studies, Specimens &c.' Notebook* (eds. Pamela Dalziel and Michael Millgate)

T   *Tess of the d'Urbervilles* (eds. Juliet Grindle and Simon Gatrell (OUP))

The following abbreviations are used to indicate the sources of quotations from secondary sources:

CT   *Thomas Hardy: The Time-Torn Man* by Claire Tomalin

GT   *The Golden Treasury (Palgrave)* (ed. Christopher Ricks)

IR   *Thomas Hardy: Interviews and Recollections* (ed. James Gibson)

MM   *Thomas Hardy: A Biography Revisited* by Michael Millgate

RP   *Thomas Hardy: A Bibliographical Study* by Richard Little Purdy (ed. Charles Pettit)

SMH   *The Second Mrs Hardy* by Robert Gittings and Jo Manton

THR   *Thomas Hardy Remembered* (ed. Martin Ray)

References not given in the text are on the same page as the previous quotation.

Preface

Nearly one-fifth of the 919 poems included by Hardy in his eight collections of poetry published between 1898 and 1928 (the year of his death at the age of eighty-seven) are concerned with his first wife, Emma.[1] The poems that make up the other four-fifths of his oeuvre present a dizzyingly diverse array of narratives and genres. Hardy liked to compare his approach to poetry to that of a Gothic architect, and perhaps the only workable analogy for prolonged immersion in the intricately patterned but bewilderingly disjunctive compendium that is *The Complete Poems* in their totality is wandering around an immense Gothic cathedral whose multifarious niches can accommodate poems on any topic under the sun, from the death of God to the infatuation of a turnip-hoer with a lady whom he rescues when the horses pulling her carriage bolt, from the feelings of a mongrel as he realizes he is being deliberately drowned by his impoverished owner to those of Edward Gibbon as he finishes *The Decline and Fall of the Roman Empire*.[2] Attempts to create a useful taxonomy of Hardy's poems, or to impose a chronological narrative of development on his eight highly miscellaneous volumes (which tend to mix up poems from widely differing phases of his writing life), founder on the monumental scale of his poetic oeuvre and the openness to contingency and multiplicity built into his *ars poetica*.

It has become routine for admirers of Hardy to marvel at the difficulty of finding a critical language or approach commensurate with the range and idiosyncrasies of his poetry. 'It is nothing short of comical', observed Donald Davie in *Thomas Hardy and British Poetry* back in 1973,

---

[1] The full titles of these eight collections are: *Wessex Poems and Other Verses* (1898), *Poems of the Past and the Present* (1901), *Time's Laughingstocks and Other Verses* (1909), *Satires of Circumstance, Lyrics and Reveries* (1914), *Moments of Vision and Miscellaneous Verses* (1917), *Late Lyrics and Earlier* (1922), *Human Shows, Far Phantasies, Songs and Trifles* (1925), and *Winter Words in Various Moods and Metres* (1928).

[2] 'God's Funeral' (CP 326–9), 'The Turnip-Hoer' (CP 703–6), 'The Mongrel' (CP 877), 'Lausanne: In Gibbon's Old Garden: 11–12 p.m.' (CP 105–6).

that a criticism which can make shift to come to terms with Ezra Pound or Apollinaire, Charles Olson or René Char, should have to confess itself unable to appraise with confidence a body of verse writing like Hardy's, which at first glance offers so much less of a challenge to tested assumptions and time-honoured procedures.[3]

The fullest and most sophisticated recent account of the difficulties posed by Hardy's verse to the would-be critic is by Marjorie Levinson. In 'Object-Loss and Object-Bondage: Economies of Representation in Hardy's Poetry' (2006), she argues that Hardy's poems are unique in their indifference to how they might be interpreted, and that this self-sufficiency leaves the reader stranded in a baffling void:

> What we have here is a body of work that appears not to solicit or even to acknowledge reading. It does not tell us how we should value it nor does it appear to care whether or not we do. It withdraws from reading without a hint of condescension, self-absorption, or even self-awareness.[4]

And yet, after wittily and eloquently staging the various dilemmas and impasses involved in attempting to assess Hardy's poetry with the techniques used by critics to assess the work of other major twentieth-century poets, both Davie and Levinson develop analyses of individual poems that are at once instructive and illuminating. There is no gainsaying, however, the overall thrust of their arguments, that Hardy's poetry and modern criticism might be compared to oil and water, a point first made by Philip Larkin in a review of some dispiriting volumes on Hardy published in 1966.[5] While critical tomes on the likes of Ezra Pound and T. S. Eliot and Wallace Stevens and Elizabeth Bishop stream from the presses, monographs devoted to Hardy's poetry have been appearing at the rate of just one a decade.[6]

The title of this book is taken from 'The Voice', which opens 'Woman much missed, how you call to me, call to me...' (CP 346). It is focused on

---

[3] Donald Davie, *Thomas Hardy and British Poetry* (London: Routledge, 1973), 13.

[4] Marjorie Levinson, 'Object-Loss and Object-Bondage: Economies of Representation in Hardy's Poetry', *ELH* 73 (2006), 550.

[5] Philip Larkin, 'Wanted: Good Hardy Critic', in *Required Writing* (London: Faber & Faber, 1983), 168–74.

[6] The most recent is Indy Clark's *Thomas Hardy's Pastoral: An Unkindly May* (London: Palgrave Macmillan, 2015). Clark's is the first book published just on Hardy's poetry since Tim Armstrong's outstanding *Haunted Hardy: Poetry, History, Memory* (London: Palgrave Macmillan, 2000).

Hardy's poetic depictions of Emma, and, more generally, on his conjugations of the concept of romance, a concept fundamental both to his vision of himself as a poet and to his understanding of human motivation. Hardy's notion of romance was shaped by his reading, by his class status, and by his early experiences of falling in love. The earliest infatuation recorded in the *Life* occurred when he was just nine or ten, and the object of his affections was nearing forty. The wealthy, childless Julia Augusta Martin had moved with her husband into the nearby manor house, Kingston Maurward, in 1844, and soon after 'took up' young Thomas:

> she had grown passionately fond of Tommy almost from his infancy—said to have been an attractive little fellow at the time—whom she had been accustomed to take into her lap and kiss until he was quite a big child. He quite reciprocated her fondness...In fact, though he was only nine or ten and she must have been nearly forty, his feeling for her was almost that of a lover.   (L 23–4)

Around 1850, however, a conflict developed between the lady of the manor and Hardy's mother over young Tommy's schooling which effectively severed relations between the two, leaving Hardy torn, as he would be for so much of his married life, between allegiance to his family and the attractions and demands of a higher-born woman. The startling impact on the young Hardy of Julia Augusta Martin's attentions and caresses can be gauged from his response to a letter that she wrote congratulating him on the publication of *Far from the Madding Crowd* in 1874, by which time she was in her sixties, and he was a married man of thirty-four:

> She was now quite an elderly lady, but by signing her letter 'Julia Augusta' she revived throbs of tender feeling in him, and brought back to his memory the thrilling 'frou-frou' of her four grey silk flounces when she had used to bend over him, and when they brushed against the font as she entered church on Sundays. He replied, but, as it appears, did not go to see her. Thus though their eyes never met again after his call on her in London [a disillusioning experience which occurred in 1862], nor their lips from the time when she had held him in her arms, who can say that both occurrences might not have been in the order of things, if he had developed their reacquaintance earlier, now that she was in her widowhood, with nothing to hinder her mind from rolling back upon her past.   (L 104–5)

There can be no doubting the formative nature of this early experience, which Hardy remodelled into the plot of his first novel, *The Poor Man and the Lady*, and which seems to have lingered in his memory as a compound of romance and trauma.[7] The episode, further, illustrates the protective forcefield thrown over her four children by Hardy's mother, Jemima, whose clannishness was so extreme that she wanted them all to remain single and live together in sibling couples. Only her eldest defied this taboo on marriage.

Hardy frequently translated the journey that he made from his humble workman's cottage in Higher Bockhampton to St Juliot rectory in Cornwall into the stuff of romantic legend, a legend primarily furnished by the popular Victorian mythology of King Arthur and the Round Table as expounded by such as Tennyson in *Idylls of the King* (1859–85) or Swinburne in *Tristram of Lyonnesse* (1882). Perhaps the most uplifting aspect of Hardy's poetic account of his chance meeting in March 1870, on what was effectively a business trip, with Emma Gifford, and of his wooing of her on his subsequent visits to the Cornish coast, is the freedom with which he figures himself as the noble knight Sir Tristram and Emma as a latter-day Iseult. I find his readiness to apply these myths to his and Emma's love story, dependent as it was on the Victorian railway network and postal system, as inspiring as John Keats's appropriation in *Endymion* of classical mythology, which led the reviewer John Gibson Lockhart to denounce him as an uppity Cockney who refused to know his station. For both Hardy and Keats romance was a vector not only for erotic fantasy but for a defiant repudiation of class conventions. What a social historian would record as the courtship by a mason's son currently employed as 'an architect's clerk'—as Hardy defined himself in the census of 1871 (MM 123)—of the dowry-less daughter of a middle-class family now fallen on hard times is transformed in Hardy's poetry into a love as legendary as that of any couple in the Western canon.

This transformation occurred, however, only after Emma's death at the age of seventy-two. In 'A Dream or No', included in his elegiac sequence 'Poems of 1912–13', Hardy ponders the 'strange necromancy' (CP 348) that draws him to St Juliot, and the phrase captures what is perhaps most

---

[7] See the poems 'Amabel' (CP 8–9) and 'The Revisitation' (CP 191–5). *The Poor Man and the Lady* was never published, and the manuscript was eventually destroyed. Extended sections of it, however, were incorporated into Hardy's first three published novels and a revised and truncated version was published in the *New Quarterly Magazine* in 1878 as 'An Indiscretion in the Life of an Heiress'.

peculiar about the poems discussed in this book. Hardy published just one poem, 'Ditty' (dated 1870 and dedicated to E.L.G. (Emma Lavinia Gifford)), that pays tribute to Emma in the three volumes that he issued when she was alive, although a handful of others can be read as refracting aspects of their marriage. All the other poems that make up his kaleidoscopic poetic portrait of Emma, from her birth in Plymouth to her burial in Stinsford churchyard, are necromantic forays into the past conducted by a man who married his second wife some thirteen months after burying his first. Death, in other words, was the portal through which Hardy gained imaginative access to Emma's emotions and experiences, as well as the source of his compulsion to recreate her life. His discovery of her caustic diaries and of her memoir *Some Recollections* in her attic room greatly fuelled this compulsion.

There are numerous essays and articles on Hardy's 'Poems of 1912–13' (see bibliography for a full listing), and excellent chapters on his poems about Emma in various monographs on elegy and on Victorian and early twentieth-century poetry, as well as in general studies of Hardy's writings.[8] This is the first book-length account, however, of the entire corpus of Emma poems,[9] as well as the first to pay attention to the role that poetry played in their courtship, both as a shared passion—as illustrated by the first of my epigraphs—and as a means of signifying his upward mobility. The majority of Hardy's poems about Emma are scattered across the four volumes that he published between 1914 and 1925 (*Satires of Circumstance, Moments of Vision, Late Lyrics and Earlier*, and *Human Shows*). Supplemented by much contextual biographical material, these poems are here used to construct a

---

[8] See in particular Peter Sacks, *The English Elegy: Studies in the Genre from Spenser to Yeats* (Baltimore: The Johns Hopkins University Press, 1985), 227–59; Jahan Ramazani, *Poetry of Mourning: The Modern Elegy from Hardy to Heaney* (Chicago: University of Chicago Press, 1994), 47–68; Melissa F. Zeiger, *Beyond Consolation: Death, Sexuality, and the Changing Shapes of Elegy* (Ithaca, NY: Cornell University Press, 1997), 43–61; Clifton R. Spargo, *The Ethics of Mourning: Grief and Responsibility in Elegiac Literature*, (Baltimore: The Johns Hopkins University Press, 2004), 165–208; Peter Howarth, *British Poetry in the Age of Modernism* (Oxford: Oxford University Press, 2005), 147–81; Jane Thomas, *Thomas Hardy and Desire: Conceptions of the Self* (London: Palgrave Macmillan, 2013), 164–91; Galia Benziman, *Thomas Hardy's Elegiac Prose and Poetry: Codes of Bereavement* (London: Palgrave Macmillan, 2018), 133–61; John Hughes, *The Expression of Things: Themes in Thomas Hardy's Fiction and Poetry* (Brighton: Sussex Academic Press, 2018), 143–66.

[9] The nearest precedent is Carl J. Weber's edition of *Hardy's Love Poems* (London: Macmillan, 1963). This comes with an extensive introduction, but one that fully bears out Larkin's complaint that Weber was prone to 'journalistic vulgarities' (Larkin, *Required Writing*, 173). See also *Unexpected Elegies: "Poems of 1912–13" and Other Poems about Emma*, selected, with an introduction by Claire Tomalin (New York: Persea Books, 2010).

web of critical readings that enable the reader to grasp with a new fullness the multifaceted complexity of his portrayals of his wife. Despite the 'deep division' and 'dark undying pain' of the last years of their marriage (CP 380), there can be no denying that Emma was utterly crucial to Hardy's success as a writer, serving as encourager and amanuensis and, on occasion, collaborator during his career as a novelist, and then as muse and source of inspiration for the poems that he composed after her death. His obsessive poetic recreations of the events of his first visit to St Juliot rectory, discussed in detail in my Prologue, reveal how he figured the moment that she 'opened the door' (CP 773) to him on the night of 7 March 1870 as the most important of his life. It was a moment rivalled for him in significance only by that of her death.

This book is in four sections of two chapters each. The first section assesses the very particular meanings and possibilities that poetry embodied for Hardy, and his attempts to describe and make sense of what he claims he always considered his primary vocation. Some six weeks before he died, Hardy's second wife, Florence, recorded the following conversation:

> Nov. 28. Speaking about ambition T. said today that he had done all that he meant to do, but he did not know whether it had been worth doing.
>
> His only ambition, so far as he could remember, was to have some poem or poems in a good anthology like the *Golden Treasury*.
>
> The model he had set before him was 'Drink to me only', by Ben Jonson.   (L 478)

Jonson's 'To Celia' perfectly exemplifies Hardy's vision of poetry as at once performing some kind of spiritual transfiguration and yet remaining wedded to the particular:

> The thirst that from the soul doth rise
>   Doth ask a drink divine;
> But might I of Jove's nectar sup,
>   I would not change for thine.   (GT 118)

This accords with the most high-romantic strains in Hardy's own verse as well as with his interest in, and talent for, lyrics that aim at the musical, many of which he subtitled 'Song'. He was also, however, acutely conscious of the unlyrical aspects of the age in which he lived and, unlike, say, Swinburne or Walter de la Mare (both of whose work he greatly admired),

Hardy evolved a poetic idiom capable of registering all manner of contemporary phenomena, from the boarding of military horses onto a naval cargo ship to the dismal life of an East End curate, from a railway station waiting room on a wet day to a second-hand suit for sale in a pawn shop.[10] The two chapters of 'What Poetry Meant to Hardy' present a wide-ranging account of the various perspectives on the poetic articulated in his fiction, in the *Life*, in his *Poetical Matter* and *Studies, Specimens &c.* notebooks and his *Personal Notebooks*, as well as in the poems that he wrote about poetry, such as 'The Vatican: Sala delle Muse', and about other poets, particularly Shelley and Keats. It is intended to create an overarching context for his poems about Emma, and to suggest the ways in which they relate to his poetic oeuvre as a whole.

The rest of the book is roughly chronological. 'Lyonnesse' is focused on Hardy's depictions of Devon and Cornwall. It uses *Some Recollections*, along with the various poems that Emma's memoir inspired, to recreate her life before she met Hardy, and examines his fascination with Charles churchyard in Plymouth, where Emma's parents and various other Giffords were buried, visits to which prompted the poems 'During Wind and Rain' and 'The Obliterate Tomb'. I also explore the classical underpinnings of his vision of Emma as the genius of the Cornish shore, and their shared interest in more homely, local forms of superstition. The second chapter in this section considers their four-and-a-half-year courtship; it draws on the many poems that present incidents from the six trips that Hardy made to Cornwall between 1870 and 1873 as well as on his Cornish novel, *A Pair of Blue Eyes* (1873). It was during the composition and serialization of this novel that Hardy, his confidence decisively bolstered by Emma's belief in his literary abilities, finally committed himself to a career as a writer rather than as an architect.

Section three, 'The Rift', follows the narrative of their marriage as developed in poems from 'Honeymoon Time at an Inn' and 'We Sat at the Window' (subtitled Bournemouth, 1875) to his imagining, in the elegy 'Your Last Drive', Emma's thoughts and feelings in the days leading up to her death. Where possible I play off Hardy's poetic, epistolary, and autobiographical accounts of the different phases of their marriage with Emma's own as expressed in letters sent to correspondents like Rebekah Owen and Elspeth Grahame as well as in her travel diaries. The move back to

---

[10] 'Horses Aboard' (CP 785–6), 'An East-End Curate' (CP 713), 'In a Waiting-Room' (CP 470), ' "A Gentleman's Second-Hand Suit" ' (CP 883–4).

Dorchester in 1883 was undoubtedly one of the primary catalysts for the eventual breakdown in their marital relations. Although being mistress of Max Gate granted Emma a certain amount of power and status, she was effectively condemned to live on Hardy's terrain and forced to experience on a regular basis the disapproval of his immediate family. Her letter of February 1896 to Hardy's sister Mary quoted at the beginning of Chapter 5 is the most signal instance of the anguish caused by proximity to Higher Bockhampton. While it is not clear how Hardy experienced the complex division of allegiances that resulted from his decision to settle permanently on the outskirts of Dorchester, as far as his writing life went it proved such a triumphant success that he was able, on the basis principally of the royalties pouring in from *Tess of the d'Urbervilles* (1891), to give up writing fiction and to devote himself to poetry.

The last section, 'Afterwards', deals with life after Emma. 'Dear Ghost' (Chapter 7) offers readings of various poems in which she appears to him as a spectre and pays detailed attention to his reconfiguration of classical precedents, in particular Virgil's Aeneas and Dido and Ovid's Orpheus and Eurydice. It is here I consider the best-known of his elegies, such as 'The Voice', 'After a Journey', and 'At Castle Boterel'. And in my final chapter, after outlining the various manoeuvres that resulted in Emma's invitation to Florence Dugdale to pay a series of extended visits to Max Gate in the second half of 1910, I assess Hardy's attempts to find a place for both 'brightsouled women' (CP 415) in the poetic narrative of his life. His last extended imaginative work, *The Famous Tragedy of the Queen of Cornwall* (begun 1916, completed 1923), transposes the menage à trois briefly attempted at Max Gate into the love triangle played out between Sir Tristram and his two Iseults, the Fair and the Whitehanded. Although Hardy can undoubtedly be accused with some justice of missing Emma in life, the extended posthumous pursuit of her traced in this book, culminating in her enthronement in the Arthurian castle of Tintagel as the legendary Queen of Cornwall, largely bears out the assertion that he made in a letter to Edward Clodd some two weeks after her funeral: 'One forgets all the recent years & differences, & the mind goes back to the early times when each was much to the other—in her case & mine intensely much' (CL IV 239).

Prologue

She Opened the Door

Of all the letters received and preserved by Thomas Hardy, it was a routine, two-sentence communication from George Crickmay, the owner of an architectural practice based in Weymouth, that had the most decisive effect on his life: 'Dear Sir,' wrote Crickmay on 11 February 1870 to his freelance employee:

> Can you go into Cornwall for me, to take a plan and particulars of a church I am about to rebuild there? It must be done early next week, and I should be glad to see you on Monday morning.   (L 66)

This was sent to the Hardy family home in Higher Bockhampton, to which Hardy had retreated from Weymouth a week or so earlier to continue work on what would become his first published novel, *Desperate Remedies* (1871). Absorbed in the intricacies of its sensational plot, which features no fewer than three young architects (one of whom becomes a bigamist and a murderer and then commits suicide, but one of whom gets to marry the heroine), Hardy initially declined this commission. 'But receiving', as he puts it in the *Life*, 'a more persuasive request from Crickmay later, and having finished the MS. of *Desperate Remedies* (except the three or four final chapters) by the beginning of March, he agreed to go on the errand' (L 67).

The nearly completed novel was dispatched to the publisher Alexander Macmillan (who would in due course reject it) on Saturday 5 March. On the Monday Hardy rose at four in the morning and walked by starlight the three and a half miles into Dorchester. His 'cross-jump journey, like a Chess-knight's move' (SR 55), as Emma later characterized it, involved catching trains from Dorchester to Yeovil, from Yeovil to Exeter, from Exeter to Plymouth, and then from Plymouth to Launceston, which he reached around four in the afternoon. That was as near as the railways could

Woman Much Missed: Thomas Hardy, Emma Hardy, and Poetry. Mark Ford, Oxford University Press.
© Mark Ford 2023. DOI: 10.1093/oso/9780192886804.003.0001

take him. For the last leg he had to hire a trap that conveyed him the 16 miles from Launceston to the rectory at St Juliot, where he was to stay.

In real time Hardy found his fourteen or fifteen hours of stop-start travelling merely 'tedious' (L 67). In poetic retrospect, however, this journey came to assume the status of a legendary quest into a remote and magical kingdom:

> When I set out for Lyonnesse,
>   A hundred miles away,
>   The rime was on the spray,
> And starlight lit my lonesomeness
> When I set out for Lyonnesse
>   A hundred miles away.
>
> What would bechance at Lyonnesse
>   While I should sojourn there
>   No prophet durst declare,
> Nor did the wisest wizard guess
> What would bechance at Lyonnesse
>   While I should sojourn there.   (CP 312)

In the *Life* Hardy recalls that the 'romantic sound' of the name St Juliot had struck his fancy the very first time that he heard it (L 66). It is not clear whether he knew before his trip to Cornwall that the dilapidated church he was to survey was only a few miles from the ruins of Tintagel, long associated with the knights of the Round Table, and in particular with the doomed lovers Tristram and Iseult, but certainly the mid-Victorian fascination with all things Arthurian pervades a number of his recreations of the momentous events of 7 March. Hardy was saturated in the poetry of Tennyson, the first instalment of whose *Idylls of the King* had appeared in 1859, and it is likely that he was also familiar with Matthew Arnold's narrative poem 'Tristram and Iseult' of 1852.

'Arrived at St. Juliot Rectory between 6 and 7,' Hardy noted in his brief diary entry for 7 March: 'Received by young lady in brown' (L 77). Although Hardy and Emma were both twenty-nine, there was clearly an element of exhilarating transgression in this first encounter. The Revd Caddell Holder was in bed suffering from gout and his wife Helen, Emma's older sister, was ministering to him. 'The dinner-cloth was laid,' Emma recalled in her memoir of her life up until she married Hardy, 'my sister had gone to her husband, who required the constant attention of his wife. At that very moment the front door bell rang and ~~he~~ [the architect] was ushered in. I had to receive him alone, and felt a curious uneasy embarrassment at receiving anyone, especially so necessary a person as the Architect. I was immediately arrested by his familiar appearance, as if I had seen him in a dream—his slightly different accent, his soft voice' (SR 55).[1] Emma also noticed a blue paper sticking out of his pocket, which she assumed to be an architectural drawing. She was surprised, however, to be informed that this blue paper was not a plan of St Juliot Church, but the draft of a poem. This was clearly an important gambit on Hardy's part. When he revealed the contents of that blue paper on that first evening, he was emphatically signalling to the young lady in brown that there was more to him than met the eye; that, despite his 'rather shabby great coat' and 'business appearance' (Emma initially wrote the rather more damning 'homely appearance') and 'yellowish beard', and the fact (not of course initially disclosed) that his father was a mason in the building trade, he had a strong claim to be considered a member of the same social class as his hostess: for he was a reader, and even a writer, of poetry (SR 55).

Repairs to the church of St Juliot were long overdue. The Revd Caddell Holder's predecessor had initiated proceedings, and the first appeal had been launched back in the 1850s. A preliminary inspection had eventually been undertaken by Hardy's first employer, John Hicks (a family friend of Holder's) in 1867; but Hicks's death two years later meant a new assessment had to be made, and new plans drawn up. There was, according to Emma, much excitement in the parish when it was confirmed that the replacement architect was finally scheduled to arrive: 'It seemed almost wonderful that a fixed date should at last be given and the work set in hand, after so many years of waiting, of difficulties and delays,' she recalled in her memoir (SR 52). It must also surely have crossed the minds of all three residents of the rectory that the long-awaited architect might possibly be a match for Emma, whose chances of meeting a suitable husband, given her age and situation, were exceedingly slim. No conclusive evidence of a plot to 'ensnare' Hardy has emerged, but it may have been no coincidence that Holder was struck down by gout just before the visiting architect's arrival, leaving his sister-in-law to welcome him alone.

----

[1] The editors of *Some Recollections* explain that 'square brackets indicate a word or words added or substituted in the manuscript by Thomas Hardy' and 'words cancelled ~~thus~~ indicate a cancellation that can certainly be attributed to Hardy' (1).

It was probably a servant rather than Emma herself who physically opened the front door of the rectory to the visiting architect that evening; but the moment of his first admission to Emma's world furnished the dominant image of the poem that, along with 'When I Set Out for Lyonnesse', most fully acknowledges the profound transformation in Hardy that this meeting would foster:

She Opened the Door

She opened the door of the West to me,
      With its loud sea-lashings,
      And cliff-side clashings
Of waters rife with revelry.

She opened the door of Romance to me,
      The door from a cell
      I had known too well,
Too long, till then, and was fain to flee.

She opened the door of a Love to me,
      That passed the wry
      World-welters by
As far as the arching blue the lea.

She opens the door of the Past to me,
      Its magic lights,
      Its heavenly heights,
When forward little is to see!

          1913   (CP 773)

This poem was one of the many that poured from Hardy in the months after Emma's death. Unlike such as 'The Going' or 'Your Last Drive', it elides the misunderstandings and antagonisms that afflicted the latter half of their marriage, instead paying fervent tribute to the glorious possibilities 'opened' for Hardy by his relationship with Emma.

The first of these was the landscape of north Cornwall, to which he returned again and again in his elegies for her, and where much of the action of his third novel, *A Pair of Blue Eyes*, is set.[2] In his 1895 preface to a

---

[2] The plot of *A Pair of Blue Eyes*, as Hardy himself pointed out, prefigures that of *Tess of the d'Urbervilles* (PBE 4). Its heroine Elfride Swancourt lives in a rectory in a fictional version of St Juliot called Endelstow. She is initially attracted to a young visiting architect, Stephen Smith,

reissue of this novel, Hardy encapsulated the dominant aspects of his depictions of this stretch of the Cornish coast:

> The place is pre-eminently (for one person at least) the region of dream and mystery. The ghostly birds, the pall-like sea, the frothy wind, the eternal soliloquy of the waters, the bloom of dark purple cast that seems to exhale from the shoreward precipices, in themselves lend to the scene an atmosphere like the twilight of a night vision.   (PBE 3)

Here in embryo is the seascape and landscape of poems such as 'After a Journey' and 'Beeny Cliff'. And as Hardy's first modern biographer, Robert Gittings, pointed out in his 1961 edition of *Some Recollections*, the first stanza of 'She Opened the Door' performs a secret linguistic commingling with Emma, appropriating or adapting an image that she deployed in her description of Tintagel in her memoir:

> Tintagel was a very remote place then, and the inhabitants expected few visitors, moreover of those who came few remained long enough to see the winter waves and foam reaching hundreds of feet high up the stern, strong dark rocks with the fantastic revellings of the gulls, puffins and rooks...   (SR 76)

Emma's 'revellings' becomes Hardy's 'revelry', a minor but signal instance of the way that his poems frequently incorporate or derive from her experiences and responses. Whether Hardy used the word deliberately or subliminally, the echo can be seen as a textual version of their shared enjoyment of the Cornish coastline to which she introduced him.

After the West comes Romance. It is striking that in this second stanza the Arthurian narrative of the knight rescuing the princess from imprisonment is reversed. The 'cell' in which Hardy pictures himself immured is that of a life without romance—a life like that of the city clerk portrayed in

---

who arrives from London to oversee repairs to Endelstow Church. When her father, Parson Swancourt, refuses the couple permission to marry because Stephen's father is a mason and his mother a housekeeper, they decide to elope and get married in London, but on arrival in Paddington lose heart and return unwed. Stephen, whose education was overseen by an older mentor friend, the literary man-about-town Henry Knight, departs for India to make his fortune as an architect. Elfride subsequently meets Knight and falls deeply in love with him. Their courtship proceeds smoothly until her relationship with a previous lover comes to light. Knight, as outraged as Angel, breaks off their engagement, to Elfride's acute distress. Like *Tess*, *A Pair of Blue Eyes* ends with the heroine's death; after wedding the local aristocrat, Lord Luxellian, Elfride dies from a miscarriage.

'Coming Up Oxford Street: Evening', whom Hardy claimed to have observed on 4 July 1872:

> Who sees no escape to the very verge of his days
> From the rut of Oxford Street into open ways;
> And he goes along with head and eyes flagging forlorn,
> Empty of interest in things, and wondering why he was born.
> (CP 717)

But when first published in *The Nation & the Athenaeum* in 1925, these lines were in the first person ('the very end of *my* days...And *I* go along...and wondering why *I* was born').[3] Only romance, and the opportunity to live life as a poet that romance makes possible, could offer release from the dreariness of such an existence; and with each rejection slip Hardy's fear of succumbing to the life of an office-bound urban drudge intensified.

Romance leads to Love, and to one of the more paradoxical aspects of Hardy's self-figurations in his poetry: while the dominant Hardy persona is of a man who never expected much and was keenly attuned to satires of circumstance, time and again in the poems inspired by Emma this wary diffidence is ruptured by expressions of the unique and triumphant power of their feelings for each other, as if their love could indeed be treated as legendary, as fit for comparison with the stories of famous literary couples such as Tristram and Iseult or Romeo and Juliet. The mere fact, for instance, of their having walked up the hill above Boscastle is presented in 'At Castle Boterel' as the most significant event that ever occurred in that hill's history:

> Primaeval rocks form the road's steep border,
> And much have they faced there, first and last,
> Of the transitory in Earth's long order;
> But what they record in colour and cast
> Is—that we two passed.   (CP 352)

Of course, the genre of the love poem tends to encourage extravagant declarations of the transcendent and superior love of the couple in question, but it is worth remembering that the poems about love that Hardy composed in the 1860s, such as the 'She, to Him' sonnets or 'Neutral Tones', nearly

---

[3] *The Nation & the Athenaeum* (13 June 1925).

always confounded such expectations. 'Neutral Tones', for example, ends with a wholly desolate summation of the different stages of disillusionment that the poem has just dramatized:

> Since then, keen lessons that love deceives,
> And wrings with wrong, have shaped to me
> Your face, and the God-curst sun, and a tree,
>   And a pond edged with grayish leaves.   (CP 12)

Whatever the nature of Hardy's entanglements with such as Eliza Nicholls, or her sister Jane Nicholls, in none of the poems that can be connected with them does Hardy articulate the vision developed in certain poems about Emma and typified by this third stanza of 'She Opened the Door', which imagines their love soaring above all 'world-welters' as effortlessly as the sky above a field.

It is hard to overestimate, or so this poem at least suggests, the extent to which Emma opened the door through which Hardy entered his life as a poet. But the opening of the poetic door into *her* life, as well as into the life that they shared together, was dependent, as this poem also implicitly admits, on her death. The last stanza of 'She Opened the Door' dramatizes the peculiar, even perverse, imaginative economy operative in any number of Hardy poems, in which poetic access to a primary experience must occur posthumously:

> She opens the door of the Past to me,
>   Its magic lights,
>   Its heavenly heights,
> When forward little is to see!   (CP 773)

Hence, poetically, Emma can often seem more alive to him as a ghost in memory than when they lived together. Indeed, this spectral Emma, in another type of paradox, updates the poem into the present tense—'She *opens* the door of the Past to me'—offering herself as a means through which he can now and ever after re-experience and recreate their shared history, its magic lights and heavenly heights, and escape the bleak, attenuated present.

Hardy's highly compressed diary entry for 7 March continues: 'Mr Holder gout. Saw Mrs Holder. The meal. Talk. To Mr Holder's room.

Returned downstairs. Music' (L 77). Later diary entries reveal that Emma and her sister performed for him on the Wednesday and Thursday evenings as well, and even record the names of a couple of the songs in their repertoire, such as 'The Elfin Call' and 'Let Us Dance on the Sands'. To these can be added 'Fall of Paris', 'Battle of Prague', and 'Roving Minstrels', which are all mentioned in the poem 'A Duettist to Her Pianoforte', a highly original elegy for Helen Holder (who died in December 1900) that takes the form of an address by Emma to the piano on which she used to play with her sister:

> Since every sound moves memories,
>   How can I play you
> Just as I might if you raised no scene,
> By your ivory rows, of a form between
> My vision and your time-worn sheen,
>   As when each day you
> Answered our fingers with ecstasy?
> So it's hushed, hushed, hushed, you are for me!   (CP 586)

Music was crucial in all sorts of ways to Hardy and Emma's relationship, both during their courtship and in their married life. On their annual sojourns for the Season in London they would frequently attend concerts together, and probably the happiest of all Hardy's marriage poems is 'To a Lady Playing and Singing in the Morning', in which he excitedly bursts out: 'Joyful lady, sing! / And I will lurk here listening, / Though nought be done, and nought begun, / And work-hours swift are scurrying' (CP 579). Conversely, the most painful and self-lacerating of the poems that he wrote about their 'deep division' (CP 380) is surely 'Lost Love', in which he recalls Emma's doomed attempts to entice him into her presence by playing on the Max Gate piano the songs with which she had originally enchanted him on his visits to Cornwall:

> I play my sweet old airs—
>   The airs he knew
>   When our love was true—
>   But he does not balk
>   His determined walk,
> And passes up the stairs.
>
> I sing my songs once more,
>   And presently hear

> His footstep near
> As if it would stay;
> But he goes his way,
> And shuts a distant door.   (CP 318)

The pathos and bitterness are only increased if these futile efforts to rekindle her husband's affection are put in the context of Hardy's responses to Emma and Helen's duets on the evenings of his initial stay at the rectory.

It is possible that these were the first occasions on which Hardy was able to assume the role of a Victorian gentleman being entertained by ladies playing music after dinner in the drawing room of an unimpeachably middle-class residence. What is more, courtesy of the reverend's gout, he was the only gentleman present. It was surely the excitement of this experience, along with all that it implied about his own prospects for moving up through the class system, that meant Hardy never forgot the sight of Emma, however un-modishly dressed, singing for him:

> But in my memoried passion
>   For evermore stands she
> In the gown of fading fashion
>   She wore that night when we,
> Doomed long to part, assembled
>   In the snug small room; yea, when
> She sang with lips that trembled,
>   'Shall I see his face again?'   ('The Old Gown', CP 585–6)

Towards the end of the *Life* Hardy alluded to his 'faculty' 'for burying an emotion in [his] heart or brain for forty years, and exhuming it at the end of that time as fresh as when interred' (L 408). A full fifty-two years had elapsed before 'The Old Gown' was published in *Late Lyrics and Earlier* (1922), and by then it was exactly half a century since Hardy had first transposed the feelings aroused in him by Emma in mid-performance into chapter 3 of the first instalment of *A Pair of Blue Eyes*. The humbly born Stephen Smith, who, it is implied, has never been entertained in this fashion before, falls in love with Elfride Swancourt as she sings a setting of Shelley's 'The Flight of Love'. The narrator prefaces his description of Elfride at the piano with what is effectively a gloss on the phrase 'memoried passion': 'Every woman who makes a permanent impression on a man is usually recalled to his mind's eye as she appeared in one particular scene, which seems ordained to be her special form of manifestation throughout the pages of his memory' (PBE 21). The paragraph that follows captures in full and fervent detail the effect made on Hardy by Emma at the piano during these after-dinner musical sessions:

> Miss Elfride's image chose the form in which she was beheld during these minutes of singing, for her permanent attitude of visitation to Stephen's eyes during his sleeping and waking hours in after days. The profile is seen of a young woman in a pale grey silk dress with trimmings of swan's-down, and opening up from a point in front, like a waistcoat without a shirt; the cool colour contrasting admirably with the warm bloom of her neck and face. The furthermost candle on the piano comes immediately in a line with her head, and half invisible itself, forms the accidentally frizzled hair into a nebulous haze of light, surrounding her crown like an aureola. Her hands are in their place on the keys, her lips parted, and thrilling forth, in a tender *diminuendo*, the closing words of the sad apostrophe:
>
> > 'O Love, who bewailest
> > > The frailty of all things here,
> > Why choose you the frailest
> > > For your cradle, your home, and your bier!'   (PBE 21)

Stephen's fixated attention in due course prompts in Elfride that tell-tale sign in Victorian fiction of erotic excitement—a blush: 'So long and so earnestly gazed he, that her cheek deepened to a more and more crimson tint as each line was added to her song' (PBE 22). Stephen and Elfride are much younger than Hardy and Emma were when they met, and the narrator frequently flags up his awareness of their naivety; but the freshness that their innocence gives to their exchanges in episodes such as this first musical evening can't help but suggest a similar kind of heady novelty was experienced by their originals.

The visiting architect had allowed himself three days in which to assess and draw up preliminary plans for the restoration of the church. The problems facing him can be gauged from the description of St Juliot Church in *Lake's Parochial History of the County of Cornwall* of 1868: 'Excepting the south aisle, extreme age has reduced this once superior church to a state of irremediable dilapidation.'[4] Its tower, which dated from the fourteenth century, was cracked and tottering, and bats and birds swooped around in the upper storeys. The tower's five bells had been placed in a transept upside down and were tolled for a funeral on the very morning that Hardy began work by a man 'lifting the clapper and letting it fall against the side' (L 77). He spent the whole of the first day drawing and measuring, and on the Wednesday, with an eye to acquiring slates for the roof, visited Penpethy quarry with Emma and Helen. There the image of Emma outlined against the green slates of the quarry, like that of her in mid-song in her old-fashioned dress, struck him vividly, again emerging half a century later in a poem that juxtaposes his original and unforgettable apprehension of her with the inevitable dispersals of time—and slate:

> It happened once, before the duller
> > Loomings of life defined them,
> I searched for slates of greenish colour
> > A quarry where men mined them;
>
> And saw, the while I peered around there,
> > In the quarry standing
> A form against the slate background there,
> > Of fairness eye-commanding.
>
> And now, though fifty years have flown me,
> > With all their dreams and duties,
> And strange-pipped dice my hand has thrown me,
> > And dust are all her beauties,
>
> Green slates—seen high on roofs, or lower
> > In waggon, truck, or lorry—
> Cry out: 'Our home was where you saw her
> > Standing in the quarry!'   (CP 712)

As John Bayley noted in his *An Essay on Hardy* (1978), this poem, despite its homely diction, heavy rhymes, and lack of authorial purposefulness, is a product of just the kind of random collision that makes certain poems, or scenes in Hardy's novels, so distinctive and memorable: one thinks of Tess

---

[4] Quoted in *St Juliot Church and Thomas Hardy* by Charles P. C. Pettit (booklet published by The Thomas Hardy Society, 2010), 2.

silhouetted in the station against the engine of the train that will take the milk from Talbothays Dairy up to London, 'the round bare arms, the rainy face and hair, the suspended attitude of a friendly leopard at pause' (T 205). 'Standing in the quarry', Emma is also suspended, a figure of mystery and possibility, not yet subject to the attritions and contingencies that the 'strange-pipped dice' of time will impose upon her. Indeed, Emma's form 'against the slate background' comes to seem as indelible—at least to those who like this kind of Hardy poem, one of many that combine anecdote and bathos with a startling central conceit—as that of Eustacia Vye against the Heath, or of Bathsheba Everdene when first spied by Oak atop her wagon.[5]

'Green Slates' also obliquely approaches the issue raised directly in poems such as 'I Found Her Out There' and 'Her Haunting-Ground' of the damage that was caused to Emma by her transplantation from her 'home' in the west; and the longing that Hardy often imputed to her ghost to return to the scenes of her pre-marital years is here transferred to the green slates. As Bayley observes: 'The sight of the girl is alive in those greenish slates, and they in their turn are as much alive as she, and more capable of speech and reminder.'[6] At the same time both slates and girl can only enter Hardy's poetry *because* they have been displaced from their home; and, further, because the dream of return can never be fulfilled. Why, Hardy often wonders in his elegies for Emma, did he never take her back to the scenes where 'her life-parts most were played' (CP 809)? In the wake of the remorseful pilgrimage to Cornwall that he made some three months after her funeral, Hardy composed numerous poems that figure her almost as the local deity of the Cornish coast, wrenched from her home like the green slates now serving as roof tiles or observed in transit. Like 'The Old Gown', 'Green Slates' travels back through the 'duller / Loomings of life' to the vision of Emma that lodged in Hardy's imagination during his first trip to St Juliot, and which then resurfaced once 'dust' were 'all her beauties'.

He seems not to have done a great deal of church surveying on the Thursday. Here is his diary entry for the day:

March 10th. Went with E.L.G. to Beeny Cliff. She on horseback—...On the cliff...'The tender grace of a day', etc. The run down to the edge. The coming home...

---

[5] Not all Hardy critics hold this poem in high esteem: in *Thomas Hardy: The Time-Torn Man* Claire Tomalin dismisses it as a 'plod' (CT 405).

[6] John Bayley, *An Essay on Hardy* (Cambridge: Cambridge University Press, 1978), 24.

In the afternoon I walked to Boscastle, Mrs H. and E.L.G. accompanying me three-quarters of the way: the overshot mill: E. provokingly reading as she walked; evening in garden; music later in evening. (L 78: the ellipses are his, and possibly indicate cuts that were made when he was selecting material from his diaries (which he later destroyed) to be copied into the manuscript of the *Life*. The 'overshot mill' was the Old Mill in Boscastle which had two overshot waterwheels.)

Emma had received her brown mare, Fanny, as a present from an eccentric old lady called Miss Robartes, with whom both she and Helen had lived respectively as an unpaid companion.[7] Her gift to Emma of the surefooted Fanny would result in the most haunting of all Hardy's posthumous figurations of his wife: as a 'ghost-girl-rider'.

> Time touches her not,
> But she still rides gaily
> In his rapt thought
> On that shagged and shaly
> Atlantic spot,
> And as when first eyed
> Draws rein and sings to the swing of the tide.   (CP 354)

Hardy didn't ride himself, and Emma's discovery of this may have alerted her to the possibility that he was not quite of the class that she had initially assumed. In *A Pair of Blue Eyes* Elfride is greatly surprised to discover the same deficiency in her love-struck swain, and 'pertly' exclaims 'Fancy a man not able to ride!' (PBE 52). Like Elfride, Emma was proud of her equestrian abilities, and clearly keen to demonstrate them to the visiting architect. In *Some Recollections* she describes 'scampering up and down the hills on my beloved mare alone, wanting no protection, the rain going down my back often and my hair floating on the wind' (SR 50). The villagers, she claims, would often stop to gaze in wonder as she sped by, and a 'butterman laid down his basket once to exclaim loudly for no one dared except myself to ride in such wild fearless fashion' (SR 51). 'Fanny and I', she asserts, 'were one creature, and very happy both of us'—and when 'hints about marrying fell upon me from the officious, I would say "I prefer my mare to any husband"' (SR 39).

---

[7] See *The First Mrs Thomas Hardy* by Denys Kay-Robinson (London: Macmillan, 1979), 15 and SR 37–9 for further details.

The trip to Beeny Cliff of 10 March 1870 was repeated by the husband for whom she eventually sacrificed her mare almost exactly forty-three years later. And the poem that resulted, 'Beeny Cliff', is pointedly subtitled 'March 1870–March 1913', as if Hardy wanted to prove to the reader his ability to exhume an emotion 'as fresh as when interred' many decades later:

> O the opal and the sapphire of that wandering western sea,
> And the woman riding high above with bright hair
>   flapping free—
> The woman whom I loved so, and who loyally loved me.
>
> (CP 350)

The extent to which Hardy felt struck by a *coup de foudre*, given that the original excursion to Beeny Cliff took place only three days after he and Emma had met, is possibly encoded in the poem's third line; but aspects of the differences between them are also subliminally present. In her later years Emma could be embarrassingly outspoken on the topic of the social superiority of the Giffords to the Hardys, whom she thought of as belonging to the 'peasant class' (MM 326), and despite Hardy's knack for producing apt poetic quotations ('the tender grace of a day' is from Tennyson's 'Break, Break, Break'), he was as acutely aware as Stephen Smith of the social gulf between the two families: the Giffords were gentry, while Hardy's parents belonged to the rural working class. Hardy's mother had been employed as a servant from her teens to her mid-twenties, and his maternal grandmother, Betty Hand (née Swetman), had been so impoverished by her disastrous marriage to a ne'er-do-well that she had been obliged to 'go on the parish', or in other words to seek poor relief (MM 15). A powerful element in Hardy's attraction to 'the woman riding high above' was analogous to that of the lowly born Will Strong to the squire's daughter in Hardy's first attempt at fiction, *The Poor Man and the Lady*, which he later adapted into 'An Indiscretion in the Life of an Heiress' (1878). Emma was by no means an heiress, indeed brought no dowry at all (clearly one of the reasons why Hardy's mother Jemima viewed the match with such disfavour), but in terms of the class stratifications that held sway in the 1870s, there is no doubt that, in courting Emma, Hardy was attempting to marry 'above' himself. A measure of tribute is duly paid in the poem to Emma's staunchness, during their courtship at any rate, in overcoming her family's prejudices and proceeding, four and a half years later, with the marriage. Had their prenuptial correspondence survived, one would know a great deal more about what was actually involved in Emma's 'loyally' loving Hardy during these years.

Like 'Beeny Cliff', Tennyson's 'Break, Break, Break' is an elegy that contrasts the eternal motions of the sea with the transience of the life of the beloved, the mourned one in Tennyson's case being his university friend Arthur Hallam.

> Break, break, break,
>> At the foot of thy crags, O Sea!
> But the tender grace of a day that is dead
>> Will never come back to me.[8]

There is, then, a minor satire of circumstance in Hardy's quotation of the first part of the third line as a means of commemorating in his diary the blossoming of his feelings for Emma as they roamed the coast together unchaperoned. Possession of books by Tennyson was a widely recognized signifier of middle-class status in the period of his laureateship, which perhaps helps explain the astonishing sales figures of a volume such as *Enoch Arden* (1864), of which 17,000 copies were purchased on the day of publication, or *The Holy Grail* (1869), for which pre-publication orders were over 26,000—and this at a time when poetry sales were in general declining. There is a good chance, accordingly, that some lines from 'Break, Break, Break' were among the 'sweet things' said by Hardy to Emma as they surveyed the waves crashing into the crags on that 'wild weird western shore' (CP 351). And his association of Tennyson's poem with Beeny Cliff is strengthened by his use of its second line ('On thy cold grey stones, O Sea') as the epigraph to chapter 21 of *A Pair of Blue Eyes*, in which Knight, Elfride's second suitor, nearly falls to his death after slipping over the edge of the Cliff without a Name, clearly based on Beeny.

'She was so *living*' (L 76)—that was how Hardy summed up in his autobiography the impression made on him by the woman in brown who had received him on 7 March, an anniversary he commemorated after her death by keeping his desk calendar set permanently to that date. It was, however, the day of his departure on the Friday that seems to have been the

---

[8] *Tennyson: A Selected Edition*, ed. Christopher Ricks (Harlow: Longman, 1989), 165 (ll. 1–4). Ricks suggests the poem was probably composed in the spring of 1834, the year after Hallam's death in 1833.

pivotal one. 'E.L.G.', he recorded in his diary, 'had struck a light six times in her anxiety to call the servants early enough' for him to set off for Launceston in time to catch the train from there to Plymouth (L 78). After his breakfast, in the half-light of dawn he went to say goodbye to Emma in the rectory garden, as recalled in 'At the Word "Farewell"', a poem included, in a letter to Florence Henniker of 7 February 1918, in a list of those collected in *Moments of Vision* (1917) that were 'literally true' (CL V 250).

> She looked like a bird from a cloud
>   On the clammy lawn,
> Moving alone, bare-browed
>   In the dim of dawn.
> The candles alight in the room
>   For my parting meal
> Made all things withoutdoors loom
>   Strange, ghostly, unreal.   (CP 432)

Emma's unpredictability, exemplified by her 'provokingly' reading during their afternoon excursion towards Boscastle of the previous afternoon, as well as the unfamiliar circumstances in which he encountered her, were crucial to Hardy's poetic fascination with antithetical aspects of her *living*ness. While many Emma-inspired poems, like 'A Duettist' or 'Lost Love', present speculative versions of her experience, transforming her inner life into the emotional and narrative stuff of a Hardy poem, others register his sense of her distance and difference from him. In these his imagination seems wholly arrested by a particular image: Emma singing in an old-fashioned gown or 'standing in the quarry', or, as in this stanza's comparison of her to a bird descended from a cloud to the 'clammy lawn' of the rectory garden, 'Moving alone, bare-browed / In the dim of dawn.'

The independence of the major heroines in Hardy's fiction nearly always ends up compromised by the plots in which he embroils them, from the humiliations inflicted on such as Bathsheba or Ethelberta or Grace Melbury to the more tragic ends suffered by Eustacia and Tess. His poetic figurations of Emma follow a roughly similar trajectory: the kiss towards which this poem builds will come, in other words, at the expense of her singularity and privacy, although the poems that he went on to write about her after her death will present his versions of both. Like 'She Opened the Door', 'At the Word "Farewell"' dramatizes the moment of his entry into the 'strange,

ghostly, unreal' world that he associated with the Cornish Emma, shows us
Hardy stepping 'through the casement to her / Still alone in the gray':

> No prelude did I there perceive
>   To a drama at all,
> Or foreshadow what fortune might weave
>   From beginnings so small;
> But I rose as if quicked by a spur
>   I was bound to obey,
> And stepped through the casement to her
>   Still alone in the gray.
>
> 'I am leaving you...Farewell!' I said,
>   As I followed her on
> By an alley bare boughs overspread;
>   'I soon must be gone!'
> Even then the scale might have been turned
>   Against love by a feather,
> —But crimson one cheek of hers burned
>   When we came in together.   (CP 432–3)

WHAT POETRY MEANT
TO HARDY

1

Votary of the Muse

Hardy's earliest surviving poem is entitled 'Domicilium', Latin for 'settled dwelling place, home, abode'. It was composed, a headnote on a manuscript copy now in the Dorset County Museum attests, between 1857 and 1860, that is between ten and thirteen years before he made his fateful trip to St Juliot. Although never collected in any of his eight individual volumes of verse, the poem was printed in its entirety as a footnote to the second paragraph of the first chapter of the *Life* (L 8–9).[1] It accordingly constitutes the first encounter with Hardy the poet to anyone approaching his life and work in chronological or biographical terms, a notion reinforced by James Gibson's decision to use it as a kind of frontispiece in his 1976 edition of Hardy's *Collected Poems*. Both the *Life* and the *Collected Poems* include on a facing page a sketch by Hardy of the Higher Bockhampton cottage depicted in the poem.

Hardy characterizes the lines as 'Wordsworthian'. With hindsight, however, one can see that they use Wordsworthian diction and blank verse to present a distinctively Hardyan drama, or anti-drama, of backward-looking curiosity, of reticence and occlusion. The opening presents the cottage as largely screened behind an irrepressible natural palisade:

> It faces west, and round the back and sides
> High beeches, bending, hang a veil of boughs,
> And sweep against the roof. Wild honeysucks
> Climb on the walls, and seem to sprout a wish
> (If we may fancy wish of trees and plants)
> To overtop the apple-trees hard by.   (CP 3)

---

[1] This was not in fact its first publication: 'Domicilium' was privately printed in 1916 in an edition of twenty-five copies by Clement Shorter 'for distribution among his friends' (RP 177), and then issued two years later by Florence as a privately printed pamphlet (again the print run was twenty-five copies) (RP 208).

Woman Much Missed: Thomas Hardy, Emma Hardy, and Poetry. Mark Ford, Oxford University Press.
© Mark Ford 2023. DOI: 10.1093/oso/9780192886804.003.0002

The inward-looking aspects of Hardy's familial culture seem subliminally figured in these arboreal and vegetative lines of defence. Change, further, is presented in the paternal grandmother's speech that makes up the poem's last lines as an inherently dubious and disruptive process.

> 'Fifty years
> Have passed since then, my child, and change has marked
> The face of all things. Yonder garden-plots
> And orchards were uncultivated slopes
> O'ergrown with bramble bushes, furze and thorn:
> That road a narrow path shut in by ferns,
> Which, almost trees, obscured the passer-by.
>
> 'Our house stood quite alone, and those tall firs
> And beeches were not planted. Snakes and efts
> Swarmed in the summer days, and nightly bats
> Would fly about our bedrooms. Heathcroppers
> Lived on the hills, and were our only friends;
> So wild it was when first we settled here.'   (CP 3-4)

The history of Hardy's extended family would prove an almost bottomless resource for the plots and characters and anecdotes developed in both his fiction and his poetry; and the 'domicilium' in Higher Bockhampton never lost for long its primary status in either his imagination or indeed in his 'life-loyalties', to borrow a term from 'In a Wood' (CP 65). But from another angle—an angle gestured towards even in this very early poem—Hardy's entire writing career can also be construed as a threat to, or even a betrayal of, the singularity and separation of the 'home' so vividly treasured in the speech here attributed to Mary Head (1772–1857). The vigorous and untrammelled riot of wildlife—snakes and efts and bats and heathcroppers—suggests a privileged closeness to nature extirpated by the conversion of bramble bushes and furze and thorn into garden plots and orchards. A path hemmed in by ferns that, like the honeysuckle of the opening lines, grew almost to the height of trees, more effectively 'obscured' the cottage from the attentions of a passer-by than its modern replacement, a road through a plantation of firs and beeches. 'Our house', Hardy's grandmother declares, 'stood quite alone': an ancestral pride in sturdy independence and self-reliant inwardness inflects the poem's use of the stock romantic ideals of pastoral solitude and a pristine relationship to nature just enough to make one feel that the poem is articulating something close to a private family creed, one passed down the generations and both embedded and embodied in the cottage at Higher Bockhampton, which was similarly handed down from one generation to the next.

While it may seem that I am over-reading a fairly generic piece of juvenilia—one characterized by Hardy himself in the *Life* as 'obvious and naïve' (L 8)—I feel the poem is both obliquely revealing of the inherent insularity of the Hardy clan and implicitly raises issues about what was involved in writing for the public about such matters. But my main reason for evoking it is because it throws into such striking relief the poems that Hardy went on to write in the mid-1860s during his five-year sojourn in London. 'Domicilium' demonstrates the appeal to the teenage Hardy of a poetry that is rooted and communal and pastoral. Hardy the Londoner, on the other hand, found himself in a wholly antithetical situation: deracinated, largely solitary, and attempting to survive in, and make sense of, the largest city on the planet. Unsurprisingly, therefore, at the moments when the Wordsworthian does resurface in early poems like the sonnet 'From Her in the Country', composed in 1866 in Hardy's lodgings near Paddington Station at 16 Westbourne Park Villas, it is only to be ruthlessly exposed and derided. The female speaker of this poem struggles with all her 'force of will' to convince herself that she is enjoying an uplifting, *Lyrical Ballads*-style relationship with 'bird, and bush, and tree', but to no avail:

> for I could not see worth
> Enough around to charm a midge or fly,
>
> And mused again on city din and sin,
> Longing to madness I might move therein!   (CP 234)

And the ballad 'The Ruined Maid' similarly upends readerly expectations of the kind fostered by the poetry of Wordsworth or the Dorset dialect poet William Barnes. Rural dialect is here deployed only to dramatize the gulf in sophistication between the fallen but now elegantly dressed and well-spoken 'Melia and her envious visitor from the country:

> —'At home in the barton you said "thee" and "thou",
> And "thik oon", and "theäs oon", and "t'other"; but now
> Your talking quite fits 'ee for high compa-ny!'—
> 'Some polish is gained with one's ruin,' said she.   (CP 159)

Indeed, far from pitying or condemning 'Melia for succumbing to the life of an urban courtesan, her childhood friend is overcome with jealousy, and, like the speaker of 'From Her in the Country', reveals herself eager to plunge into the 'din and sin' of city life:

> —'I wish I had feathers, a fine sweeping gown,
> And a delicate face, and could strut about Town!'—
> 'My dear—a raw country girl, such as you be,
> Cannot quite expect that. You ain't ruined,' said she.

It was during his residence of over five years in London (from April 1862 to July 1867) that Hardy discovered himself to be 'a votary of the muse' (LLI 7). The phrase comes from the short story 'An Imaginative Woman' published in *The Pall Mall Magazine* in 1894 and collected in *Wessex Tales* of 1896 and then in the Wessex Edition of *Life's Little Ironies* of 1912. The imaginative woman or votary of the muse in question is Ella Marchmill, an 'impressionable palpitating creature' obsessed with poetry, which she herself writes and occasionally gets published under the pseudonym of 'John Ivy'. She is also, however, the mother of three small children and unhappily married to a midlands gun-manufacturer whose 'soul', as Hardy puts it with deft irony, 'was in that business always'. The opposition between the poetic or 'imaginative' and the economic and practical that recurs so frequently in Hardy's fiction is mordantly enacted in the tale. Ella is particularly enamoured of the poetry of Robert Trewe—altered from Crewe in the manuscript, to heighten his contrast to the industrializing Marchmill—and she is delighted when it turns out that her husband has by chance rented for a family holiday in Solentsea (based on Southsea in Hampshire) the very rooms that Trewe occupies for most of the year, but vacates during the summer months, for reasons that the landlady outlines to Ella:

> 'You see he's a different sort of young man from most—dreamy, solitary, rather melancholy—and he cares more to be here when the Southwesterly gales are beating against the door, and the sea washes over the Parade, and there's not a soul in the place, than he does now in the season.'   (LLI 9–10)

Trewe is a compound of clichés derived from popular Victorian conceptions of the poet and was probably loosely based on one of the most ostentatiously poetic figures of the era, Dante Gabriel Rossetti, from whose sonnet 'Stillborn Love' the story quotes at a climactic moment. Nevertheless, Hardy invests Ella's fantasy of an aesthetic, spiritual, and indeed—although she never actually meets him—erotic relationship with the sensitive and reclusive Trewe with a considerable degree of pathos. The daughter of an unsuccessful man of letters, it is only through poetry that Ella can 'find a congenial channel in which to let flow her painfully embayed emotions, whose former limpidity and sparkle seemed departing in the stagnation caused by the routine of a practical household and the gloom of bearing children to a commonplace father' (LLI 11). When shown by the landlady some of Trewe's scribblings on the wall above the bed ('My belief is that he wakes up in the night, you know, with some rhyme in his head, and jots it down there on the wall lest he should forget it by the morning' (LLI 13)), she is unable 'to conceal a rush of tender curiosity', and finds herself flushing. She dresses up in his clothes, kisses his photograph, and caresses his pencilled phrases until 'it seemed as if his very breath, warm and loving, fanned her cheeks from those walls' (LLI 19).

While there is undoubtedly an element of satire in Hardy's depiction of the doleful poet—we are told that his 'large dark eyes' convey 'an unlimited capacity for misery' (LLI 18)—as well as of his swooning acolyte, the story is also a transposition of precisely the dilemma that confronted Hardy when he was seized, in his mid-twenties, by the conviction that he was at heart a poet. 'A sense of the truth of poetry, of its supreme place in literature, had awakened itself in me,' he wrote in a passage excerpted in the *Life* recalling his overwhelming sense of poetic vocation during his time in London; 'At the risk of ruining all my worldly prospects I dabbled in it…was forced out of it…' (L 415—the ellipses are Hardy's). Although Trewe enjoys more success with magazine editors and poetry publishers than the young Hardy ever did, and suffers from no money worries, being in receipt of a private income that proves enough, as his landlady puts it, 'to write verses on' (LLI 10), he too finds the life of a poet in Victorian England to be unsustainable. Trewe is 'forced out of it', however, not by the indifference or the conservatism of those in charge of the poetry industry, but by the lack of a 'tenderly devoted' female friend (LLI 27).

'An Imaginative Woman' not only makes inventive narrative use of Hardy's unending fascination with the dichotomy between the poetic and the worldly; it also extends the increasingly bleak diagnosis carried out in his fiction of the 1890s of a related polarity—that of the war between the spirit and the flesh. Robert Trewe and William Marchmill, like Angel and Alec of *Tess of the d'Urbervilles*, or Sue and Arabella of *Jude the Obscure*

(1895), pull in wholly antithetical directions, and Ella, like Tess and Jude, falls victim to the resulting tug of war. After learning that her husband won't be returning until the next day from a boat trip, she allows herself to indulge in her fantasy of communing with Trewe. Lying in his bed, surrounded by his verses, both as printed in his books and as drafted in pencil on the wall above her, brushing his photograph with her lips, she gives her poetic-erotic reverie full rein:

> She thought how wicked she was, a woman having a husband and three children, to let her mind stray to a stranger in this unconscionable manner. No: he was not a stranger! She knew his thoughts and feelings as well as she knew her own; they were, in fact, the selfsame thoughts and feelings as hers; which her husband distinctly lacked; perhaps luckily for himself, considering that he had to provide for family expenses...And now her hair was dragging where his arm had lain when he secured the fugitive fancies: she was sleeping on a poet's lips, immersed in the very essence of him, permeated by his spirit as by an ether.
>
> While she was dreaming the minutes away thus a footstep came upon the stairs, and in a moment she heard her husband's heavy step on the landing immediately without.
>
> 'Ell! where are you?'   (LLI 19–20 [my ellipsis])

He has returned early, somewhat drunk, and determined to assert his connubial rights, a determination made clearer in the manuscript, in which Ella hears him pulling off his clothes, than in the bowlderized version published in *The Pall Mall Magazine* and subsequent printings. Even after these cuts, however, the text is unambiguous: 'I wanted to be with you tonight,' Marchmill asserts, after stooping and kissing his wife.

The vision of poetry as romance cherished by Ella, and by Hardy himself in his twenties, is brought into crude collision with the realist novelist's depiction of marriage as a commercial transaction devised as a means of sanctioning or procuring sex. Marchmill is surprised to discover the next morning that he has been sleeping on top of the photograph of some unknown 'bloke', although he subsequently comes to believe that the child conceived by Ella that night has been physically, as well as imaginatively, fathered by Trewe. This is not possible since, despite a series of near-misses, the ideal poet-lovers never actually meet in the flesh; and yet the narrative ingeniously manages to intimate that they inadvertently cause each other's deaths. Trewe shoots himself in the head shortly after reading a vicious review of his recently published volume of verse, 'Lyrics to a Woman Unknown'. In a letter to a friend written shortly before his suicide and read out at the inquest, he suggests that the main reason, however, that he will be taking this drastic step is the absence from his life of the imaginary woman to whom his passionate lyrics are addressed—a woman, as his letter makes clear, exactly like Ella Marchmill:

> I have long dreamt of such an unattainable creature, as you know; and she, this undiscoverable, elusive one, inspired my last volume; the imaginary woman alone; for in spite of what has been said in some quarters there is no real woman behind the title. She has continued to the last unrevealed, unmet, unwon.   (LLI 27)

'O,' Ella bursts out on reading this, 'if he had only known of me—known of me—me!...O if I had only once met him—only once; and put my hand upon his hot forehead—kissed him—let him know how I loved him...' It is highly appropriate that the only individual poem by Trewe mentioned in the story is a ballad entitled 'Severed Lives' (LLI 16).[2]

Some months later Ella herself dies while giving birth to the child conceived on the night that Marchmill interrupted her poetic-erotic fantasies of Trewe, the implication being that it was these fantasies that made conception possible. And some years later, in a further twist, the remarried Marchmill comes across the photograph of Trewe, along with a lock of his hair obtained for Ella from the corpse of the poet by his Solentsea landlady, and finds himself pondering the looks of the child, now a noisy toddler, who caused his first wife's death:

> [H]e took him on his knee, held the lock of hair against the child's head, and set up the photograph on the table behind, so that he could closely

---

[2] Dante Gabriel Rossetti's sonnet 'Severed Selves' expresses longings similar to Ella Marchmill's. Its octet runs:

> Two separate divided silences,
> Which, brought together, would find loving voice;
> Two glances which together would rejoice
> In love, now lost like stars beyond dark trees;
> Two hands apart whose touch alone gives ease;
> Two bosoms which, heart-shrined with mutual flame,
> Would, meeting in one clasp, be made the same;
> Two souls, the shores wave-mocked of sundering seas...

(Dante Gabriel Rossetti, *Collected Poetry and Prose*, ed. Jerome McGann (New Haven: Yale University Press, 2003), 145).

compare the features each countenance presented. By a known but inexplicable trick of Nature there were undoubtedly strong traces of resemblance to the man Ella had never seen; the dreamy and peculiar expression of the poet's face sat, as the transmitted idea, upon the child's, and the hair was of the same hue.   (LLI 32)[3]

'Then she *did* play me false with that fellow at the lodgings!' he exclaims angrily, before turning on the child that he now believes was begotten by Trewe: 'Get away, you poor little brat! You are nothing to me!'

Robert Trewe and Ella Marchmill are the last of the poet-figures to appear in Hardy's fiction. It is striking to note that their predecessors, Ethelberta Petherwin of *The Hand of Ethelberta* (1876) and George Somerset of *A Laodicean* (1881), are similarly 'forced out' of poetry (L 415). Ethelberta publishes a volume of verse entitled 'Metres by Me' (changed to 'Metres by E.' in later editions) which leads to her being disinherited by her wealthy mother-in-law and having to turn herself into a professional storyteller to support her extended family. Somerset, on the other hand, spends two years in his twenties composing 'in every conceivable metre except an original one, and on every conceivable subject, from Wordsworthian sonnets on the singing of his tea-kettle to epic fragments on the fall of Empires',[4] but fails to get any of his work into print at all; he accordingly returns to his original profession, that of architect. The links between the experiences of these characters and those of their creator would not have been apparent to contemporary readers of these novels, although a poem of Hardy's, 'The Fire at Tranter Sweatley's' (later retitled 'The Bride-Night Fire'), had been published in the *Gentleman's Magazine* in 1875. Hardy clearly derived a lugubrious

---

[3] In his Prefatory Note to *Life's Little Ironies* of May 1912 Hardy suggests that 'medical practitioners and other observers of such manifestations' are aware of the 'trick of Nature' that has made Ella give birth to a child who resembles her imaginary lover rather than the child's biological father (LLI 3). Hardy's source for this somewhat implausible phenomenon was probably the final chapter of August Weismann's *Essays on Heredity and Kindred Biological Problems*, Vol. 1 (1891), in which Weismann asserts: 'But it cannot be denied that there are a few undoubtedly genuine observations upon cases in which some character in the child reminds us in a striking manner of a deep psychical impression by which the mother was strongly affected during pregnancy' (*Essays on Heredity and Kindred Biological Problems*, Vol. 1 (Oxford: Clarendon Press, 1891), 456–7). Entry 1281 in Hardy's *Literary Notebooks*, Vol. 1 (ed. Lennart A. Bjork (New York: New York University Press, 1985)) is concerned with Weismann's theories (148).

[4] *A Laodicean*, ed. John Schad (London: Penguin, 1997), 5.

pleasure from inserting into his fiction covert references to the failure of his early poetic ambitions. Trewe, we are informed, 'perpetrated sonnets in the loosely-rhymed Elizabethan fashion, which every right-minded reviewer said he ought not to have done' (LLI 11): of the thirty Hardy poems composed between 1865 and 1867 that survive, over a third are sonnets richly indebted to the Elizabethans, and their loose, or at least surprising, rhymes include 'call to me / ecstasy' (CP 9), 'them less / listlessness' (CP 11), 'I will / domicile' (CP 15) 'debtor says / forgetfulness' (CP 234). And we are told that Ethelberta's debut volume concludes with a 'whimsical and rather affecting love-lament' that suggests the influence of Sir Thomas Wyatt;[5] its title, 'Cancelled Words', is surely a private joke on magazine editors' responses to the young Hardy's attempts to get his own effusions into print.

'By as early as the end of 1863,' Hardy records in the London chapter of the *Life*, 'he had recommenced to read a great deal—with a growing tendency towards poetry' (L 49). This tendency would—or at least as he tells it in his autobiography—develop into a mania and prove a major factor in the breakdown of his health in the summer of 1867. Although it is possible that the *Life* exaggerates his addiction to poetry during his London years, as part of its overall strategy of celebrating Hardy the instinctive poet over Hardy the professional novelist, there is no doubt that he engaged in an intense and deeply personal perusal of a significant number of English and Scottish poets during these years. The range of his reading is most fully illustrated by his '*Studies, Specimens &c.*' notebook, in use mainly between 1865 and 1867. Into this he copied out lines and passages from poets such as Spenser, Shakespeare, Lodge, Milton, Wordsworth, Coleridge, Scott, Burns, Byron, Shelley, Ingelow, Tennyson, and Swinburne, as well as verses from the Bible. On occasion the chosen extracts are followed by reformulations, or 'concoctions' to use his own term, of lines or images to create curious composite phrases, or riffs on given words, as if he were learning a foreign language: 'her / lips slack with sorrow : if time would slack / a little : his love is slacked…hasty pants : hasty / treads : hasty heart : marches of pleasure, march / into death, the grave : march through the years, / march through your beauty…' (SS 70–1). This obsessive word-spinning suggests the high stakes involved in Hardy's commitment to poetry during these years: since, as he put it in the *Life*, he had come to believe that 'in verse was concentrated the essence of all imaginative and emotional literature, to read verse and

---

[5] *The Hand of Ethelberta*, ed. Tim Dolin (London: Penguin, 1996), 26.

nothing else was the shortest way to the fountain-head... And in fact for nearly or quite two years he did not read a word of prose except such as came under his eye in the daily newspapers and weekly reviews' (L 51).

About half of the thirty poems that Hardy composed between 1865 and 1867 and later published depict or refract a relationship between a man and a woman. With a few exceptions, such as 'Her Definition' and 'The Musing Maiden', they rigorously avoid allowing the reader to feel that the relationship that they dramatize has any chance of prospering. As Hardy later pointed out in 'After Reading Psalms XXXIX, XL, etc.', 'At my start by Helicon / Love-lore little wist I' (dated 187-, CP 697). The keynotes struck are disappointment, disillusionment, evasion, recrimination, and unreturned or thwarted desire; to nearly all could be affixed the title of Trewe's ballad, 'Severed Lives'. There is, then, a startling mismatch between Hardy's exalted figurations of poetry as essential or 'supreme', as the 'heart of literature' (PW 246), as the surest path to the 'fountain-head' of meaning, and the drab, embittered diagnoses of failed romance that one finds in early poems such as 'Amabel' (prompted by his disappointing reunion with Julia Augusta Martin) or 'At a Bridal' or 'Neutral Tones'. From the outset Hardy was drawn to scenarios and tableaux that undermine belief in 'heroism and worth', and work instead to foster 'visions ghast and grim' (CP 829), to borrow terms from 'Discouragement' (dated 1863–7, and so the earliest begun of Hardy's London poems). 'Her Dilemma' of 1866 is a good example of the thoroughness with which the early Hardy set about conjugating the discouraging aspects of existence:

> The two were silent in a sunless church,
> Whose mildewed walls, uneven paving-stones,
> And wasted carvings passed antique research;
> And nothing broke the clock's dull monotones.
>
> Leaning against a wormy poppy-head,
> So wan and worn that he could scarcely stand,
> —For he was soon to die,—he softly said,
> 'Tell me you love me!'—holding hard her hand.
>
> She would have given a world to breathe 'yes' truly,
> So much his life seemed hanging on her mind,
> And hence she lied, her heart persuaded throughly
> 'Twas worth her soul to be a moment kind.

But the sad need thereof, his nearing death,
So mocked humanity that she shamed to prize
A world conditioned thus, or care for breath
Where Nature such dilemmas could devise.   (CP 13–14)

The poem registers the shock attendant upon Hardy's loss of religious faith
in the mid-1860s in a manner at once daring and vehement. The sunless
church's 'mildewed walls, uneven paving-stones', 'wasted carvings', and
'wormy poppy-head' read like a series of emblems of the decay and collapse
of Christianity, which the poem figures as inevitably succumbing to the march
of time, the 'clock's dull monotones'. Hardy himself, the evidence suggests,
did not conclusively abandon his hopes of going to Cambridge and then
taking up holy orders until the summer of 1865, and it is surely no coincidence
that his poetry mania began shortly afterwards ('he wrote constantly', he
records in the *Life*, 'through the years 1866 and most of 1867' (L 51)). His
poetic ambitions may have reached the pitch they did in this period because
he was on the rebound, so to speak, from the breakdown of his religious
beliefs; and the dilemma that his apostasy caused him is surely mirrored in
the dilemma here imposed on the woman who must pretend to her dying
admirer that she returns his love.[6] Beneath the far-fetched, even melodramatic narrative developed in the poem looms an existential question that
Hardy's writing, however attentive to specifics or contingencies, never avoids
for long: how best to live in 'a world conditioned thus'?

One answer was—by writing poetry. Thirty years after composing 'Her
Dilemma', and two years before it appeared in *Wessex Poems* in 1898, Hardy
observed in a diary entry:

Poetry. Perhaps I can express more fully in verse ideas and emotions
which run counter to the inert crystallized opinion—hard as a rock—
which the vast body of men have vested interests in supporting. To cry out
in a passionate poem that (for instance) the Supreme Mover or Movers,
the Prime Force or Forces, must be either limited in power, unknowing, or

---

[6] This poem, like 'Coming Up Oxford Street: Evening', was one in which Hardy switched
when revising from first to third person. The manuscript has 'We two were silent...holding
long my hand...I would have given a world', and so on (CPVE 14).

cruel—which is obvious enough, and has been for centuries—will cause them merely a shake of the head; but to put it in argumentative prose will make them sneer, or foam, and set all the literary contortionists jumping upon me, a harmless agnostic, as if I were a clamorous atheist, which in their crass illiteracy they seem to think is the same thing...If Galileo had said in verse that the world moved, the Inquisition might have let him alone.   (L 302)

Poetry is here imagined affording Hardy a licence to voice unpalatable truths, which, because presented in verse, will occasion merely 'a shake of the head' rather than the uproar caused by a novel such as *Jude the Obscure*, published the previous year. He is careful not to suggest that his 'ideas and emotions' will alter 'inert crystallized opinion' if expressed in poetry, positing only that there they will have the freedom to 'run counter' to it. Hardy here implies that the cultural assumptions surrounding the genre of poetry, which had been steadily marginalized during the Victorian era, allied with the pleasures of rhyme and metre, will serve to suspend any objections that the reader might have to the vision of life expressed by the poem. Without quite suggesting that poetry 'makes nothing happen',[7] as Auden would put it in his elegy for W. B. Yeats, he yet sees poetry as able to approach 'ideas and emotions' from an angle that makes polemical attack or ideological protest more difficult. An earlier note, of 22 July 1883, applies a musical analogy to the same issue: 'Poetry versus reason: e.g., A band plays "God save the Queen", and being musical the uncompromising Republican joins in the harmony: a hymn rolls from a church-window, and the uncompromising No-God-ist or Unconscious-God-ist takes up the refrain' (L 167).[8]

The concept of freedom frequently features in Hardy's ruminations on the appeal of poetry. Despite the amount of quotidian detail contained in his poetic oeuvre—more, surely, than in any other poet in English—Hardy enjoyed borrowing from romantics such as Shelley and Keats in his figurations of poetry as an abstract or spiritual realm beyond the everyday: 'Christmas Day [1890].—While thinking of resuming "the viewless wings of

---

[7] 'In Memory of W. B. Yeats', *The English Auden*, ed. Edward Mendelson (London: Faber & Faber, 1977), 242 (l. 36).

[8] This notion recurs in an idea for a poem to be called 'The Sceptic's Doom' outlined in Hardy's *'Poetical Matter' Notebook*: 'Jan 1899. Poem. "The Sceptic's Doom" He is compelled by his passion for church music to go continually to Cathedrals & churches, & sing & sing & sing, unable to leave off. (He may relate this in the manner of The Ancient Mariner)' (PM 30).

poesy" before dawn this morning, new horizons seemed to open and worrying pettinesses to disappear' (L 241). Bound up with this freedom was a sense of the opportunities for camouflage or reticence afforded by poetry, although he could speak on both sides of the equation when it came to determining whether his poetry was or wasn't a means of self-revelation. He had Florence reply to a letter enquiring about the biographical sources of *Jude the Obscure* with a tart assertion that there was 'not a scrap of personal detail in it', before advising his impertinent correspondent that 'there is more autobiography in a hundred lines of Mr Hardy's poetry than in all the novels' (L 425). And yet in the prefaces included before each of his first three volumes (all published, it's worth noting, before he had composed the obviously personal poetry occasioned by the death of Emma), Hardy pointedly insisted on the 'dramatic or personative' nature of his poems (CP 6): 'Of the subject-matter of this volume—even that which is in other than narrative form—much is dramatic or impersonative even where not explicitly so,' he wrote in the Preface to *Poems of the Past and the Present* (1901, CP 84), and in that to *Time's Laughingstocks* (1909): 'the sense of disconnection, particularly in respect of those lyrics penned in the first person, will be immaterial when it is borne in mind that they are to be regarded, in the main, as dramatic monologues by different characters' (CP 190). He was, analogously, anxious to make clear that the poems gathered in each volume did not articulate his own particular 'philosophy of life' and were best approached as a series of 'unadjusted impressions' that conveyed 'little cohesion of thought' (CP 84).

Hardy's private reflections on his own poetry, as well as his public pronouncements about how it should be read, often suggest the fascinating tension between the active and the passive that was fundamental to what was involved for him in being a 'votary of the muse'. In his 1911 General Preface to the Wessex Edition he makes the usual disclaimers that no 'objectless consistency' is being aimed at, and that all his poetry can offer are 'mere impressions of the moment, and not convictions or arguments' (PW 49), before outlining his hope that his poetry might eventually come to constitute a kind of Balzacian *comédie humaine*, a 'comprehensive cycle' of volumes in which poems 'in dramatic, ballad and narrative form should include most of the cardinal situations which occur in social and public life, and those in lyric form a round of emotional experiences of some completeness' (PW 49–50). One must square, to put it another way, the invigorating sweep and scope of the poet who planned and composed *The Dynasts* with the unobtrusive humility of the poet who wrote 'Any Little Old Song':

Any little old song
        Will do for me,
Tell it of joys gone long,
        Or joys to be,
Or friendly faces best
        Loved to see.

Newest themes I want not
        On subtle strings,
And for thrillings pant not
        That new song brings:
I only need the homeliest
        Of heartstirrings.   (CP 702)

Hardy was clearly proud, as the *Life* often demonstrates, of his lack of the kind of drive associated with many Victorian success stories. A typical diary entry—this one made some eight months after settling in Tooting in 1878—runs: 'November 28. Woke before it was light. Felt that I had not enough staying power to hold my own in the world' (L 127). And in the mid-1890s, at the height of his commercial success, he abandoned his habit of jotting down 'memoranda' on the grounds that he no longer felt the details of his life worth preserving: 'His personal ambition in a worldly sense, which had always been weak, dwindled to nothing, and for some years after 1895 or 1896 he requested that no record of his life should be made' (L 328). Only poetry was exempt from this temporary ban on writing—'his verses being kept going from pleasure in them'. And, in line with these self-figurations, his poetry was not to be considered as an act of will, but as a yielding to a '*tendency*':

> Thomas Hardy was always a person with an unconscious, or rather unreasoning, *tendency*, and the poetic tendency had been his from the earliest. He would tell that it used to be said of him at Sir Arthur Blomfield's [the London architect in whose offices he worked from 1862 to 1867]: 'Hardy, there can hardly have been anybody in the world with less ambition than you.'   (L 415)

But, for all such protestations, Hardy's sense of being a chosen and dedicated votary of the muse also finds its way into his poetry. At times his knowledge of his poetic election is treated like an intensely private secret that irradiates his everyday experience, but needs to be guarded from prying eyes:

> In the seventies I was bearing in my breast,
> > Penned tight,
> Certain starry thoughts that threw a magic light
> On the worktimes and the soundless hours of rest
> In the seventies; aye, I bore them in my breast
> > Penned tight.   ('In the Seventies', CP 459)

These 'starry thoughts' and 'magic light' were bound up during the years on which this poem reflects with his burgeoning love for Emma as well as his sense of being a literary man of destiny. Both romance, however, and his inner conviction of his vocation had to remain, for the moment, 'penned tight' or 'locked' in him, 'immuned', as he puts it, 'from the chillings of misprision'. Although neighbours, and even his friend (possibly a reference to Horace Moule) shake their heads and reflect 'Alas, / For his onward years and name unless he mend', Hardy here presents himself as triumphantly sustained by a 'vision' that 'nought could darken or destroy', despite the barriers that it erects between the poet-in-waiting and those around him.

At other moments his separation is more starkly expressed. In 'Wessex Heights', for instance, of 1896, written in the wake of the scandal caused by *Jude the Obscure* and the collapse of his hopes of a romantic relationship with Florence Henniker, Hardy figures himself as a derided outcast: 'In the lowlands I have no comrade, not even the lone man's friend— / Her who suffereth long and is kind [i.e. Charity]' (CP 319).[9] Down in these lowlands, by which he means society at large, 'nobody thinks as I', and accordingly he is vilified by all and sundry. Gothic phantoms, who seem a compound of prying journalists with their 'weird detective ways' and friends that he can no longer trust, pursue him through the towns, 'and they say harsh heavy things— / Men with a wintry sneer, and women with tart disparagings'. His response is to assume the mantle of a prophet in the wilderness, and to flee (metaphorically at least) to the Wessex Heights, symbolized by Ingpen Beacon, Wylls-Neck, Bulbarrow, and Pilsdon Crest.[10] Only while roaming around these modest elevations can he preserve belief in his 'liberty', along with a sense of the 'simple self that was'.

---

[9] 'Charity suffereth long and is kind' (1 Corinthians 13:4).

[10] Bulbarrow Hill (5 miles west of Blandford Forum) retains its original name, but the others have been slightly altered: Inkpen Beacon is in Berkshire, Will's Neck in the Quantocks in Somerset, and Pilsdon Pen (4 miles west of Beaminster) in Dorset.

Such moments of explicit defiance are relatively rare in Hardy, and 'Wessex Heights' is probably the closest he comes to adopting the pose of a Shelleyan prophet-victim—'I fall upon the thorns of life! I bleed!'[11] He was, however, frequently drawn to the image of a courageous individual delivering a vatic speech to a multitude, like St Paul in 'In the British Museum', 'Facing the crowd, / A small gaunt figure with wasted features, / Calling out loud' (CP 382), or the Paul imagined preaching to passing Londoners on the steps of the cathedral named after him in 'In St Paul's a While Ago', lifting 'his hand / In stress of eager, stammering speech', only to be dismissed by those who pause to listen as an 'epilept enthusiast'(CP 717).[12]

The prophet Elijah was another embattled biblical figure whose story meant much to Hardy. His first surviving letter, written from London to his sister Mary on 17 August 1862, opens ' "After the fire a still small voice"—I just come from the evening service at St. Mary's Kilburn & this verse, which I always notice, was in the 1st Lesson' (CL I 1). In the chapter in Kings in question, the still small voice follows a series of cataclysmic upheavals wrought by wind, earthquake, and fire, and is the Lord demanding of the prophet, 'What doest thou here?'[13] In 'Quid Hic Agis?' (originally titled 'In Time of Slaughter'), published in the *Spectator* in August 1916, Hardy reflects on the very personal importance that these verses would end up accruing for him. Part I recalls a service in the church at Lesnewth (a village near St Juliot) during the first summer of his courtship of Emma at which this passage was read; being unable to see into the future, the eager young lover cannot

>   apprehend
>   As I sat to the end
>   And watched for her smile
>   Across the sunned aisle,
>   That this tale of a seer

[11] 'Ode to the West Wind', *Shelley's Poetry and Prose*, eds. Donald H. Reiman and Sharon B. Powers (New York: Norton, 1977), 223 (l. 54).

[12] For a more detailed discussion of Hardy's identification with St Paul, see my *Thomas Hardy: Half a Londoner* (Cambridge, MA: Harvard University Press, 2016), 244–51.

[13] 1 Kings 19:13. 'An Imaginative Woman' also evokes the poetic powers that Hardy associated with the Old Testament prophet: 'The mantle of Elijah,' Ella Marchmill remarks after she has donned Trewe's mackintosh and waterproof cap; 'Would it might inspire me to rival him, glorious genius that he is!' (LLI 15). The Thomas Hardy Memorial Window in Stinsford Church, designed by Douglas A. Strachan and unveiled two years after Hardy's death, depicts Elijah, robed in purple, listening to the Lord's still small voice.

> Which came once a year
> Might, when sands were heaping,
> Be like a sweat creeping,
> Or in any degree
> Bear on her or on me!   (CP 441)

Part II expands on the nature of this private significance, for here Hardy recalls a later service at Lesnewth at which he read this particular lesson himself, as his partial avatar, Henry Knight, does, in *A Pair of Blue Eyes* (PBE 169)—although F. B. Pinion has persuasively argued that here the poem may also have strayed into fiction, since Hardy was not in fact in Cornwall on any subsequent Sundays when this lesson was read.[14] Nevertheless, being entrusted with readings at services by Emma's brother-in-law, the Revd Caddell Holder, was clearly a token of respect, and possibly even interpreted by Hardy as confirmation of his suitability as a prospective husband for Emma.[15] The passage's association with the parched days of August is proleptically developed in this second section of the poem into a metaphor for the 'drought' that would later afflict their relationship:

> I did not see
> What drought might be
> With me, with her,
> As the Kalendar
> Moved on, and Time
> Devoured our prime.   (CP 442)

By the time of the last part of this triptych, which is set in the present, Emma is dead, and Hardy finds himself, like Elijah, 'spiritless / In the wilderness'. The wind, earthquake, and fire of the chapter in Kings now summon up the artillery barrages of the First World War, and the still small voice seems to be admonishing the poet for his inactivity in this desperate crisis. As Elijah took to his cave in the wilderness but was found there by the Lord's still small voice, so Hardy has evaded the prophetic role that,

[14] 'Hardy's Visits to Cornwall' by F. B. Pinion, in *New Perspectives on Thomas Hardy*, ed. Charles P. C. Pettit (Basingstoke: Macmillan, 1994), 204.

[15] Hardy's Bible and prayerbook reveal that on 8 September 1872 he read both lessons (Jeremiah 36 and Romans 9) at the afternoon Sunday service of the recently reopened St Juliot Church (MM 135).

the poem implies, he ought somehow to be fulfilling. 'But now', the poem concludes,

> I shrink from sight
> And desire the night,
> (Though, as in old wise,
> I might still arise,
> Go forth, and stand
> And prophesy in the land),
> I feel the shake
> Of wind and earthquake,
> And consuming fire
> Nigher and nigher,
> And the voice catch clear,
> 'What doest thou here?'

While the form that this prophetic mission might take is not revealed, the poem's stirring conclusion harks back to the earnestness with which the blinded Clym Yeobright of *The Return of the Native* adopts the role of an itinerant open-air preacher after he too has become a widower. Clym's sermons or addresses, we are told, were 'sometimes secular, and sometimes religious, but never dogmatic'.[16] Like, say, 'The Oxen' or 'Afternoon Service at Mellstock', 'Quid Hic Agis?' reveals how adeptly Hardy's poetry fuses the secular and the religious, managing to model and inhabit narratives of belief and commitment, without itself believing in or committing to those narratives. Not the least of the attractions of poetry to Hardy was the way it allowed him to remain 'churchy' (L 407), despite his scepticism, in a manner that had become impossible for him in prose.

Although in 'Wessex Heights' he represents himself as a simple country soul at the mercy of unscrupulous urban sophisticates, as a pariah whose sufferings, like those of Clym, have forced him to abandon the conventions and dictates of society, Hardy was acutely aware that he was anything but simple. Indeed, as the *Life* often makes clear, he keenly relished the extent

[16] *The Return of the Native*, ed. Simon Gatrell (Oxford: Oxford University Press, 2005), 389.

to which his seeming simplicity successfully cloaked his true thoughts and feelings:

> [N]one of the society-men who met him suspected from his simple manner the potentialities of observation that were in him. The unassertive air, unconsciously worn, served him as an invisible coat almost to uncanniness. At houses and clubs where he encountered other writers and critics and world-practised readers of character, whose bearing towards him was often as towards one who did not reach their altitudes, he was seeing through them as though they were glass.   (L 408)

Unlike those who sneer at him in 'Wessex Heights', however, or its tartly disparaging women, Hardy refrained from making public his views of these writers and critics who patronized him: 'He set down', he tells us, 'some cutting and satirical notes on their qualities and compass, but destroyed all of them, not wishing to leave behind him anything which could be deemed a gratuitous belittling of others.'

The title poem of Hardy's fifth collection develops in rich and complex detail what was involved in seeing through people 'as though they were glass' and constitutes his most determined attempt to articulate and assess the role that poetry might play in the shaping of consciousness. 'Moments of Vision' conjugates the standard Renaissance trope of art as a mirror, probing the implications of the image in relation to the quest for self-knowledge, as well as in relation to the impulse to evade it. The issues are framed, however, in a manner that is insistently modern: in the absence of God, who is there to make ultimate sense of the account that art's mirroring, or indeed any act of self-reflection, tallies up and presents? And where, the poem asks, in a move that dizzyingly widens the scope of its enquiry, do our assumptions about such matters come from? To use its own imagery, who is the one lifting and holding the mirror in which we trace and judge our lives, and, given that there is no divinity or afterlife, what status can such tracings and judgements possibly have?

> That mirror
> Which makes of men a transparency,
> Who holds that mirror
> And bids us such a breast-bare spectacle see
> Of you and me?

That mirror
Whose magic penetrates like a dart,
Who lifts that mirror
And throws our mind back on us, and our heart,
Until we start?

That mirror
Works well in these night hours of ache;
Why in that mirror
Are tincts we never see ourselves once take
When the world is awake?

That mirror
Can test each mortal when unaware;
Yea, that strange mirror
May catch his last thoughts, whole life foul or fair,
Glassing it—where?   (CP 427)

The magic inner light of 'In the Seventies' is here transformed into a piercing dart, or pang of self-recrimination, that takes the heart by surprise. The moment of vision is depicted as dramatically arriving in a manner beyond the poet's control, and as delivering the kind of truth that the active or daytime mind avoids or suppresses. The 'breast-bare spectacle' that the poet sees in the mirror is a discomfiting one, and the poem proceeds wholly to undo any romantic implications that readers may bring to its title. Whereas a Wordsworthian moment of vision or spot of time will put the poet in touch with mysterious energies that seem to fuse the natural, the human, and the divine, Hardy's flash of insight seems to involve experiencing an acute and unsettling personal guilt, which, the poem then goes on to suggest, there is no supernatural power to acknowledge or forgive.

'Moments of Vision' is a good example of Hardy's reconfiguration of the ideas and idioms that he inherited from the romantic poets whose work he read so intensively during his years in London. The word 'vision', for instance, glossed as 'the faculty divine' by Wordsworth, and used to describe the magical trance inspired in Keats by the nightingale ('Was it a vision, or a waking dream?'),[17] occurs repeatedly in Hardy's poetry, but the term is

---

[17] *The Excursion*, Book I, 'The Wanderer', in *William Wordsworth: The Poems*, Vol. 2, ed. John O. Hayden (Harmondsworth: Penguin, 1977), 42 (l. 79); 'Ode to a Nightingale' in *The Poems of John Keats*, ed. Miriam Allott (London: Longman, 1970), 532 (l. 79).

frequently imbued with either a hint of wistfulness or with the kind of ironical humour that plays around the depictions of Robert Trewe and Ella Marchmill in 'An Imaginative Woman': St Paul's 'vision-seeing mind' (CP 716), for instance, is comically at odds with the culture of mid-Victorian capitalism on display in the adjacent market that also bears his name, while the momentary 'kindling vision' that the poet experiences in the cathedral's Whispering Gallery is, notwithstanding his hopes that it might be a sign of 'transcending things', in fact the result of an acoustical trick (CP 522). The word is more brutally deployed still in 'They Would Not Come', which reads as a mocking riposte to elegies such as 'After a Journey' and 'At Castle Boterel'. In this poem Hardy again records travelling to St Juliot and the Cornish coast in quest of Emma's spirit, but this time in vain:

> Where the ocean had sprayed our banquet
>   I stood, to recall it as then:
>   The same eluding again!
> No vision. Shows contingent
> Affrighted it further from me
>   Even than from my home-den.   (CP 641)

Hardy, in other words, would have had more chance of communing with Emma's ghost had he stayed at home in Max Gate. And 'vision' receives what might be called its *coup de grâce* in 'We Are Getting to the End', the penultimate poem of his final volume, *Winter Words* (1928), which opens 'We are getting to the end of visioning / The impossible within this universe' (CP 929). This bleak sonnet proceeds to renounce even modest hopes for progress, arguing—all too presciently, in the event—that the 'demonic force' that led to the outbreak and frenzied prosecution of one war probably means that another war is not too far off. 'Yes', it concludes, as if to tidy away once and for all the follies of romantic idealism, 'We are getting to the end of dreams!'

Which is not to say that Hardy did not strike a note of extreme reverence in his poetic commemorations of his most idolized romantic forebears, Shelley and Keats. In 'Shelley's Skylark', for instance, composed while journeying through the Livorno region during his trip to Italy with Emma in the spring of 1887, he broods in characteristically literal fashion on the exact whereabouts of the remains of the blithe spirit that had inspired Shelley's ode:

> Somewhere afield here something lies
> In Earth's oblivious eyeless trust
> That moved a poet to prophecies—
> A pinch of unseen, unguarded dust:
>
> The dust of the lark that Shelley heard,
> And made immortal through times to be;—
> Though it only lived like another bird,
> And knew not its immortality:
>
> Lived its meek life; then, one day, fell—
> A little ball of feather and bone;
> And how it perished, when piped farewell,
> And where it wastes, are alike unknown.
>
> Maybe it rests in the loam I view,
> Maybe it throbs in a myrtle's green,
> Maybe it sleeps in the coming hue
> Of a grape on the slopes of yon inland scene.   (CP 101)

While clearly an ardent tribute to 'our most marvellous lyrist' (L 22), it is worth noting that the poem plays off the spiritual against the material, or the aesthetic against the physical, as ruthlessly as does 'An Imaginative Woman'. Romantic birds are often figured as living forever ('Thou wast not born for death, immortal Bird!', as Keats put it in 'Ode to a Nightingale', compounding the individual with the species), while Hardy's focus is on the bird as a 'ball of feather and bone' that after death has been absorbed into the soil or the vegetation that grows from it.[18] This is the Darwinian immortality dramatized in poems such as 'Voices from Things Growing in a Churchyard' or 'Proud Songsters', in which nothing ever dies but is simply

---

[18] *Poems of John Keats*, 529 (l. 61). Keats's sleight of hand is most explicitly refuted in 'The Selfsame Song':

> A bird sings the selfsame song,
> With never a fault in its flow,
> That we listened to here those long
>   Long years ago.
>
> A pleasing marvel is how
> A strain of such rapturous rote
> Should have gone on thus till now
>   Unchanged in a note!
>
> —But it's not the selfsame bird.—
> No: perished to dust is he...
> As also are those who heard
>   That song with me.   (CP 598)

transformed into some different aspect of nature; and it is set alongside the radiant but immaterial literary immortality conferred by Shelley's ode upon his skylark as if to render explicit the gulf separating the romantic from the late Victorian poet.

The poem in which Hardy most directly presents himself as a votary of the muse also derived from his 1887 trip to Italy. The third of his poems set in Rome, 'The Vatican: Sala delle Muse', recounts an imaginary colloquy between Hardy and a composite Muse figure, called by the poem 'an essence of all the Nine' (CP 104). The Sala delle Muse houses a series of sculptures found in the Villa of Cassius near Tivoli that purportedly represent Calliope, Clio, Erato, Euterpe, Melpomene, Polyhymnia, Terpsichore, Thalia, and Urania.[19] Hardy records 'nearly falling asleep' (L 196) in this gallery during an exhausting day in the Vatican, and the poem takes the form of 'a vision, or a waking-dream':

> I sat in the Muses' Hall at the mid of the day,
> And it seemed to grow still, and the people to pass away,
> And the chiselled shapes to combine in a haze of sun,
> Till beside a Carrara column there gleamed forth One.
>
> She looked not this nor that of those beings divine,
> But each and the whole—an essence of all the Nine;
> With tentative foot she neared to my halting-place,
> A pensive smile on her sweet, small, marvellous face.
>
> 'Regarded so long, we render thee sad?' said she.
> 'Not you,' sighed I, 'but my own inconstancy!
> I worship each and each; in the morning one,
> And then, alas! another at sink of sun.
>
> 'To-day my soul clasps Form; but where is my troth
> Of yesternight with Tune: can one cleave to both?'   (CP 103–4)

Hardy's dithering when it comes to choosing between the Muses maps directly on to his fickle—and seemingly largely imaginary—pursuit of a series of girls as described in the last section of chapter 1 of the *Life*, where he recalls falling successively in love during his early teens with a girl who passed him on horseback, with a girl who had moved to Dorchester from

---

[19] The Muses, respectively, of epic poetry, history, love poetry, music, tragedy, hymns, dance, comedy, and astronomy.

Windsor (but had not, disappointingly, read Harrison Ainsworth's *Windsor Castle*), with a gamekeeper's daughter (addressed in 'To Lizbie Browne'), and finally with the wealthy farmer's daughter Louisa Harding (commemorated in 'To Louisa in the Lane' and 'Louie' and 'The Passer-by') (L 29–30). The equally enticing range of female muse-figures gathered in the gallery constitute a telling analogue for the fusion of poetry and romance that had made the young Hardy risk all his 'worldly prospects' (L 415) for the sake of his own poethood some twenty years before 'Sala delle Muse' was composed.

The Muse's answer, however, collapses the poetic-erotic fantasy as conclusively as the arrival of her husband deflates that of Ella Marchmill. For she effectively disavows her own existence. None of the muse-figures that he would woo, she insists, including that of the composite form that she herself assumed, exists outside the poet's own projections. However fervently he commits to whichever figure excites him, he can never, or so this poem implies, escape his own subjectivity. The post-romantic votary of the muse, in other words, must end up discovering that the shrine at which he worships is that of his own imagination: 'Nay, wooer,' she answers, 'thou sway'st not. These are but phases of one':

> 'And that one is I; and I am projected from thee,
> One that out of thy brain and heart thou causest to be—
> Extern to thee nothing. Grieve not, nor thyself becall,
> Woo where thou wilt; and rejoice thou canst love at all!'   (CP 104)

2

The Other Side of Common Emotions

On 17 July 1868, about a year after returning from London to Higher Bockhampton, Hardy observed in his notebook: 'Perhaps I can do a volume of poems consisting of the *other side* of common emotions' [his italics]. The notebook in which this gnomic ambition was recorded does not survive, for it was among those filleted by Hardy for the *Life*, and afterwards destroyed either by Hardy himself or by his literary executors (his second wife, Florence, and Sydney Cockerell). Evidently the remark struck him in 1917, the year that he and Florence began work on his third-person autobiography, as worth preserving, but he also reports finding himself somewhat baffled by it: 'What this means', he reflects, 'is not quite clear' (L 59).

The first version of the title of the novel that Hardy dispatched to Alexander Macmillan just over a week after making his cryptic diary entry was:

> *The Poor Man and the Lady.*
> *A Story with no plot;*
> *Containing some original verses.* (L 58)

This was later amended to *The Poor Man and the Lady; By the Poor Man*, and the 'original verses' that Hardy planned to include were either never composed or discarded. The first title of his first novel suggests that from the outset of his writing career Hardy was fascinated by the possibility of combining poetry and fiction to create a new literary compound, and in his biography we often find him brooding on the dialectic between the two, asserting, for instance, in the chapter covering the years 1897–8 in which he bids farewell to fiction, that as a novelist he had always tried 'to keep his narratives close to natural life, and as near to poetry in their subject as the conditions would allow' (L 309).

Hardy was no doubt aware of, and impressed by, Shelley's dramatic assertion in *A Defence of Poetry* that the 'distinction between poets and

Woman Much Missed: Thomas Hardy, Emma Hardy, and Poetry. Mark Ford, Oxford University Press.

prose writers is a vulgar error,[1] but, as a novelist writing to support a middle-class but dowry-less wife, was never able to take quite such a lofty view of the matter as that espoused by his hero. He found an early, if mainly symbolic, solution to the gulf between his exalted vision of himself as a poet and the exigencies of the fictional marketplace of the 1870s by 'dissolving', to use his term, lines from his early London poems, and the whole of the sonnet 'She, to Him II', into passages of *Desperate Remedies*. Some forty years later it was clearly important to him that readers recognize the ingenuity with which he'd kept a foot in the poetry camp even while writing a Wilkie Collins-style thriller, for in his 1912 Preface to the Wessex Edition reissue of *Desperate Remedies* he goes out of his way to draw attention to this early attempt to broker a rapport between his poetic '*tendency*' (L 415) and the genre of the popular novel:

> The reader may discover, when turning over this sensational and strictly conventional narrative, that certain scattered reflections and sentiments therein are the same in substance with some in the *Wessex Poems* and others, published many years later. The explanation of such tautology is that the poems were written before the novel, but as the author could not get them printed, he incontinently used here whatever of their content came into his head as being apt for the purpose—after dissolving it into prose, never anticipating at that time that the poems would see the light.
>
> (DR 388)

The division between poetry and prose, here displayed, in a kind of hey presto! moment, as porous, is one of the numerous polarities that shape the dynamics of Hardy's imagination. The process of crossing to, or viewing from, 'the *other side*' assumes numerous forms and guises in Hardy, and can be construed in opposition to the idealized, transcendent, and unifying impulse underlying the concept of being a Shelleyan or Trewe-like 'votary of the muse' committed to creating 'Forms more real than living man, / Nurslings of immortality', to borrow the lines from Shelley's *Prometheus Unbound* quoted in 'An Imaginative Woman' (LLI 19). It is striking that the first words of the poem chosen by Hardy to open his first collection, *Wessex Poems*, as well as to open the various editions of his *Collected Poems* that he saw through the press, point in precisely the opposite direction to that of

---

[1] 'A Defence of Poetry', *Shelley's Poetry and Prose*, eds. Donald H. Reiman and Sharon B. Powers (New York: Norton, 1977), 484.

'immortality'. 'Change and chancefulness in my flowering youthtime' (CP 7) begins 'The Temporary the All' and change and chancefulness prove indeed to be the presiding deities of the poems that follow, operating as de facto and irrefutable givens, and often consigning the poet to a dispassionate observer's role in relation to the 'common emotions' that the poems refract. Contingency rules, Hardy's inaugural poem declares, and the means and ability to record and accept contingency are frequently depicted as both a poetic credo and a modus vivendi: for the 'road to a true philosophy of life', as he put it in the Preface to *Poems of the Past and the Present*, 'seems to lie in humbly recording diverse readings of its phenomena as they are forced upon us by chance and change' (CP 84).

Equally important for Hardy, however, was the urge to do justice to his innate resistance to chance and change. The poem 'Childhood among the Ferns', collected in *Winter Words*, recreates an experience that Hardy had previously described in chapter 1 of the *Life* (where he suggests that he was just under eight when it occurred), and had also transferred to the young Jude Fawley:

> I sat one sprinkling day upon the lea,
> Where tall-stemmed ferns spread out luxuriantly,
> And nothing but those tall ferns sheltered me.
>
> The rain gained strength, and damped each lopping frond,
> Ran down their stalks beside me and beyond,
> And shaped slow-creeping rivulets as I conned,
>
> With pride, my spray-roofed house. And though anon
> Some drops pierced its green rafters, I sat on,
> Making pretence I was not rained upon.
>
> The sun then burst, and brought forth a sweet breath
> From the limp ferns as they dried underneath:
> I said: 'I could live on here thus till death;'
>
> And queried in the green rays as I sate:
> 'Why should I have to grow to man's estate
> And this afar-noised World perambulate?'   (CP 864)

Like 'Domicilium', this poem treasures privacy and separation, fostering an image of the young Hardy as a creature of the ferny 'lea', even its *genius loci*, snug and content in his makeshift den. As in his elegies for Emma, transplantation comes to seem a self-evident wrong, and indeed the 'green rays' that surround him in this poem function somewhat like the 'green slates' of the poem recalling the just-met Emma 'standing in the quarry' in Penpethy (CP 712). The boy's pride in his improvised shelter is mirrored in the neat triple rhymes as well as in the precision and enjoyment that the poem takes in hyphenated adjectives such as 'spray-roofed' and 'afar-noised', which communicate both his individual perceptions and the inventive sufficiency of his coinages (both are surely unique to Hardy) in relation to the descriptive task at hand.[2] Further, his future vulnerability, so like that of the figure of Emma in 'Green Slates', to the 'afar-noised' world's incursions, is movingly heightened by the completeness of his identification, like that of a camouflaged animal, with his habitat. Hardy figures his younger self as enjoying a 'personalized loneliness', to borrow a phrase from *A Pair of Blue Eyes* (PBE 198).

Part of the appeal of Hardy's poetry, an appeal gestured towards in his concept of articulating 'the *other side* of common emotions', derives from the unlikeliness of the angles from which he chooses to depict experiences, narratives, or ideas. 'How typical of Hardy!' can seem the only appropriate response to monologues delivered by, say, an aged newspaper or by a hare contemplating a milestone or by a set of musical instruments housed in a museum or by a sundial or by a love letter, or to lyrics addressed to a sea cliff, to a sooty tree in London, to a bunch of flowers sent to Max Gate from Italy in winter. The freedom with which Hardy inhabits or animates such a diverse range of phenomena—phenomena that, although common enough in themselves, register as outré or bizarre when used by Hardy as *materia poetica*—seems intimately connected with the lack of ambition that he first recognized, textually at any rate, in the course of this childhood experience. For, bound up with this unwillingness to grow up is an instinctive, one might say childlike, curiosity, as well as the sort of imaginative ingenuity that can transform the fronds of a fern into 'green rafters'.

In the prose versions of the same incident, or of one markedly similar to it, the young Hardy's and the young Jude's carapace is a straw hat rather than ferns, and there is no rain. It is the version told in the *Life* that establishes most clearly its significance in relation to Hardy's conception of his innate selfhood:

One event of this date [*c*.1847] or a little later stood out, he used to say, more distinctly than any. He was lying on his back in the sun, thinking

---

[2] Neither appears in the OED.

how useless he was, and covered his face with his straw hat. The sun's rays streamed through the interstices of the straw, the lining having disappeared. Reflecting on his experiences of the world so far as he had got he came to the conclusion that he did not wish to grow up. Other boys were always talking of when they would be men; he did not want at all to be a man, or to possess things, but to remain as he was, in the same spot, and to know no more people than he already knew (about half a dozen). Yet this early evidence of that lack of social ambition which followed him through life was shown when he was in perfect health and happy circumstances.

Afterwards he told his mother of his conclusions on existence, thinking she would enter into his views. But to his great surprise she was very much hurt, which was natural enough considering she had been near death's door in bringing him forth. And she never forgot what he had said, a source of much regret to him in after years.   (L 20)

His mother's distress was also, of course, an index of precisely what Hardy claims that he himself lacked—ambition. Earlier in the chapter Hardy describes her as endowed with 'unusual ability and judgment, and an energy that might have carried her to incalculable issues' (L 12). She had initially, he goes on, 'resolved to be a cook in a London club-house; but her plans in this direction were ended by her meeting her future husband', whom she married, in a shotgun wedding, some six months before Hardy's birth. The disjunction between the child's self-delighting experience of freedom and belonging and his mother's stern sense of reality can be mapped, I think, onto Hardy's concept of a poetry that is drawn to discovering perspectives that indulge the invigorating sense of lawlessness dramatized in 'Childhood among the Ferns', while also observing the inescapable laws of chance and change inculcated by his mother.

In an entry dated 'about 1906' in his *Poetical Matter* notebook,[3] Hardy returned again to the concept of writing poems that approach their subject matter from unsuspected or unusual angles:

[3] This notebook is one of the few working notebooks not destroyed by Hardy or his executors. Its entries were, a heading reveals, '[m]ostly copied from old notes of many years ago' (PM 3). It covers the full span of his career: its earliest entry is from 26 August 1868 and the last from shortly before his death. For further details, see the Introduction to *Thomas Hardy's 'Poetical Matter' Notebook*, eds. Pamela Dalziel and Michael Millgate (Oxford: Oxford University Press, 2009).

Poems about <u>the other side of the story</u>. i.e. the other side of things generally: before & after the usually chief incident, seems a pregnant
idea.   (PM 54)

This notebook itself contains numerous examples of scenarios that would
involve relating the 'chief incident' through the narrative prism of some
convoluted, distancing irony:

<u>Man asleep</u> under sheaves in the heat. Messenger, say a child, arrives to tell
him that his dearly loved wife & child are dead, or that she has eloped. The
others (reapers?) watch, & don't wake him...   (PM 23)

People heard indoors rejoicing at the news that they have come into a fortune, or that the son is not dead. Somebody comes up. The news is untrue.
Outsiders peep through hole in shutter: what shall they do? when
tell?   (PM 23)

A person sitting alone in a coach, a room, &c. The <u>faces</u> of people look in,
& bring tragic news scrap by scrap. Mode might be K. of Rav^n [i.e. the
ballad 'Keith of Ravelston']   (PM 65–6)

Indeed, the tableaux and anecdotes preserved in this notebook often convey
even more strongly than the poems that Hardy completed and published
the element of the perverse in his imagination. Both when considering
possible topics for poems and when pondering the points of view that any
given poem might deploy, he is time and again revealed as instinctively
drawn to the truncated and the oblique, the far-fetched and the
disconcerting. Some dramatically estranging means of reconfiguring the
commonplace clearly often constituted his initial moment of inspiration:

Highway closely lined with ruts. Each pair of ruts connected with some
family history   (PM 12)

<u>The Hand</u> (short poem) A hand seen lying on a rail, gate, or what not, by
moonlight. The owner not seen.   (PM 23)

[A] driver will not ask a man to ride: finds it is himself many years
earlier: at first he does not recognize that it is the same one he keeps
passing   (PM 28)

—A man goes among people who see him as a ghost, though he does not
himself know that he has died & is one.   (PM 37)

A room as viewed by a mouse from a chink under skirting: or a person by a fly: or householders by bird in nest—'They do not see me'.   (PM 39)

Cerne Abbey…Give names of Abbots, monks, & great personages, who are now kicked about by the cows in the Abbey field—'This clod was William Beyminster'—'I am W.B', &c.   (PM 40)

—A poem of little children with matured faces.

—A poem on a dinner-table (Gr—y's [i.e. Granny's] old one)

…on a card table—(the table loq. [i.e. speaks])   (PM 43)

Imagine everything a person, with a character: e.g. 'Fiddler June'.   (PM 59)

The entries that focus on what he calls 'process' (PM 42) or 'Meth' (i.e. method, PM 47) analogously indicate the importance for Hardy of creating an awareness of related but differing poetic perspectives on the same experience, implying that he saw it as the task of the poem to mediate between the two, without, however, necessarily unifying them: ' "How it was" versus "How it seemed" ' or ' "What I saw & what I felt" ' or ' "Backgrounds & Foregrounds" ' (PM 42). The relationship between either side of these antitheses might be compared to that outlined in the vignette quoted above in which a driver keeps failing to stop to pick up a passenger, who then turns out to be his own earlier self.

'Imagine everything a person…' Some particularly intriguing entries made shortly after Hardy had re-devoted himself to poetry in the mid-1890s point to the sources of the animism that is so distinctive a feature of his imaginative world. 'I cannot help noticing', he observes in early 1897, 'countenances in objects of scenery. e.g. trees, hills, houses, &c.' (PM 21). 'All things speak incessantly; will keep on addressing; cannot escape them' (PM 22), runs a more elliptical note of February of the following year, making Hardy briefly sound like a Beckettian narrator assailed by mysterious external voices, unable to tune out 'the revel of quick-cued mumming' (to borrow a phrase from ' "According to the Mighty Working" ' (CP 571)) that surround him in Wessex. Some three years earlier he drafted a scenario that explored in revealing detail this propensity, and even offered a tentative explanation for it:

A person, or family, may be abnormally developed on the imaginative side. They not only imagine ghosts & personalities in every sound & sight, but converse with them, or about them. Their belief may be that all the world is so many forms of thought & emotion, choosing, or compelled to choose, these infinite varieties of expression. Their attitude imparted by fear of life.   (PM 20)

The connection posited here between a rampant imagination and 'fear of life' inevitably summons up the image of the young Hardy crouching in the dripping ferns and deciding he would rather not grow up, or Jude coming to the same conclusion under his straw hat: to be 'abnormally developed on the imaginative side' is also to be abnormally vulnerable to the disappointments that attend an approach to life as 'so many forms of thought & emotion'. It is not clear if Hardy drafted this outline with the intention of developing it in poetry or prose, but it is followed by an idea for a poem to be called 'What does it mean?' that would present the confusions of 'a puzzled, ignorant, groping creature…'. And this is followed by an intriguing list of possible titles. Like those that Hardy considered for *Jude the Obscure* (*The Simpletons*, *Hearts Insurgent*, and *The Recalcitrants*),[4] these oscillate between figuring the condition of hyper-sensitivity as a new kind of spirituality that looks forward to more enlightened modes of being, and a glum acceptance that the likes of Jude and Sue or members of the abnormally imaginative family who see 'ghosts & personalities in every sound & sight' are irredeemably unsuited to the social conditions of late nineteenth-century England.

Titles. The Lightseekers: The Life-Learners: The Anticipators: The Wrath-Fleers: The Etherealists: The Ecstatics: The Erratics: The Flutterhearts. The Emotionalists: The Life-Fearers.   (PM 20)

One of the most excruciating aspects of the sensibility bestowed by Hardy on Jude and Sue is their shared anxiety that—despite their highly developed sense of difference from all around them—their own emotions are in fact relatively commonplace. Hardy seems to have associated this anxiety with a line from Shelley's *The Revolt of Islam* (1818), 'All shapes like mine own self, hideously multiplied', which Sue quotes as 'Shapes like our own selves hideously multiplied' after she and Jude have balked a second time at marrying (JO 276). Hardy alludes to Shelley's line again in a *Poetical Matter* notebook entry of 1917 ('Self "hideously multiplied", or others' (PM 28)). In this context the ideal of a poetry capable of expressing 'the *other side* of

---

[4] 'The Recalcitrants' was eventually used as the title of a poem (CP 389).

common emotions' can be seen as a crucial element in Hardy's dream of resisting the standardizing forms of industrial capitalism, and preserving, if only through some sleight of hand equivalent to his transplantation of lines from early poems into the prose of *Desperate Remedies*, a vision of his own uniqueness and autonomy.

It is a telling irony, further, that the poem most fully incorporated into Hardy's first published novel is precisely *about* the compression of an individual's distinctive and multifaceted 'Whole Life' into a commonplace cliché. The sonnet 'She, to Him II' records the decline of affection in a male lover, and the pain caused by his rejection of her:

> Perhaps, long hence, when I have passed away,
> Some other's feature, accent, thought like mine,
> Will carry you back to what I used to say,
> And bring some memory of our love's decline.
>
> Then you may pause awhile and think, 'Poor jade!'
> And yield a sigh to me—as ample due,
> Not as the tittle of a debt unpaid
> To one who could resign her all to you—
>
> And thus reflecting, you will never see
> That your thin thought, in two small words conveyed,
> Was no such fleeting phantom-thought to me,
> But the Whole Life wherein my part was played;
> And you amid its fitful masquerade
> A Thought—as I in your life seem to be!   (CP 15)

The first line characteristically posits her own death as one of the conditions necessary for recapturing the attention of her ex-lover, although here the posthumous moment of mutual understanding that concludes so many of Hardy's elegies for Emma ('And saying at last you knew!' (CP 586)) is sternly withheld. According to the poem's somewhat baroque conceit, it is her resemblance to some chance-met woman that she imagines triggering her ex-lover's memories of her, a notion that emphasizes that it is not her distinctiveness that surfaces in his mind, but rather the characteristics that she shared with an anonymous other. And the hackneyed epithet with which he then commemorates, or rather inters, their radically unequal relationship in the second quatrain, 'Poor jade!', again reduces her to the commonplace. On the other hand, the poem itself can be read as a potent act of resistance to his derisory encapsulation of her existence, for its intricate and elaborate argument serves to illustrate the sophistication and complexity of her character.

It is important to note, however, that it is only after, or indeed *through* her citation of his derogatory dismissal that she can launch her counter-offensive and articulate the utter disparity between his 'thin thought, in two small words conveyed' and her 'Whole Life', a phrase movingly expanded by Hardy in the speech based on this poem given to Cytherea Graye—who is on the point of forced marriage to the evil libertine Aeneas Manston—in *Desperate Remedies*:

> 'they will not feel that what to them is but a thought, easily held in those two words of pity, "Poor girl," was a whole life to me; as full of hours, minutes, and peculiar minutes, of hopes and dreads, smiles, whisperings, tears, as theirs: that it was my world...'   (DR 236)

The density and idiosyncrasy of individual experience emerge with great vividness in the seemingly awkward 'minutes, and peculiar minutes', a phrase which opens a fascinating vista into Cytherea's private life, and into her own sense of its distinctiveness, however 'common' the emotions she feels might seem to others when put into words. And while her list dramatizes what 'She, to Him II' calls life's 'fitful masquerade', it also asserts her right to experience in her own being and on her own terms the emotions that it catalogues, infusing the generic 'hopes and dreads, smiles, whisperings, tears' with what is 'peculiar' to her, and is therefore hers alone.

That Hardy experienced a comparable threat to his sense of self around the time that he floated the idea of composing 'a volume of poems consisting of the *other side* of common emotions' can be deduced from a note that he made some two and a half weeks earlier, and included in the *Life*:

> On July 1 [1868] he writes down—in all likelihood after a time of mental depression over his work and prospects:
> 'Cures for despair:
>   To read Wordsworth's "Resolution and Independence".
>   "   " Stuart Mill's "Individuality" in *Liberty*
>   "   " Carlyle's "Jean Paul Richter".'   (L 59)

Clearly that summer Hardy found himself, like Wordsworth's traveller on the moor in 'Resolution and Independence', 'Perplexed, and longing to be comforted'.[5] All three of the works listed as antidotes to the prolonged loss of self-confidence that he experienced in the period after he had beaten his retreat from London around a year earlier present uplifting celebrations of singularity. 'Eccentricity', writes Mill,

> has always abounded when and where strength of character has abounded; and the amount of eccentricity in a society has generally been proportional to the amount of genius, mental vigour, and moral courage it contained. That so few now dare to be eccentric marks the chief danger of the time.[6]

The wholesale rejection of the poems dispatched to magazine editors during his last years in London had evidently set him pondering the relationship between the narrow prejudices of cultural orthodoxy and the eccentricities of 'genius'.[7]

Even more influential than Mill, however, on Victorian notions of the *Übermensch* was Thomas Carlyle, and with hindsight one can read Carlyle's 1827 review-essay on Jean Paul Friedrich Richter as offering almost a template for the literary career that Hardy would himself go on to develop. Indeed, Carlyle's soaring paean to originality in this essay was possibly the source for Hardy's related notion of approaching the commonplace from some estranging distance:

> Originality is a thing we constantly clamour for, and constantly quarrel with; as if, observes our Author himself [i.e. Jean Paul Richter], any originality but our own could be expected to content us! In fact, all strange things are apt, without fault of theirs, to estrange us at first view; unhappily scarcely anything is perfectly plain, but what is also perfectly common. The current coin of the realm passes into all hands; and be it gold, silver, or copper, is acceptable and of known value: but with new ingots, with foreign bars, and medals of Corinthian brass, the case is widely different.[8]

---

[5] William Wordsworth, *Selected Poems*, ed. John O. Hayden (London: Penguin, 1994), 157 (l. 117).

[6] *Utilitarianism* by John Stuart Mill, ed. Mary Warnock (Glasgow: Collins, 1979), 196–7.

[7] It was in 1866, or so Hardy recounts in the *Life*, that he took to sending off his poems to magazines for publication. All, he somewhat bitterly records, were 'rejected by editors' (L 49). No evidence, it should be said, of these submissions has come to light.

[8] Thomas Carlyle, 'Jean Paul Friedrich Richter', first published in *Edinburgh Review*, 91 (1827), collected in *Critical and Miscellaneous Essays*, Vol. 1 (London: Chapman and Hall, 1888), 10.

It is intriguing to learn from Carlyle that the originality of Richter's idiom in part derived from his deployment of precisely those linguistic habits of which so many reviewers of Hardy's poetry would in due course complain: 'he presents himself', Carlyle comments admiringly, 'with a professed and determined singularity: his language itself is a stone of stumbling to the critic... [he] invents hundreds of new words, alters old ones, or, by hyphen, chains, pairs, and packs them together into most jarring combination; in short produces sentences of the most heterogeneous, lumbering, interminable kind' [my ellipsis]. One catches an echo, too, in a note made by Hardy somewhat later in 1868, of Carlyle's discussion of Richter's humour: 'by a single stroke', observes Carlyle, 'he can change a laughing face into a sad one. But in his smile itself a touching pathos may lie hidden, a pity too deep for tears.'[9] Hardy characteristically presents this from 'the other side': 'How people will laugh in the midst of a misery! Some would soon get to whistle in Hell' (L 61).[10]

The relationship between eccentricity and humour that Carlyle explores in such detail in his essay on Richter is unquestionably central to the distinctive tone and effects of much of Hardy's poetry. As Eric Griffiths persuasively argued in *The Printed Voice of Victorian Poetry*, in Hardy's verse even 'emotions such as deep grief are subject to odd "vicissitudes of passion" [the phrase is from Johnson's 'Preface' to *Shakespeare*], gusts of indifference, absent-heartedness, laughter in the midst of misery'.[11] Hardy instinctively imparted his particular style of wry humour to the interplay between the comic and the tragic in his poems; and while the result in a rural ballad such as, say, 'The Slow Nature' (which is subtitled 'An Incident of Froom Valley' and dated to 1894) might verge on eccentricity, the narrative and characters lodge firmly, if unobtrusively, in the memory precisely because pathos and bathos are so inextricably fused:

> 'Thy husband—poor, poor Heart!—is dead—
>   Dead, out by Moreford Rise;
> A bull escaped the barton-shed,
>   Gored him, and there he lies!'

---

[9]   Ibid. 13.

[10]   Towards the end of the essay, Carlyle returns to this theme: 'On the whole, Genius has privileges of its own; it selects an orbit for itself; and be this never so eccentric, if it is indeed a celestial orbit, we mere stargazers must at last compose ourselves; must cease to cavil at it, and begin to observe it, and calculate its laws' (17).

[11]   Eric Griffiths, *The Printed Voice of Victorian Poetry* (Oxford: Oxford University Press, 1989), 215.

—'Ha, ha—go away! 'Tis a tale, methink,
          Thou joker Kit!' laughed she.
'I've known thee many a year, Kit Twink,
          And ever hast thou fooled me!'

—'But, Mistress Damon—I can swear
          Thy goodman John is dead!
And soon th'lt hear their feet who bear
          His body to his bed.'

So unwontedly sad was the merry man's face—
          That face which had long deceived—
That she gazed and gazed; and then could trace
          The truth there; and she believed.

She laid a hand on the dresser-ledge,
          And scanned far Egdon-side;
And stood; and you heard the wind-swept sedge
          And the rippling Froom; till she cried:

'O my chamber's untidied, unmade my bed,
          Though the day has begun to wear!
"What a slovenly hussif!" it will be said,
          When they all go up my stair!'

She disappeared; and the joker stood
          Depressed by his neighbour's doom,
And amazed that a wife struck to widowhood
          Thought first of her unkempt room.

But a fortnight thence she could take no food,
          And she pined in a slow decay;
While Kit soon lost his mournful mood
          And laughed in his ancient way.   (CP 69–70)

Singularity can often teeter on the edge of the ridiculous, as instanced by, say, Lewis Carroll's parody of 'Resolution and Independence' in 'The White Knight's Song' in *Through the Looking-Glass*. Hardy's poetic idiom is less easy to guy because it so often already incorporates a perspective from 'the other side' on the incidents related; the joker Kit, so to speak, is already present in the poem, and no consoling moral of the kind that Wordsworth derives from the leech-gatherer can be gleaned from this anecdote. Indeed, although Hardy's numerous encounter poems deliver up any number of characters as quirky and difficult to parse as the leech-gatherer, they almost never provide the kind of uplifting nugget of sustaining wisdom with which Wordsworth's poem concludes: '"God," said I, "be my help and stay secure; / I'll think of the leech-gatherer on the lonely moor!"'[12]

Hardy's personal quest for resolution and independence, as it comes down to us through the *Life* and his surviving notebooks, often involved the use of quasi-religious terms such as *soul* and *spiritual*. A diary entry of June 1877 transferred to the *Life* neatly encapsulates the opposition between the 'mechanical' and the 'spiritual' that so powerfully shaped Hardy's concept of the value of art, and especially of poetry:

> So, then, if Nature's defects must be looked in the face and transcribed, whence arises the *art* in poetry and novel-writing? which must certainly show art, or it becomes merely mechanical reporting. I think the art lies in making these defects the basis of a hitherto unperceived beauty, by irradiating them with 'the light that never was' on their surface, but is seen to be latent in them by the spiritual eye.   (L 118)

In practice Hardy was rarely drawn to the transcendental or the mystical implicit in the concept of 'the light that never was', instead using his 'spiritual eye' to figure ghosts or souls speaking or acting with unnerving literalness. Here, in its original form in the *Poetical Matter* notebook, is his description of 9 March 1888 of souls adrift in the British Library Reading Room:

> Souls gliding about in the B. M. They are in a sort of dream, screened by their bodies somewhat, but imaginable. Dissolution is gnawing at them all, slightly hampered by renovation. Time, in the great circle of the library, looking into Space. Coughs floating in the same great vault, mixed with the rustle of book-leaves & the touches of footsteps on the floor…Or souls of the authors—midnight—   (PM 16)

This last idea is reprised in an entry on the very last pages of the notebook, which imagines a kind of literary séance, at which the phantoms of Swinburne, Browning, Tennyson, Moore, Wordsworth, Scott, Byron,

---

[12] Wordsworth, *Selected Poems*, 158 (ll. 139–40).

Shelley, Keats, Milton '(faint)' and Shakespeare '(very faint)' appear to a child who has imbibed some gin or wine (PM 81). The visits paid by Hardy's teeming cast of ghosts or souls from 'the other side' allow his poetic Wessex often to assume the lineaments of a Dantescan Divine Comedy, in which the dead and living cohabit in a crepuscular, intermediary realm: 'Time', as he puts it in the entry describing souls gliding through the British Library, 'looking into Space'.

From the outset of his career as a writer, Hardy clearly figured poetry as affording the fullest access to the spiritual, as he understood and defined it in his 'peculiar' way, to pick up the word used by Cytherea in her anguished reflections on the eve of her marriage. Notebook entries frequently emphasize the importance of the 'peculiar' or 'eccentric' to the expressive power of other art forms too, as in his celebration of the 'much-decried, mad, late-Turner' land- and seascapes which present 'the deeper reality underlying the scenic, the expression of what are sometimes call abstract imaginings' (L 192). Hardy's own sense of a 'deeper reality' was anything but abstract, as he perhaps most fully acknowledged in a letter of 1915 in which he discusses his responses to the philosophy of Henri Bergson, whom he pits as a representative of modernity against more superstitious kinds of 'abstract imaginings':

> Half my time—particularly when writing verse—I 'believe' (in the modern sense of the word) not only in the things Bergson believes in, but in spectres, mysterious voices, intuitions, omens, dreams, haunted places, etc, etc. But I do not believe in them in the old sense of the word any more for that... (L 400)

If this suggests a certain defensiveness on Hardy's part—he believes in them 'when writing verse' because they help him to write good poems but is in fact as modern and unillusioned as Bergson—it was probably because for him the stakes were so high. For involved in believing in 'spectres, mysterious voices, intuitions' etc. was a commitment not only to the traditions and stories passed down to him by his parents and grandparents, that is, to the atavistic sources of his own imagination, but to the 'peculiar' nature of experience itself. In a revealing metaphor used in his 1912 introduction to the Wessex Edition of *Wessex Tales*, he compares the way our 'imperfect memories insensibly formalize the fresh originality of living fact—from whose shape they slowly depart' to the way 'machine-made castings depart by degrees from the sharp hand-work of the mould' (PW 22).

Paradoxically, then, the multiple estranging techniques developed in Hardy's poetry can be read as a means of recovering the 'fresh originality' of experiences, as a form of resistance to the standardizing processes of memory, here shown as replicating the erosion of distinctions inherent in industrial manufacturing. It was far better the past assume the form of some gothic spectre who will keep him company as he carries out his everyday chores:

> We two kept house, the Past and I,
>   The Past and I;
> Through all my tasks it hovered nigh,
>   Leaving me never alone.
> It was a spectral housekeeping
>   Where fell no jarring tone,
> As strange, as still a housekeeping
>   As ever has been known.
>
> As daily I went up the stair
>   And down the stair,
> I did not mind the Bygone there—
>   The Present once to me;
> Its moving meek companionship
>   I wished might ever be,
> There was in that companionship
>   Something of ecstasy.   ('The Ghost of the Past', CP 308)

The past is 'latent', to borrow the word used in the 1877 diary entry (L 118), in the present, and its 'companionship' infuses pattern and meaning into passing time and the routines of the day, but in due course this ghost itself shrinks and fades, dwindling into a spectral skeleton, as imperfect memory hollows out and abrades the 'fresh originality of living fact':

> And then its form began to fade,
>   Began to fade,
> Its gentle echoes faintlier played
>   At eves upon my ear
> Than when the autumn's look embrowned
>   The lonely chambers here,
> When autumn's settling shades embrowned
>   Nooks that it haunted near.

> And so with time my vision less,
> > Yea, less and less
> Makes of that Past my housemistress,
> > It dwindles in my eye;
> It looms a far-off skeleton
> > And not a comrade nigh,
> A fitful far-off skeleton
> > Dimming as days draw by.   (CP 308–9)

The aura of this idealized 'housemistress' is shown gradually leeching away, marooning the past in the 'common emotion' of disillusioned bitterness.

J. I. M. Stewart once wittily observed that the only phrase bearing any relation to the truth in T. S. Eliot's ad hominem denunciation of Hardy in one of the lectures collected in *After Strange Gods* were the words 'the late Thomas Hardy'.[13] 'He seems to me to have written', complained Eliot, 'as nearly for the sake of "self-expression" as a man well can; and the self which he had to express does not strike me as a particularly wholesome or edifying matter of communication.'[14] Eliot's attack probably had its source in his dislike of Hardy's religious scepticism and his secularizing vision for the future of the Church of England, but it is not impossible that there may have also been an element of 'hypocrite lecteur!—mon semblable,—mon frère!' in Eliot's aversion to Hardy's work.[15] The idea of using poetry for 'self-expression' was, of course, as much an anathema for Hardy as it was for Eliot, although it must be acknowledged that a wide theoretical gulf exists between Hardy's claims in his prefaces that his poems were 'dramatic or personative' (CP 6) and Eliot's concept of the objective correlative or discussion of 'impersonality' in 'Tradition and the Individual Talent'. But, stepping back a little, it is surely impossible to think of two poets whose work elicits such intense and seemingly irresistible biographical speculation, or indeed of two poets whose unhappy marriages played such a crucial role in inspiring their best known

[13] Quoted by Cecil Day Lewis in his lecture 'The Lyrical Poetry of Thomas Hardy', reprinted in *Thomas Hardy: Poems*, eds. James Gibson and Trevor Johnson (Basingstoke: Macmillan, 1979), 148.

[14] T. S. Eliot, *The Complete Prose: The Critical Edition*, Vol. 5: *(1934–39)*, eds. Iman Javadi, Ron Schuchard, and Jayme Stayer (Baltimore: Johns Hopkins University Press, 2017), 40.

[15] This phrase of Baudelaire's is the last line of 'The Burial of the Dead' in *The Waste Land* (*The Poems of T. S. Eliot*, Vol. 1, eds. Christopher Ricks and Jim McCue (London: Faber & Faber, 2015), 57 (l. 76)).

and most obviously heartfelt works. What female muse-figures rival in potency, in poetry in English, Vivien and Emma? Possibly only Shakespeare's Dark Lady. And for all his sophistication and critical acumen, Eliot ends up not much clearer than Hardy when it comes to explaining how the individual talent might express age-old and widely shared feelings in an original way: 'The business of the poet is not to find new emotions, but to use the ordinary ones and, in working them up into poetry, to express feelings which are not in actual emotions at all.'[16] Behind the smoke and mirrors of such a passage (how does one distinguish between 'emotions' and 'feelings'?), as behind Hardy's concept of 'the *other side* of common emotions', lurks the urge to use poetry as a means of 'self-expression', or even confession, bound up with a rigorous taboo on attempting any such thing.

Towards the end of his life Robert Lowell revealed to Grey Gowrie that the two poets who had meant most to him were Ezra Pound and Thomas Hardy—'because of the heart-break'.[17] Lowell, at least after composing the poems collected in *Life Studies* in the late 1950s, had no compunction about using details from his personal life, and from the lives of his family, lovers, and friends, in his poetry. Hardy was far more cautious and instinctively secretive yet also seems to have found it impossible to avoid scattering clues about his private life throughout his eight collections, and it was surely these autobiographical strands of narrative that had such an effect on Lowell, as well as on Hardy's vast army of critic-sleuths, who, however outlandish their speculations, are also responding to prompts and conundrums secreted in the poetry. As Cytherea laid claim to her 'peculiar minutes' in a rhetorical act of resistance to the pressures menacing her individuality, so poetry enabled Hardy to view with a 'spiritual eye' anything that caught his attention, from a pair of new boots to the skeleton of a sunshade, from lovers glimpsed on Tooting Common to faint markings on a whitewashed wall.[18] Curiosity and distance, eccentricity and humour, combine in unstable quotients in any given Hardy poem, while an element of the posthumous or ghostly often suffuses the narrative and characters. Indeed, Hardy the poet exercising his 'spiritual eye' is closely allied to Hardy 'the dead man walking', to borrow the title of one of many poems in which

---

[16] *Selected Prose of T. S. Eliot*, ed. Frank Kermode (London: Faber & Faber, 1975), 43.

[17] Grey Gowrie, *The Italian Visitor* (Manchester: Carcanet, 2013), 105.

[18] 'The New Boots (CP 902), 'The Sunshade' (CP 490), 'Beyond the Last Lamp' (CP 314–15), 'The Whitewashed Wall' (CP 685–6).

he imagines himself as a 'corpse-thing' (CP 219), as having died in the midst of life:

> They hail me as one living,
>> But don't they know
> That I have died of late years,
>> Untombed although?
>
> I am but a shape that stands here,
>> A pulseless mould,
> A pale past picture, screening
>> Ashes gone cold.   (CP 217–18)[19]

As in Eliot ('I am Lazarus, come from the dead, / Come back to tell you all, I shall tell you all'),[20] so in Hardy the lure of such self-figurations insistently makes itself felt. For it is death that creates the fullest awareness of the '*other side*' of any story, and as Hardy observed in a notebook entry of 29 May 1871: 'The most prosaic man becomes a poem when you stand by his grave & think of him' (PN 10).

---

[19] This poem echoes the following notebook entry from June 1888: 'For my part, if there is any way of getting a melancholy satisfaction out of life it lies in dying, so to speak, before one is out of the flesh; by which I mean putting on the manners of ghosts, wandering in their haunts, and taking their views of surrounding things. To think of life as passing away is a sadness; to think of it as past is at least tolerable. Hence even when I enter into a room to pay a simple morning call I have unconsciously the habit of regarding the scene as if I were a spectre not solid enough to influence my environment, only fit to behold and say, as another spectre said: "Peace be unto you"' (L 218).

[20] 'The Love Song of J. Alfred Prufrock', Eliot, *The Poems*, 8 (ll. 94–5).

LYONNESSE

3

Emma's Devon and Cornwall

Some seven weeks after Emma's death of a heart attack, her eventual successor, Florence Dugdale, wrote to Edward Clodd from Max Gate:[1]

> [H]is life here is *lonely* beyond words, & he spends his evenings in reading & re-reading voluminous diaries that Mrs H. has kept from the time of their marriage. Nothing could be worse for him. He reads the comments upon himself—bitter denunciations, beginning about 1891 & continuing until within a day or two of her death—& I think he will end by *believing* them.   (LEFH 75)

Newman Flower, a notoriously unreliable witness, claimed in a memoir of 1950 that Hardy also found among Emma's papers two book-length manuscripts: one was entitled 'The Pleasures of Heaven and the Pains of Hell' and the other 'What I think of my Husband'.[2] Whether true or not, the latter title does seem pretty much to capture the tenor of the so-called Black Diaries. It goes without saying that these multi-volume diaries, characterized by Florence in a letter of January 1916 to Rebekah Owen as 'full of venom, hatred & abuse of him & his family' (LEFH 114), were in due course fed to the flames. In Emma's attic rooms Hardy also, however, discovered the small paperbound volume in which she had set down not only her memories of her childhood in Plymouth and of her fourteen years in Cornwall, but had recorded as the climactic moment of her life her meeting with her man of destiny, 'the one intended for me' (SR 50), the writer whom, twelve years before the convergence of the twain, a fortune-telling servant of the Giffords called Ann Tresider Chappel had predicted that she would marry:

> A hot day in June of 1858—Midsummer day, [as] it was bound to be—at twelve o'clock precisely, we went out on the front lawn at Bedford Terrace

---

[1] For a full account of Emma's final illness, see *Hardy the Physician: Medical Aspects of the Wessex Tradition* by Tony Fincham (Basingstoke: Palgrave Macmillan, 2008), 58–60.

[2] Newman Flower, *Just As It Happened* (London: Cassell, 1950), 96.

and she [i.e. Ann] brought out three tumblers of cold water, full up—one for my sister, one for me, and one for the parlour-maid. We all liked this proceeding immensely. Into one of these tumblers set before us we each broke an egg, letting the white only drop into the water, then watching what form it would take which should signify the occupation of our future spouses. My sister began the charm eagerly—a church with a tower arose very plainly.

'You will marry a Clergyman Ann said—which she did.

I hesitated, the maid broke hers in a hurry, a ship in full sail as plainly appeared also.

'You will marry a sailor', said Ann authoritatively, which she did. Ann gazed a longer time into the glass when my turn came, then she pronounced it to be a very large ink-bottle and an immense quill pen stretching across the water—all agreed it was so quite plainly. Ann said firmly, 'You will marry a writer'. And so I did! Now how did those eggs reveal it all? A most mysterious matter that!   (SR 40–1)

At the time of writing (the manuscript is dated 4 January 1911), Emma was in her most fiercely evangelical Christian phase, so it is intriguing to find her willing to recall without negative comment just the sort of belief in folk superstition that occurs in so many Hardy novels, stories, and poems. That said, in the memoir's concluding paragraph Emma insists—in the teeth of all the evidence amassed in the Black Diaries—that 'an Unseen Power of great benevolence directs my ways' (SR 61). And its final sentences are about as far as one could get from the philosophy of the husband whom she so vehemently chided for his religious scepticism:

I have some philosophy and mysticism, and an ardent belief in Christianity and the life beyond this present one, all which makes any existence curiously interesting. As one watches *happenings* (and even if should occur *unhappy happenings*) outward circumstances are of less importance if Christ is our highest ideal. A strange unearthly brilliance shines around our path, penetrating and dispersing difficulties with its warmth and glow.   (SR 61)

Despite Florence's fear that Hardy would end up '*believing*' what Emma wrote about him, many letters suggest that he at least partially attributed her 'bitter denunciations' to mental instability. In a letter to Florence Henniker of 17 December 1912 he talks of 'certain painful delusions she suffered from at times' (CL IV 243), and on 29 January 1913 he wrote to Florence, whom he would marry the following year: 'I am getting through E's papers…It was, of course, sheer hallucination in her, poor thing' (CL IV 255). In a further letter on the subject to Florence Henniker he describes Emma as 'a little unhinged at times' (CL V 19), while to Emma's cousin Kate Gifford he explained that in her 'later years an unfortunate mental aberration for which she was not responsible altered her much' (CL V 64). Hardy did not, of course, need to read Emma's fulminations to know that summer gave them sweets, but autumn wrought division. Because he later destroyed them, one can only guess at how much the kinds of self-reproach voiced in poems like 'Lost Love' or 'The Haunter' related to specific complaints or incidents recorded by Emma. It is, however, possible to see how *Some Recollections* filtered into the deepest springs of Hardy's imagination, opening the poetic door to the West, to Romance, to Love, and to the Past (CP 773).

A rich and irresistible alchemy transformed Hardy's shock at Emma's death and his reading of her memoir into a compulsion to re-enter her 'olden haunts' (CP 349). This drove him to return to St Juliot and the coast around Boscastle, as well as to her native city Plymouth, on the pilgrimage that he made with his brother Henry (6–11 March 1913), and to compose numerous poems that incorporate details from Emma's descriptions of her life in Devon and Cornwall, both before and after she met him.

The earliest memory set down in *Some Recollections* is of being taken into the country to see daisies: 'my surprise and joy', she writes, 'were very great when I saw a whole field of them, I can never forget the ecstatic state it put me in' (SR 3). Both flowers and rapture infuse the elegiac trope used in the last stanza of 'Rain on a Grave', which imagines Emma's posthumous life in nature in Stinsford churchyard:

> Soon will be growing
>   Green blades from her mound,
> And daisies be showing
>   Like stars on the ground,
> Till she form part of them—
> Ay—the sweet heart of them,
> Loved beyond measure
> With a child's pleasure
>   All her life's round.   (CP 341–2)

The comforting trope of representing Emma in death as a child is repeated in the last lines of 'I Found Her Out There' ('And joy in its throbs / With the heart of a child' (CP 343)), and then taken to a bizarre extreme in 'The Clock of the Years', in which the poet agrees to the offer of a Spirit to make time go backwards, only to have to watch Emma change from dead to 'woman-grown' to 'child-fair' to 'babyhood' until, to his great chagrin, she 'smalled till she was nought at all' (CP 529): 'Better,' he complains, 'She were dead as before! The memory of her / Had lived in me; but it cannot now!'

In the poems inspired by *Some Recollections* Hardy generally avoids conceits of this kind, preferring to imagine her as 'a real girl in a real place', to borrow a phrase of Philip Larkin's.[3] Her birth and early years in Plymouth are recreated in the first two stanzas of 'Places' with the reverence due to a saint, although a saint whom no one else knows about:

> Nobody says: Ah, that is the place
> Where chanced, in the hollow of years ago,
> What none of the Three Towns cared to know—
> The birth of a little girl of grace—
> The sweetest the house saw, first or last;
>> Yet it was so
>> On that day long past.
>
> Nobody thinks: There, there she lay
> In a room by the Hoe, like the bud of a flower,
> And listened, just after the bedtime hour,
> To the stammering chimes that used to play
> The quaint Old Hundred-and-Thirteenth tune
>> In Saint Andrew's tower
>> Night, morn, and noon.   (CP 352–3)

St Andrew's Church features also in 'The West-of-Wessex Girl', inspired, like 'Places', by Hardy's brief stays in Plymouth on his journeys to and from Boscastle in March 1913. This visit served as an inspiring catalyst for his enchanted vision of Emma 'In a room by the Hoe, like the bud of a flower', or walking the 'marbled ways' of Plymouth, 'That in her bounding early days / Were friendly with her feet' (CP 572). Chronologically, the myth of Emma's life in Hardy's poetry begins in these two poems, along with 'The

---

[3] 'Lines on a Young Lady's Photograph Album', Philip Larkin, *Collected Poems*, ed. Anthony Thwaite (London: Faber & Faber, 1988), 71 (l. 25).

Marble-Streeted Town', in which, again, Plymouth's indifference to the 'brightest of its native souls' is a source of wonder to the sorrowing poet:

> The place seems not to mind
>> That she—of old
> The brightest of its native souls—
>> Left it behind!
> Over this green aforedays she
>> On light treads went and came,
>>> Yea, times untold;
> Yet none here knows her history—
>> Has heard her name.   (CP 681)

Hardy's lyrics about Emma's Plymouth (to which he made another pilgrimage with a baffled and resentful Florence in 1914, and then again in 1917)[4] slide from observation of quotidian detail back through time to imagine Emma participating, sixty years earlier, in the scenes that the poems depict:

> I reach the marble-streeted town,
>> Whose 'Sound' outbreathes its air
>>> Of sharp sea-salts;
> I see the movement up and down
>> As when she was there.
> Ships of all countries come and go,
>> The bandsmen boom in the sun
>>> A throbbing waltz;
> The schoolgirls laugh along the Hoe
>> As when she was one.   (CP 681)

---

[4] This second pilgrimage to various Gifford-related sites in Plymouth was caustically described by Florence in a letter to Sydney Cockerell: 'We arrived in Plymouth about mid-day on Saturday & had a tiring & rather depressing time there. To me there is nothing more dismal than visiting wretched decayed houses, with the plaster falling from the walls, where people, now dead, were born & lived more than 70 years ago, & graves with broken coping & weeds,— a thick crop of groundsel grown over one—& half-obliterated names. How much better to have no neglected little plot of ground to testify to the indifference of grand-children to their grand-parents' memory. In one case where my husband had sent money for a grave to be kept in order the relative—a great-niece—had obviously never been near it' (LEFH 134).

This reconfigures some enthusiastically scatty passages from *Some Recollections*, imposing the discipline and distance of verse elegy onto the spirited vivacity of Emma's disjointed stream of memories. And it was surely the very disjointedness of Emma's text—as of her conversation—that so appealed to Hardy. Reading *Some Recollections* enabled him to recover the experience of surrendering, during their courtship, to the unpredictable excitements and vagaries of a consciousness so different from his own, an experience replicated and extended by his surrender to the 'region of dream and mystery' (to quote from the 1895 Preface to *A Pair of Blue Eyes* (PBE 3)) where he chanced to meet her, and onto descriptions of which he transferred the intense, if contradictory, feelings that Emma aroused in him. In *A Pair of Blue Eyes* itself, the naïve, impulsive, impressionable, but fatally passive Stephen Smith is the vector for Hardy's urge to surrender, while the more worldly Henry Knight, although equally attracted to Elfride's 'freshness', finds in her much to instruct and correct. The Knight-like disciplinarian aspect of Hardy's responses to Emma can be traced not only in the way these poems shape and mould, and make scan and rhyme, her more Molly Bloom-style mode of recalling her childhood and adolescence in Plymouth, but in his editing, and on occasion rewriting, of *Some Recollections* itself. As its editors point out in their introduction, Hardy's emendations, 'while sometimes adding to the clarity of the original, detract from its spontaneity, introducing, almost comically, a literary and pedantic tone' (SR xiii). The unstable mixture of uncontrollable fascination and the antithetical—or possibly consequent—urge to punish, which plays itself out in Knight's doomed courtship of Elfride, is present in many of Hardy's elegies for Emma, particularly in those that depict her in her coffin, such as the posthumously published 'The Sound of Her', which recreates the noise ('creak, creak' (CP 955)) of the screws being driven into its lid.

The discovery of *Some Recollections* granted Hardy inspiring access to the young Emma's observations and emotions. It also reminded him of her snobbish family who had so scorned him and were now powerless to prevent him from brooding over their graves. In a characteristically Hardyan twist of fate, the Gifford family vault in Charles churchyard had been damaged so badly during a church restoration that Emma, who attended—without her husband—her father's funeral there in 1890, had decided that she no longer wished to be buried in the same graveyard as her parents (L 387).

Hardy's rooting around in Charles churchyard in search of the graves of his wife's relatives resulted in two poems that balance a strain of vindictive triumphalism over the entire Gifford clan against the urge to offer expiation for the disastrous breach with her immediate family that was occasioned by Emma's decision to accept her 'low-born' suitor (LEFH 78). 'The Obliterate Tomb', collected in *Satires of Circumstance* (1914), concerns a 'man of means' who is prompted to seek out, like Hardy in Charles churchyard, the burial place of his enemies:

> 'More than half my life long
> Did they weigh me falsely, to my bitter wrong,
> But they all have shrunk away into the silence
> Like a lost song.
>
> 'And the day has dawned and come
> For forgiveness, when the past may hold it dumb
> On the once reverberate words of hatred uttered
> Half in delirium . . .
>
> 'With folded lips and hands
> They lie and wait what next the Will commands,
> And doubtless think, if think they can: "Let discord
> Sink with Life's sands!"
>
> 'By these late years their names,
> Their virtues, their hereditary claims,
> May be as near defacement at their grave-place
> As are their fames.'
>
> —Such thoughts bechanced to seize
> A traveller's mind—a man of memories—
> As he set foot within the western city
> Where had died these
>
> Who in their lifetime deemed
> Him their chief enemy—one whose brain had schemed
> To get their dingy greatness deeplier dingied
> And disesteemed.
>
> So, sojourning in their town,
> He mused on them and on their once renown,
> And said, 'I'll seek their resting-place to-morrow
> Ere I lie down,

> 'And end, lest I forget,
> Those ires of many years that I regret,
> Renew their names, that men may see some liegeness
>   Is left them yet.'   (CP 383–4)

The next night, equipped with a lantern (this is Hardy in gothic mode), he succeeds in finding their sadly defaced graves, on which their names are now barely legible, and resolves to repair them, only to be confronted by a mysterious stranger who claims not only to be a member of the family, but to have himself journeyed from the 'Pacific coast' precisely in order to restore the ruined resting places of his ancestors. Crestfallen, 'as one bereft / Of some fair object he had been moved to cherish' (CP 386), the man of memories retires, and is that night further depressed by a dream in which the 'phantoms of the ensepulchred' appear to him, accusing him of wanting to obliterate altogether the legends engraved on their tombstones, thus wiping them from the historical record forever. When, a year later, he returns, he finds the tomb still 'Untouched, untended, crumbling, weather-stained' (CP 387), and eventually begins to wonder if the mysterious relative was himself a phantom…He dies, his good deed unaccomplished, and in due course church restorers briskly resolve to demolish the tomb in order to broaden the church path:

> 'Their names can scarce be read;
> Depend on't, all who care for them are dead.'
> So went the tomb, whose shards were as path-paving
>   Distributed.
>
> Over it and about
> Men's footsteps beat, and wind and waterspout,
> Until the names, aforetime gnawed by weathers,
>   Were quite worn out.
>
> So that no sage can say
> In pensive progress near where they decay,
> 'This stone records a luminous line whose talents
>   Told in their day.'   (CP 387–8)

As in so many Hardy poems, the whirligig of time brings in its revenges, in despite, on this occasion, of the good intentions of the man of memories towards the last remnants of his foes. It is worth pointing out, however, that the poem's narrative, in alliance with the attritions of the passing years, ends up fulfilling precisely the vindictive plot that the protagonist was accused of hatching by his enemies in his dream.

And this alliance between the poem's progress and the workings of time also underpins the more complex tension between imaginative sympathy and covert retaliation that governs the development of the other poem inspired by Hardy's visit to Charles churchyard:

During Wind and Rain

They sing their dearest songs—
He, she, all of them—yea,
Treble and tenor and bass,
   And one to play;
With the candles mooning each face...
   Ah, no; the years O!
How the sick leaves reel down in throngs!

They clear the creeping moss—
Elders and juniors—aye,
Making the pathways neat
   And the garden gay;
And they build a shady seat...
   Ah, no; the years, the years,
See, the white storm-birds wing across!

They are blithely breakfasting all—
Men and maidens—yea,
Under the summer tree,
   With a glimpse of the bay,
While pet fowl come to the knee...
   Ah, no; the years O!
And the rotten rose is ript from the wall.

They change to a high new house,
He, she, all of them—aye,
Clocks and carpets and chairs
   On the lawn all day,
And brightest things that are theirs...
   Ah, no; the years, the years;
Down their carved names the rain-drop ploughs.   (CP 495–6)

The Gifford-related aspects of this poem only became apparent with the publication of *Some Recollections* in 1961. The details given in the first five lines of each stanza derive fairly directly from Emma's accounts of her family's life in Plymouth, and even the short first line of the ballad-like refrain that makes us aware that these scenes happened a long time ago, and that those depicted, for all their vitality and hopes and schemes, are now dead and buried, had its origins in Emma's text, as did the rain of its title and of its last line. It is without doubt the Hardy poem that illustrates most fully his ability to exploit, poetically, her writings and consciousness while also concealing the fact, for none of the relevant passages from *Some Recollections* were among those included in the *Life*:

For the first stanza:

My Father played the violin and my mother could play beautifully on the piano and sing like a professional. Her musical abilities were much enjoyed by us all as we stood round her piano to hear the Battle of Prague—Mary Queen of My Soul, and pieces and songs then in vogue. They taught us to sing harmony and our four voices went well together. (My youngest [brother] could not sing, though fond of music.) We sang rounds, such as 'See our Oars with feathered Spray' and 'Wisdom is better than silver or gold.' etc. A brother's alto was particularly melodious. Sometimes my Mother and my Father sang their old songs together as in their youth.

(SR 14–15)

For the second stanza:

This garden had fine fruit trees in full bearing, besides a large kitchen garden and many flower beds. An unusual possession for a house in a street was a magnificent Elm tree of great age and girth showing itself high above the houses. We could see it in after years after we had removed to the north of the Town. But it has long since been cut down; all has been changed with the oncoming years ['Ah, no; the years O!']; a street is now in our old garden. Underneath the tree were on each side of it long garden seats with long tables and a circular seat encircling it, nothing could have been better arranged by our elders, a most delightful spot it was for happy childhood—nearby were the flower beds, and a strange old sweet-scented jessamine with deep-coloured thick blossoms such I have never met with since.   (SR 5–6)

For the third stanza:

At one end of our garden we had a poultry-house put up, and a choice selection of poultry was bought, for there was a mania at that time for keeping handsome fowls, and particularly Cochin-Chinas and Brahma-Pouters, Speckled Hamburgs, Black Spanish, and pretty Bantams; we loved and admired them all... (SR 6)

For the fourth stanza:

Bedford Terrace, North Road, [Tavistock Road] was our next pleasant home. It was a fine Terrace with handsome houses and flights of steps, stone front parade with the houses all standing high above the wide terrace...(SR 30) Our upper front windows had glorious views over Plymouth. It stood so high that we could see right beyond the intervening houses to the Sound and harbour... (SR 32)

This move Hardy conflates with the Giffords' final departure from Plymouth after the death of John Attersoll Gifford's mother, and the revelation that they had been living off her capital rather than the interest that they thought it had been accruing, and accordingly found themselves much poorer than they had anticipated. Grandmother Gifford died in February 1860, and in May that year Emma's father was admitted to the Cornwall County Asylum in Bodmin in quest of a cure for problems that seem to have been related to hereditary schizophrenia compounded with alcoholism, and which forced him to abandon his career as a solicitor.[5] It was therefore her mother who

---

[5] The extracts from the medical reports of the various doctors who assessed John Attersoll Gifford included in Andrew Norman's chapter on the Gifford family in *Thomas Hardy: Behind the Mask* (Stroud: The History Press, 2011) vividly convey the seriousness of his problems: 'Occasional great excitement and restlessness—uncontrollable desire for intoxicating drinks—which when indulged in leads him to commit acts of violence to others and [to display] great eccentricity of manner'; 'I was informed by his Mother and Wife that he was extremely violent without any sufficient motive and that they were afraid of personal injury unless he were placed under restraint'; 'Manner irritable and violent, conversation incoherent and natural disposition and habits totally perverted'; 'has broken the windows of his home, injured the furniture, is very excitable and requires restraint' (150). The report also reveals that his father was a victim of a similar condition, as was Emma's older brother Richard Ireland Gifford. Richard was also admitted to Cornwall County Asylum in 1888 after attempting to commit suicide. He died in Warneford Asylum in Headington, Oxford, in 1904 having spent—like his brother-in-law—years working on an epic poem about the Napoleonic Wars (148). For further details see Norman's chapter, 'The Troubled Lives of the Giffords' (144–52); Stephen Mottram's 'Hardy,

had to organize and oversee the move. The family set off from Plymouth railway station during a raging storm, having sent ahead the hapless Willie Gifford to decide which of two possible houses they should rent:

> My second brother was sent on first…and had taken the smaller of the two which proved impossible to get into, as his masculine inaptitude for domestic affairs had caused him to forget the fact that our furniture was very large and we had much of it.   (SR 34–5)

In the context of these extracts from *Some Recollections*, 'During Wind and Rain' can be seen as balancing a potent fascination with the doings of the Giffords, as recounted by Emma in such delightful detail, with a more saturnine insistence that none of the appurtenances of their middle-class life will save them from death or even, as in 'The Obliterate Tomb', the erosion of their funerary monuments. And while Hardy's use of ostentatiously literary exclamations such as 'yea' and 'Aye', or a word such as 'maidens', can make the poem feel like a generalized elegy for the material comforts and ideological assumptions of bourgeois Victorian culture (which Hardy's writings could hardly be said to champion), the poem only permits the indulgence of such feelings of nostalgia because all involved are dead.

Further, the choric framing of the vignettes of the Giffords' life in Plymouth by a seemingly prophetic voice that refutes four times the glimpses of familial happiness transplanted from Emma's memoir makes the poem into a stylized enactment of exactly the emotional forces in play in their courtship and marriage: her 'unhesitant energy', to borrow a phrase from Philip Larkin's review of *Some Recollections*,[6] on display in her singing, her gardening, her playing with her 'pet fowl', clearly attracts and delights him, yet also calls forth a Tiresian resentment at her unselfconsciousness. The doom intoned in the reprise of each stanza possibly had its source in Emma's own forebodings on leaving Plymouth, which remained her favourite of all the towns and cities that she ended up living in:

> The heavens poured down a steady torrent on our farewells, and never did so watery an omen portend such dullness, and sadnesses and sorrows as

Emma and the Giffords: A Re-Appraisal', *The Hardy Society Journal* 8, 1 (2012), 24–46; and Fincham, *Hardy the Physician*, 73–4.

 6 Philip Larkin, *Required Writing* (London: Faber & Faber, 1983), 143.

they did for us. Cornwall was very strange at first, after we had had to leave our very pleasant home. [And] Soon troubles began.   (SR 34)

'Ah, no' interrupts each stanza's depiction of communal family activity with the incantatory force of a spell or curse, terminating the Giffords' leisurely middle-class routines by abruptly intruding the folkloric, atavistic traditions of a very un-middle-class art form—the tragic ballad.

'Thus from the past,' declares Merlin in the epilogue to *The Famous Tragedy of the Queen of Cornwall*,

> the throes and themes
> Whereof I spake—now dead as dreams—
>   Have been re-shaped and drawn
> In feinted deed and word, as though
> Our shadowy and phantasmal show
> Were very movements to and fro
>   Of forms so far-off gone.   (FTQC 77)

The phrase 'dead as dreams' encapsulates the paradoxes inherent in Hardy's poetics of necromancy: if 'During Wind and Rain' resurrects the Giffords from Emma's text only to bury them, they yet live in the dream of the poem, and the poem itself testifies to their power to haunt Hardy's fantasies, despite their deaths and rigorous exclusion from his autobiography. 'Their mirth', Merlin continues, 'crimes, fear and love begat / Your own, though thwart their ways.' 'Thwart' sums up many aspects of Hardy's relationship with Emma and her family, as of hers with his. Equally the word might be applied to describe the experience of moving from the ellipsis in which each fifth line of 'During Wind and Rain' tails off, to the emblems of mortality presented in its four refrains, culminating amid the Gifford graves in Charles churchyard in Plymouth:

> Ah, no; the years, the years;
> Down their carved names the rain-drop ploughs.

Emma's family lived for only a short while in Bodmin itself. The house they rented there was situated, she complained, 'practically in the churchyard, the larder looking into it and below the level, therefore quite unfit for food' (SR 35). To heighten the gothic atmosphere further, 'Owls of every kind and voice assailed our ears the whole night long.' By the end of 1861 they had moved from these insalubrious quarters into Kirland House, an impressive Regency residence located about a mile south of Bodmin, where they lived in a style as close to that of landed gentry as their 'impoverished circumstances' (SR 36) would allow. Quite how they managed the rent is not clear, for Kirland House boasted 'a panelled hall and staircase…a splendid matured walled garden well stocked with fruit trees, a lawn sloping down to a pretty rivulet and bathing pool; an old orchard, worn out but beautiful, where musrooms grew plenteously' (SR 35–6). Nevertheless, her mother, Emma plaintively recorded, 'was always longing to get back to Plymouth, as indeed we all were' (SR 37).

It was Devon rather than Cornwall that assumed for Hardy's West-of-Wessex girl, at work on her memoir in her attic a year or so before she died, the legendary aura of a lost paradise: 'no county has ever been taken to my heart like that one [of Devon]: its loveliness of place, its gentleness, and the generosity of the people are deeply impressed upon my memory' (SR 34). Further, the 'gentleness' of the Devonians that she recalled from her childhood years clearly stood in stark contrast to the 'guile' displayed by her husband's relatives in treacherous Dorset: '*My* beloved country is Devon', she pointedly writes in a letter of around a decade earlier to the Hardy-worshipping and Wessex-obsessed Rebekah Owen, 'my beloved people the gentle, good-hearted Devonians—without guile any of them, & altogether lovely' (LEFH 18).

Emma found life in rural Cornwall tedious. *Some Recollections* describes the Cornish working class as 'dull, aggressive' (SR 59), as 'primitive' and 'evil-speaking' (SR 46, 47): 'I never have liked the Cornish working orders', she confides, 'as I do Devonshire folk, the so-called independence of character was most disagreeable to live with and usually amounted to absence of kindly interest in others, of gratitude and of affection' (SR 58). However, unknown to her, the 'Unseen Power of great benevolence' that she celebrates at her memoir's conclusion would soon be stirring. The 'dullness' of life in Kirland House, as well as financial 'necessity' (SR 37), eventually impelled Emma's older sister Helen to take on the role of companion to an elderly lady called Miss Robartes, who lived in Tintagel; and it was in Miss Robartes's house that Helen one day met a sixty-five-year-old widower with grown-up children in search of a helpmeet to assist with parish duties relating to the church of St Juliot, to which he had just been appointed rector. '[I]t seems as if all had been arranged in orderly sequence for me,' reflects Emma, 'link after link occurring in a chain of movements to bring me to the point where my own fortunes came on' (SR 46).

Superstition and the supernatural feature in many of Hardy's poetic evocations of Emma in Cornwall. He returned from his first trip to Lyonnesse with 'magic in his eyes' (CP 254), and the magician Merlin—'a phantasmal figure', as the stage direction puts it, equipped 'with a white wand' (FTQC 5)—presides over the poetic drama that he composed over half a century later, and which can be read as his most elaborate and far-fetched transposition of their Cornish love story into legend. In his Prologue to the play, a scene to be staged in crepuscular gloom, the wizard to the court of King Arthur explains that he is about to conjure up the past:

> I come, at your persuasive call,
> To raise up in this modern hall
> A tragedy of dire duresse
> That vexed the Land of Lyonnesse:—
> Scenes, with their passions, hopes, and fears
> Sunk into shade these thousand years;
> To set, in ghostly grave array,
>   Their blitheness, blood, and tears,
> Feats, ardours, as if rife to-day
>   Before men's eyes and ears.   (FTQC 5)

The phantasmal Merlin here figures himself as answering some equally spectral 'persuasive call', just as the uncanny opening lines of 'After a Journey' prompt the unanswerable question of who is summoning whom:

> Hereto I come to view a voiceless ghost;
>   Whither, O whither will its whim now draw me?   (CP 349)

The agency implicit in the original version of the poem's first line, 'Hereto I come to interview a ghost' (CPVE 349), is brilliantly evaded by Hardy's revision, which, as so often happens in his Cornish elegies, presents the poet as compulsively surrendering to bewitching forces beyond his control. The supernatural elements in these poems can be seen as echoing 'across the dark space' between estranged husband and dead wife the various prophetic encounters with fortune-telling types described in Emma's *Some Recollections*. As well as the servant who predicted her future by breaking eggs into a glass of water, she meets 'a gipsy woman' who 'suddenly started up from the road-side, a little out of Bodmin, catching hold of my bridle and making me listen to her—a great deal of her prophesying came true' (SR 39–40). Further, 'Twice afterwards my fortune was told in an amazing way by cards which an old friend of the family laid out mysteriously' (SR 40). In addition, she recalls hearing 'various queer tales' and much that was 'strange…fresh, peculiar' (SR 51) from Cornish country-folk whom she visited during her rambles around the parish of St Juliot. In the third stanza of 'A Man Was Drawing Near to Me' (a poem spoken by Emma), Hardy refers glancingly to her fascination with such tales, using the allusion to stress her unawareness that she is herself on the verge of participating in a story that will prove much more momentous, although just as 'queer' and 'strange':

> I thought of nobody—not of one,
> But only of trifles—legends, ghosts—
> Though, on the moorland dim and dun
>> That travellers shun
>> About these coasts,
> The man had passed Tresparret Posts.   (CP 580)

Her untrammelled innocence is starkly contrasted with the irresistible forces driving towards St Juliot the man of her 'destiny', whom the poem's aura of foreboding converts into a weirdly ominous figure, someone more like her 'sinister mate', to use the term applied to the iceberg in 'The Convergence of the Twain', than her future redeemer. 'Alien they seemed to be', Hardy wrote in his 'Lines on the loss of the Titanic', 'No mortal eye could see / The intimate welding of their later history' (CP 307). Both poems culminate in impressively orchestrated tableaux of *sturm und drang*, the one cosmic ('Till the Spinner of the Years / Said "Now!" And each one hears, / And consummation comes, and jars two hemispheres'), the other domestic. Indeed, 'The Convergence of the Twain' can itself be read as the poetic 'sinister mate' of 'A Man Was Drawing Near to Me':

> There was no light at all inland,
> Only the seaward pharos-fire,
> Nothing to let me understand
>> That hard at hand
>> By Hennett Byre
> The man was getting nigh and nigher.

> There was a rumble at the door,
> A draught disturbed the drapery,
> And but a minute passed before,

With gaze that bore
My destiny,
The man revealed himself to me.   (CP 580)

The topographical precision on display in 'A Man Was Drawing Near to Me'
serves to fuse the biographical and realistic dimensions of the poem with its
gothic elements and feel of mesmeric inexorability. As Hardy noted in his
1895 Preface to *A Pair of Blue Eyes*, Emma's Cornwall exuded for him 'an
atmosphere like the twilight of a night vision' (PBE 3), yet at the same time
her presence there magnetized for him even the most quotidian incidents
and ordinary details, as demonstrated by poems such as 'Green Slates', 'The
Sundial on a Wet Day' (spoken by the sundial in the rectory at St Juliot), or
'The Frozen Greenhouse', subtitled 'St Juliot':

'There was a frost
Last night!' she said,
'And the stove was forgot
When we went to bed,
And the greenhouse plants
Are frozen dead!'

By the breakfast blaze
Blank-faced spoke she,
Her scared young look
Seeming to be
The very symbol
Of tragedy.

The frost is fiercer
Than then to-day,
As I pass the place
Of her once dismay,
But the greenhouse stands
Warm, tight, and gay,

While she who grieved
At the sad lot
Of her pretty plants—
Cold, iced, forgot—
Herself is colder,
And knows it not.   (CP 736–7)

It was during his first visit to St Juliot in March 1870 that this minor calamity occurred in the rectory greenhouse. Emma's blank-faced despair is recreated in the poem's first two stanzas with an earnestness and respect that make the scene as distinct as that of her standing in the quarry in 'Green Slates', and in both poems the startling freshness of the incident recalled is undiminished by the necromantic route that Hardy must take to reach it.

Among the Latin poets that Hardy records reading during his intense phase of self-education in the classics when he was sixteen is Ovid, and Emma's presence in the Cornish landscapes of his elegies for her insistently invokes the kind of interplay between character and nature that is dramatized in the *Metamorphoses*. Hardy himself can often seem in these poems like Apollo or Zeus discovering an untouched nymph in some remote and beautiful nook, and falling instantly in love with her:

> I found her out there
> On a slope few see,
> That falls westwardly
> To the salt-edged air,
> Where the ocean breaks
> On the purple strand,
> And the hurricane shakes
> The solid land.   (CP 342)

And as in Ovid, contact with the visitant from 'shires unknown' (CP 579) inevitably results in transformation, although not into a bird or beast, but into the twin antitheses of ghost, as in 'After a Journey', or loam, as in 'I Found Her Out There':

> I brought her here,
> And have laid her to rest
> In a noiseless nest
> No sea beats near.
> She will never be stirred
> In her loamy cell
> By the waves long heard
> And loved so well.

Further, the link forged in his fantasy between Emma's presence and the Cornish coast was so potent that, in a move that mirrors the Ovidian compensation of metamorphosis of the ravished nymph into flower or stream or tree, Hardy imaginatively restores her in death to her 'haunting-ground', the land- and seascapes where, for him at any rate, 'her life-parts most were played' (CP 809):

> So she does not sleep
> By those haunted heights
> The Atlantic smites
> And the blind gales sweep,
> Whence she often would gaze
> At Dundagel's famed head,
> While the dipping blaze
> Dyed her face fire-red;
>
> And would sigh at the tale
> Of sunk Lyonnesse,
> As a wind-tugged tress
> Flapped her cheek like a flail;
> Or listen at whiles
> With a thought-bound brow
> To the murmuring miles
> She is far from now.
>
> Yet her shade, maybe,
> Will creep underground
> Till it catch the sound
> Of that western sea
> As it swells and sobs
> Where she once domiciled,
> And joy in its throbs
> With the heart of a child.   (CP 342–3)

Like 'Green Slates' and 'The Frozen Greenhouse', 'I Found Her Out There' mediates between Hardy's awareness of the exiled corpse of Emma in her distant 'loamy cell' and the transformative powers of imaginative memory which can return her to her youth and Cornwall. The poem's last three stanzas are themselves haunted by a single sentence of *Some Recollections*, which was converted by Hardy, in an act of textual metamorphosis, into his reanimating vision of Emma at one with the elements on the 'haunted heights' of the Cornish coast:

> Scarcely any author and his wife could have had a much more romantic meeting with its unusual circumstances, in bringing them together from two different though neighbouring counties to this one at this very remote spot, with beautiful sea-coast, and the wild Atlantic ocean rolling in with its magnificent waves and spray, its white gulls and black choughs and grey puffins, its cliffs and rocks and gorgeous sunsettings sparkling redness in a track widening from the horizon to the shore.   (SR 50)

The 'unhesitant energy' of her prose is channelled into Hardy's excited recollection of her 'fire-red face' and 'wind-tugged tress', the compound adjectives working to fuse her with the setting sun and the wind, while it is the 'murmuring miles' of the sea that make her brow 'thought-bound'. As in so many of his elegies set in Cornwall, Emma is recreated as the local deity of the coast where he 'found her', while his success in wooing her and then transplanting her from her natural habitat is figured as the catalyst for her death.

The oblique but insistent parallels suggested by these poems with the transformations of Greek and Roman mythology make it seem plausible that the expansion of his horizons released by meeting Emma on some level connected with the ambitions generated by his self-education in the classics. The past, in other words, to which she opened the door included fuller access than one finds elsewhere in his poetry to classical landscapes and myth, which he fused with Arthurian legend to generate the 'magical' aura of his poetical Cornwall. In particular, he seemed never to tire of reliving the moment of discovery, which he conjugates in ways that frequently recall the initiation of some amorous adventure in the *Metamorphoses*. In 'A Dream or No' he remembers

> how, coastward bound on a night long ago,
> There lonely I found her,
> The sea-birds around her,
> And other than nigh things uncaring to know.   (CP 348)

Emma is here presented as an innocent recluse as happily indifferent to the world beyond as an Ovidian sea nymph, although *Some Recollections* makes clear that she was by no means content with her lot as a subordinate relative in her married sister's household and often felt frustrated by the lack of social opportunities available in remote St Juliot. A related poem, 'The Discovery', engineers a pivot from one classical realm to another. In the first of its two stanzas the poet wanders 'to a crude coast / Like a ghost' (CP 332) and seems initially to have entered the ominous realms of epic strife:

> Upon the hills I saw fires –
> Funeral pyres
> Seemingly—and heard breaking
> Waves like distant cannonades that set the land shaking.

These fires would have been started by farmers to clear gorse and bracken but seem to be used by Hardy to summon up the martial worlds of Virgil or Homer. In the poem's second stanza, however, his apprehension is converted into delight, for, instead of approaching a battlefield, he finds his journey ending in a pastoral love nest:

> And so I never once guessed
> A Love-nest,
> Bowered and candle-lit, lay
> In my way,
> Till I found a hid hollow,
> Where I burst on her my heart could not but follow.   (CP 333)

The poems which recreate Emma's Cornwall dramatically contradict, then, the philosophical implications of Hardyan stoicism, the notion that life offers only 'neutral-tinted haps' as he puts it in 'He Never Expected Much' (CP 886). Saturated with meaning and legend, they fearlessly employ the hyperbolic and extreme.

The most intense and radically divided of Hardy's 'discovery-of-Emma' poems is 'The Wind's Prophecy', in which his fateful trip to Cornwall of 7 March 1870 is transformed into a scene which might have been conjured up by the witches on the heath in *Macbeth*. Just as in 'A Man Was Drawing Near to Me' Emma was shown to be unconscious of her impending appointment with destiny, so in 'The Wind's Prophecy' the travelling poet is unaware that he is on the verge of exchanging his black-haired lover, who is based in a city in the east, for one with 'tresses flashing fair' who lives in rural seclusion on a western coast. The emotional division that will be caused by this exchange results in one of the most extravagant deployments of the pathetic fallacy since Ruskin invented the term. Here are the last three stanzas:

> From tides the lofty coastlands screen
> Come smitings like the slam of doors,
> Or hammerings on hollow floors,
> As the swell cleaves through caves unseen.
> Say I: 'Though broad this wild terrene,
> Her city home is matched of none!'
> From the hoarse skies the wind replies:
> 'Thou shouldst have said her sea-bord one.'
>
> The all-prevailing clouds exclude
> The one quick timorous transient star;
> The waves outside where breakers are
> Huzza like a mad multitude.
> 'Where the sun ups it, mist-imbued,'
> I cry, 'there reigns the star for me!'
> The wind outshrieks from points and peaks:
> 'Here, westward, where it downs, mean ye!'
>
> Yonder the headland, vulturine,
> Snores like old Skrymer in his sleep,
> And every chasm and every steep
> Blackens as wakes each pharos-shine.
> 'I roam, but one is safely mine,'
> I say. 'God grant she stay my own!'
> Low laughs the wind as if it grinned:
> 'Thy love is one thou'st not yet known.'   (CP 494–5)

Old Skrymer is a legendary Norse giant, and the allusion is in keeping with the poem's primitive, epic energies, as is Hardy's use of the archaic-sounding 'pharos-shine' for the beams of a lighthouse. It is odd that this elemental strife, which is being used to dramatize (if one recalls the actual nature of the journey that it transfigures in biographical terms) an imminent shift in the affections of an architectural clerk travelling mainly by rail on business, results not in bathos but an almost Wagnerian grandeur and drive, and an intense foreboding that recalls an Aeschylean tragic chorus.

Hardy gives no hint in the *Life* as to the identity of this dark and soon to be abandoned lover, although within his poetic oeuvre it seems reasonable to assume that she is also the speaker of 'The Shiver', whose man returns from a journey to the west and brutally explains:

> 'It's hard for your bearing, alas!
>
> 'But I've seen, I have clasped, where the smart ships plough,
>> One of far brighter brow.
> A sea-goddess. Shiver not. One far rarer
> In gifts than I find thee; yea, warmer and fairer:—
> I seek her again; and I love you not now.'   (CP 782)

Emma in this poem is transmuted into a pagan sea goddess (a warm one, fortunately), and in several of his Cornish elegies she is similarly depicted in mythological terms, as a hybrid being who inhabits a different plane of existence from that of her amazed admirer. Her horse Fanny often plays a part in this, elevating Emma above her non-riding suitor, as in 'The Going', in whose third stanza she assumes the power to scrutinize and speculate, reversing the gendered roles of courtship of the time. The poet is reduced to being the passive object of her gaze, while her alliance with features of the coastal scenery seems to grant her powers like those of an Ovidian deity:

> You were she who abode
> By those red-veined rocks far West,
> You were the swan-necked one who rode
> Along the beetling Beeny Crest,
>> And, reining nigh me,
>> Would muse and eye me,
> While Life unrolled us its very best.   (CP 338)

As in the opening lines of 'After a Journey', the vividness of the moment derives from the suspension of Hardy's sense of selfhood and agency. The 'red-veined rocks', characteristic of the coast around Boscastle, seem almost as alive as its 'swan-necked' inhabitant, who is here shown imperiously orchestrating their romance on what is definitively her terrain.

The metamorphic tendencies of Hardy's figurations of Emma in Cornwall are made most explicit in a poem called 'A Woman Driving'. She is not in this astride Fanny but instead depicted piloting a cart and horses up and down the perilous coastal roads around Boscastle, and even, or so it is rumoured, across the Atlantic itself:

> Some said her silent wheels would roll
> > Rutless on softest loam,
> And even that her steeds' footfall
> > Sank not upon the foam.   (CP 682)

In such a poem Emma has moved beyond Hardy's scope and understanding altogether, transformed into a half-glimpsed Cornish divinity, one released in its final verse not into the processes of nature, but into the ethereal and supernatural:

> Where drives she now? It may be where
> > No mortal horses are,
> But in a chariot of the air
> > Towards some radiant star.

Distance and difference are crucial to the development of romance throughout Hardy's poetry and fiction, and in his poems about Emma this is repeatedly marked geographically by his insistence that Cornwall is in the far west, although the journey from Dorchester to St Juliot could be accomplished in a day. There is not a great deal of evidence to suggest that Emma pined particularly intensely for Cornwall during the thirty-eight years of their marriage, but Hardy frequently pictured her doing so:

> Stretching eyes west
> Over the sea,
> Wind foul or fair,
> Always stood she
> Prospect-impressed;
> Solely out there
> Did her gaze rest,
> Never elsewhere
> Seemed charm to be.   (CP 448)

And in 'The Woman Who Went East' the journey is depicted as utterly ruinous. This poem imagines Emma as having returned to her western haunts and engaging in a ballad-like dialogue with a former lover who fails to recognize her. In the last two stanzas she unveils herself, and attributes the loss of all her former charms to her disastrous decision to abandon her native region:

'O unforgotten day long back,
  When, wilful, east she sped
From you with her new Love. Alack,
Her lips would still be ripe and red
  Had she not eastward sped!

'For know, old lover, dull of eyes,
  That woman, I am she:
This skeleton that Time so tries
Your rose of rareness used to be;
  Yes, sweetheart, I am she.' (CP 917)

Another dialogue poem, 'Fetching Her', dramatizes the same dilemma from the perspective of the eastern-dwelling husband who had assumed that by marrying a 'pure product', to borrow William Carlos Williams's phrase,[7] of the Cornish coast he would be importing into his own realm 'the pure brine breeze, the sea, / The mews—all her old sky and space' (CP 637). Alas, as the friend who speaks the poem points out, these high hopes fast prove illusory:

  —But time is prompt to expugn,
    My friend,
  Such magic-minted conjurings:
    The brought breeze fainted soon,
  And then the sense of seamews' wings,
    And the shore's sibilant tune.

  So, it had been more due,
    My friend,
  Perhaps, had you not pulled this flower
    From the craggy nook it knew,
  And set it in an alien bower;
    But left it where it grew! (CP 637)

These, along with ghost poems such as 'Her Haunting-Ground' and 'My Spirit Will Not Haunt the Mound' which present Emma's shade as returning to the Cornish coast as instinctively as a migrating bird, can be read as belated acts of propitiation, firstly for making Emma move east, and then

[7] William Carlos Williams, 'To Elsie', Selected Poems, ed. Charles Tomlinson (Harmondsworth: Penguin, 1976), 55 (l. 1).

for failing to return her in death to the 'surfy shore' (CP 636) on which he had found her.

'We grew much interested in each other,' Emma observed in *Some Recollections* of her visiting architect, 'and I found him a perfectly new subject of study and delight, and he found a "mine" in me, he said' (SR 58). She could not have known, when she wrote this less than two years before her death, that Hardy's excavation of the 'mine' that he found in her had, in the event, barely begun. From the moment that Emma died Hardy set about reanimating her as a 'phantom of his own figuring' (CP 354), recreating the scenes and landscapes of their courtship, in defiance of the present. And although he claimed in the last lines of 'At Castle Boterel' that he would 'traverse old love's domain / Never again' (CP 352), poem after poem revisits Beeny and Bos, St Juliot and Valency, or pleads with Emma's ghost to return her beleaguered, grieving, penitent widower to the sacred sites of their Cornish romance.

4

Courtship

As mentioned in the Preface, the only poem celebrating the momentous events of 7–11 March 1870 to appear in Emma's own lifetime was 'Ditty'. It was published in *Wessex Poems* of 1898, perhaps in the hope that it might mitigate the ill-feeling caused by poems self-evidently about other women, such as 'Thoughts of Phena', 'At an Inn', 'I Look Into My Glass' or 'In a Eweleaze Near Weatherbury', not to mention all the sonnets of the 1860s inspired by her predecessors in Hardy's affections, or indeed by 'The Ivy-Wife', which, as a letter of 1899 to Rebekah Owen makes clear, Emma read as a direct attack: '[P]erhaps you admire "The Ivy Wife",' she wrote to Hardy's American aficionado; 'Of course my wonder is great at any admiration for it, & SOME others *in the* same collection' (LEFH 19).

If only she could have seen in print the belated but unstinting efforts of her husband to recapture the magical effect of his meeting with her, characterized in 'An Experience' as 'a new afflation— / An aura zephyring round / That care infected not' (CP 616). Hardy frequently attempted to replicate this 'zephyring aura' by writing poems that verged on the musical, such as 'When I Set Out for Lyonnesse', which was given a magnificent orchestral setting by Gerald Finzi, or 'As 'Twere Tonight', one of the many subtitled 'Song':

> As 'twere to-night, in the brief space
>   Of a far eventime,
>   My spirit rang achime
> At vision of a girl of grace;
> As 'twere to-night, in the brief space
>   Of a far eventime.
>
> As 'twere at noontide of to-morrow
>   I airily walked and talked,
>   And wondered as I walked
> What it could mean, this soar from sorrow;
> As 'twere at noontide of to-morrow
>   I airily walked and talked.

Woman Much Missed: Thomas Hardy, Emma Hardy, and Poetry. Mark Ford, Oxford University Press.
© Mark Ford 2023. DOI: 10.1093/oso/9780192886804.003.0005

> As 'twere at waning of this week
> >   Broke a new life on me;
> >   Trancings of bliss to be
> In some dim dear land soon to seek;
> As 'twere at waning of this week
> >   Broke a new life on me!   (CP 582)

It is interesting to contrast the self-consciously virtuoso metaphors and literary diction deployed in pre-Emma love poems such as the 'She, to Him' sonnets with the more anonymous lyricism of a song-poem like this, which yet encodes a private experience that transformed at a stroke virtually every aspect of Hardy's life, or such is the implication of 'As 'Twere Tonight', as of so many of the poems that he wrote about his courtship of Emma. Hardy's *vita nuova* began that week, and the poem's lilting rhythms and rhymes—it is itself all 'achime'—both pay implicit homage to Emma's captivating musical abilities and illustrate the harmonies that she released in him.

Between 1870 and 1873 Hardy returned six times to the 'dim dear land' where he had discovered his 'girl of grace'. As far as one can tell, he spent around fifteen weeks in the company of Emma in the course of their courtship, but these visits were supplemented by a correspondence that Hardy liked to compare to that of Robert Browning and Elizabeth Barrett, according, at any rate, to Florence, who, in December 1931, wrote to the Hardy enthusiast Harold Bliss:

> With regard to the letters written by T.H. to E.L.G.—afterwards ELH—it was *she* who burned his letters, & he told me he much regretted that at the time, & since. She asked him for her letters to him which he had carefully preserved, & she burned those too. He told me he thought the letters quite as good as the Browning letters, & they might have been published.   (LEFH 312)

The only fragments that survive are a few sentences from two of Emma's missives that Hardy transcribed into his *Memoranda I* notebook:

> E's letter of yesterday: '--- this dream of my life—no, not dream, for what is actually going on around me seems a dream rather....I take him (the reserved man) as I do the Bible; find out what I can, compare one text with another, & believe the rest in a lump of simple faith.'   (PN 6)

The second sentence quoted is put pretty much directly into the mouth of Elfride in chapter 19 of *A Pair of Blue Eyes*, in which she tells Knight: 'I suppose I must take you as I do the Bible—find out and understand all I can; and on the strength of that, swallow the rest in a lump, by simple faith' (PBE 173–4). The extent to which their correspondence was 'mined' for the novel based on their courtship will never be known, but the transposition of Emma's words to Elfride is undoubtedly of a piece with the collaborative nature of the composition of the novel as a whole.

The second extract that Hardy copied out, from a letter of July 1874, some three months before they married, indicates that he was less willing to share with her progress on its successor, *Far from the Madding Crowd*, which was largely written in Higher Bockhampton, and made use of his terrain and family rather than hers:

> July 1874. E.L.G.'s letter. 'My work, unlike your work of writing, does not occupy my true mind much...
>
> 'Your novel seems sometimes like a child all your own & none of me.'   (PN 17)

A passage in the *Life* makes it clear that he had not shared with Emma even the outlines of his most successful early novel before it began appearing in the *Cornhill*: 'It can be imagined how delighted Miss Gifford was to receive the first number of the story, whose nature he had kept from her to give her a pleasant surprise, and to find that her desire of a literary course for Hardy was in fair way of being justified' (L 100).

Hardy commemorated his various visits to Cornwall in a poem included in *Late Lyrics and Earlier* called 'The Seven Times'. It uses a very characteristic Hardyan conceit. As he advances through 'thick dark', its speaker discovers trotting beside him a boy 'with uncertain air', who proceeds to unfold his tale:

> 'I reached—'twas for the first time—
> A dwelling. Life was clogged in me with care;
> I thought not I should meet an eyesome maiden,
> But found one there.
>
> 'I entered on the precincts for the second time—
> 'Twas an adventure fit and fresh and fair—
> I slackened in my footsteps at the porchway,
> And found her there.   (CP 687)

And so on. Hardy in fact skips over one of his courtship journeys to St Juliot, for the seventh visit is the one made in March 1913 with Henry after Emma's death:

> 'I went again—long after—aye, the seventh time;
>   The look of things was sinister and bare
> As I caught no customed signal, heard no voice call,
>   Nor found her there.   (CP 688)

Baffled by the amount of 'loving, loss, despair' that one so young claims to have experienced, the narrator turns his lantern on his youthful interlocutor, only to discover:

> His head was white. His small form, fine aforetime,
>   Was shrunken with old age and battering wear,
> An eighty-years long plodder saw I pacing
>   Beside me there.

As in 'An Experience', the sudden relief from 'care', from feeling 'cob-webbed, crazed' (CP 616) or 'clogged', forms an essential part of the process of falling in love as depicted by Hardy in his courtship poems. The soaring seven-beat line and triple rhyme scheme of 'Beeny Cliff' most dramatically enact this exhilarating feeling of escape into another world in which dream and reality, as in the passage Hardy quoted from Emma's letter of October 1870 ('for what is actually going on around me seems a dream rather'), appear merged in some glorious, uplifting, ever-shifting new compound or medium:

> I
>
> O the opal and the sapphire of that wandering western sea,
> And the woman riding high above with bright hair flapping
>   free—
> The woman whom I loved so, and who loyally loved me.
>
> II
>
> The pale mews plained below us, and the waves seemed
>   far away
> In a nether sky, engrossed in saying their ceaseless
>   babbling say,
> As we laughed light-heartedly aloft on that clear-sunned
>   March day.

III

A little cloud then cloaked us, and there flew an irised rain,
And the Atlantic dyed its levels with a dull misfeatured stain,
And then the sun burst out again, and purples prinked the
    main.   (CP 350–1)

As F. B. Pinion has pointed out, in his description of purples prinking the
main Hardy is recycling an image from Thomas Gray's 'The Progress of
Poesy', 'The bloom of young Desire and purple light of Love' (GT 194). He
would have read Gray's poem in Palgrave's *Golden Treasury*, and he quotes
from it also in chapter 4 of *A Pair of Blue Eyes*: 'She [i.e. Elfride] looked so
intensely *living* and full of movement as she came into the old silent place
that young Smith's world began to be lit by "the purple light" in all its defi-
niteness' (PBE 27).[1] Hardy's rapturous enjoyment in 'Beeny Cliff' of the
unpredictability of the weather mirrors his fascination with Emma's
refusal, or inability, to conform to his expectations. His previous romances
had been conducted, it is worth remembering, with women such as Eliza
Nicholls or his cousin Tryphena Sparks, who were obliged to work for a
living, whereas Emma occupied a somewhat undefined position as a
dependant in the Caddell Holder household. Her freedom from the practical and economic concerns that dogged Hardy and the wage-earning
women whom he had up to this point courted was most strikingly
embodied for him in the experience of watching her, to quote from *Some
Recollections*, 'scampering up and down the hills' on her beloved mare (SR 50).
'[T]he moment she was on a horse she was part of the animal' (L 77), he
wistfully recalled in the *Life*, whereas he—despite his depiction of himself
in 'Fetching Her' as having 'saddled' (CP 636) up before setting out for
Lyonnesse—always accompanied her on foot. In terms of social history,
Emma's skilled horsewomanship can be seen as deriving from, and dramatizing, her superior class status. In the writings about their courtship of
both, however, the image of the skilful 'girl-rider' galloping on Fanny
along the Cornish coast, her 'bright hair flapping free', incarnated the ideal

---

[1] I largely agree with F. B. Pinion's assessment of Donald Davie's much-celebrated essay,
'Hardy's Virgilian Purples' (first published in *Agenda: Thomas Hardy Special Issue* (1972), 138–56
and reprinted in *The Poet in the Imaginary Museum* (Manchester: Carcanet, 1977), 221–35).
In 'Hardy's Visits to Cornwall', in *New Perspectives on Thomas Hardy*, ed. Charles P. C. Pettit
(Basingstoke: Palgrave Macmillan, 1994), Pinion describes Davie's essay as an 'intoxicating
tour de force founded on false assumptions' (206). Thomas Gray's 'The Progress of Poesy', rather
than Virgil's use of *purpureus* in book VI of the *Aeneid* (l. 641), is undoubtedly the origin of
Hardy's references to purple in both *A Pair of Blue Eyes* and 'Beeny Cliff'.

of an escape into an idyllic realm beyond the 'rut' (CP 717) of financial pressures and social conventions. Indeed, the poem's dizzying vistas should perhaps be read as a sublimation of the anxieties of which the lovers are momentarily relieved, or as a glorious dispersal of them amid the fickle energies of the weather and the ever-changing Atlantic.

The most important of the 'unusual circumstances' (SR 50) of their meeting by chance in a remote part of Cornwall was the release that it afforded from the contexts of their families and, accordingly, from inherited assumptions and inhibitions. Roaming with Emma on Beeny Cliff licensed a release in Hardy, as both reader and writer, of the 'poetic' that verged on a flood. It inspired him while there with Emma on 10 March 1870 to quote 'Break, break, break, / On thy cold grey stones, O Sea!', and when he returned forty-three years later to compose (perhaps partially under the influence of the Dover cliff episode in *King Lear*) a poem that more exuberantly than any other emancipates the lovers from their given historical circumstances and particular social and familial identities. The best gloss on the transposition of emotions onto sea and sky and cliff achieved in the first three stanzas of this poem is his attempt to characterize the effects of certain watercolours by Turner: 'a landscape *plus* a man's soul' (L 225). And yet 'Beeny Cliff' also leaves traces of what has to be suppressed or sublimated for the soul to achieve the state of 'flapping free'. As mentioned in the Prologue, 'loyally' in the last line of the first stanza ('The woman whom I loved so, and who loyally loved me') glances obliquely at all that menaced the burgeoning relationship, and the 'dull misfeatured stain' can possibly be linked to the threat of ancestral madness that Hardy in time came to believe Emma had inherited, and which he presents as dogging her in poems such as 'At the Piano', 'The Blow', 'At a Fashionable Dinner', and 'The Interloper'. Certainly, the latter's epigraph, which was invented by Hardy for the final printing of this poem after some probing by Vere Collins in an interview of December 1920, seems to echo the term 'misfeatured': 'And I saw the figure and visage of Madness seeking for a home' (CP 488). This minor premonition or 'shiver' vanishes almost at once, yet possibly instigates the cut from March 1870 to March 1913, from self-forgetful, exhilarated recollection to the chastening question-and-answer rituals of elegy:

IV

—Still in all its chasmal beauty bulks old Beeny to the sky,
And shall she and I not go there once again now March is nigh,
And the sweet things said in that March say anew there by and by?

V

What if still in chasmal beauty looms that wild weird
    western shore,
The woman now is—elsewhere—whom the ambling
    pony bore,
And nor knows nor cares for Beeny, and will laugh there
    nevermore.

Hardy set off on his second visit to St Juliot, which would last around three weeks, on 8 August 1870. On arrival he found 'the "young lady in brown" of the previous winter—at that time thickly muffled from the wind—to have become metamorphosed into a young lady in summer blue, which suited her fair complexion far better' (L 81). The weather, for the first fortnight at least, was glorious. In a footnote (that he later tried to erase) to Emma's discussion of his visits to the rectory in *Some Recollections* Hardy asserted that this second sojourn there was 'by invitation of Mr Holder' (SR 56), meaning that it can be seen as his debut as a houseguest. In due course Hardy would be invited to stay at an impressive variety of stately homes, such as Eggesford House (by Lady Portsmouth), Vice-Regal Lodge in Dublin (by Lord Houghton), and Rushmore (by General Augustus Lane Fox Pitt-Rivers), but there was clearly some awkwardness in his initial attempts to adapt to this role. These emerge most clearly in chapter 7 of *A Pair of Blue Eyes*, which describes Stephen Smith's return to Endelstow Rectory. When he and Elfride play chess, she is puzzled by his peculiar handling of the pieces, and then amazed to be told that he taught himself the game wholly from books and has in fact never actually played it before. 'This was a full explanation of his mannerism,' Elfride reflects; 'but the fact that a man with the desire for chess should have grown up without being able to see or engage in a game astonished her not a little' (PBE 48). Stephen then partially redeems himself by accurately completing, and translating, a quotation from Horace delivered by Parson Swancourt, only to be informed by the parson that his pronunciation of the Latin is 'grotesque' (PBE 49). Hardy claimed in the *Life* that Stephen's method of acquiring Latin entirely through correspondence with his mentor, Knight, was based on a story related to him by the original of Parson Swancourt, the Revd Caddell Holder, and yet, having explained in such detail his own autodidactic feats in chapter 2 of his autobiography, one can't help reading this as one of Hardy's sly pleasantries. Like his alter ego, Hardy was both proud of his strenuous efforts at self-education and aware that they rendered him vulnerable.

A year or so after it was issued as a book, Hardy was delighted to receive a letter from Coventry Patmore praising *A Pair of Blue Eyes* but admitting that he 'regretted at almost every page that such unequalled beauty and power should not have assured themselves the immortality which would have been impressed upon them by the form of verse' (L 107–8). The novel is, indeed, studded with quotations from Hardy's favourite poets: Elfride and Stephen flirt by exchanging quotations from Keats's 'La Belle Dame Sans Merci' (PBE 53–4), and each of its forty chapters is introduced with an epigraph from such as Wyatt, Marlowe, Shakespeare, Milton, Gray, Burns, Scott, Wordsworth, Byron, and Tennyson, all of whom feature in Hardy's *Studies, Specimens &c.* notebook, compiled during his nights of study in his room in 16 Westbourne Park Villas in London.

Poetry, further, played an important role not only in his courtship novel but in the courtship itself. In 'An Ancient to Ancients', a poem which, like 'During Wind and Rain', elegizes the passing of High Victorianism, he devotes a stanza to the nook in the rectory garden to which he and Emma would retreat to read their favourite poems and passages by the poet laureate:[2]

> The bower we shrined to Tennyson,
>> Gentlemen,
> Is roof-wrecked; damps there drip upon
> Sagged seats, the creeper-nails are rust,
> The spider is sole denizen;
> Even she who voiced those rhymes is dust,
>> Gentlemen!   (CP 696)

This probably recalls 18 August, the day of the battle of Gravelotte in the Franco-Prussian War, for on that day, Hardy records in the *Life*, 'they were reading Tennyson in the grounds of the rectory' (L 81). He continues:

It was at this time and spot that Hardy was struck by the incident of the old horse harrowing the arable field in the valley below, which, when in far later years it was recalled to him by a still bloodier war, he made into the little poem of three verses entitled 'In Time of "The Breaking of Nations"'.

---

[2] For an illuminating account of Hardy's poetic relationship to Tennyson, see Helen Small, 'Hardy's Tennyson', in *Tennyson among the Poets*, eds. Robert Douglas-Fairhurst and Seamus Perry (Oxford: Oxford University Press, 2009), 356–74.

The maid and wight of this poem's final verse can on one level be seen as Darwinian victors whose DNA will be passed down the generations and hence survive when the First World War itself will have vanished into cloudy remoteness, and yet something of the legendary potency that Hardy ascribed to the 'story' of the love that he shared with Emma surely also creeps into this image. As in 'At Castle Boterel', where he asserts that what the primeval rocks bordering the road up from Boscastle primarily record is that he and Emma 'passed' there (CP 352), so in 'In Time of "The Breaking of Nations"' the sublime sweep of history is evoked as a means of framing the still more sublime triumph of the love of the maid and her wight:

> Yonder a maid and her wight
> Come whispering by:
> War's annals will cloud into night
> Ere their story die.   (CP 543).

History, in such poems, functions rather as sea and sky and nature did in 'Beeny Cliff'. And in this wartime poem (it is dated 1915), the defiantly archaic terms 'maid' and 'wight' liberate these lovers just as effectively from their given social identities, allowing them to assume the generic power of archetypes.

His three-week stay in St Juliot in August of 1870 was undoubtedly decisive in Hardy's understanding of the direction in which his relationship with Emma was heading. By the autumn of that year he felt himself to be 'virtually if not distinctly engaged to be married to a girl with no money' (he is here recounting his financial prospects) 'except in reversion after the death of relatives' (L 86). The phrasing neatly captures his sense of Emma's status: she is herself penniless but comes from a family that belonged to a stratum of society in which fortunes, or even estates, might be passed 'in reversion' to descendants. The delicate relationship between class and money here broached resonates throughout *A Pair of Blue Eyes*. In chapter 10 Stephen Smith's mother confronts her infatuated son so directly on the issue of Elfride's penury that one wonders how Emma responded to this episode:

'I knew she was after 'ee, Stephen—I knew it.'

'After me! Good Lord, what next!'

'And I really must say again that you ought not to be in such a hurry, and wait for a few years. You might go higher than a bankrupt pa'son's girl then.'   (PBE 86)

More wounding still must have been a gibe delivered by Mrs Smith later in the conversation: 'She'd most likely have died an old maid if you hadn't turned up.'

Emma herself avoided reflecting on the sordid business of ways and means in the memories of this second visit of Hardy's that she set down in *Some Recollections*:

> I rode my pretty mare Fanny and he walked by my side and I showed him some [more] of the neighbourhood—the cliffs, along the roads, and through the scattered hamlets, sometimes gazing down at the solemn small shores [below] where the seals lived, coming out of great caverns very occasionally. We sketched and talked of books; often we walked down the beautiful [Vallency] Valley to Boscastle harbour where we had to jump over stones and climb over a low wall by rough steps, [or] get through by narrow path-ways to come out on great wide spaces suddenly, with a sparkling little brook going the same way, into which we once lost a tiny picnic-tumbler, and there it is to this day no doubt between two small boulders.　(SR 57)

The poem based on this last incident, 'Under the Waterfall', was positioned by Hardy just before the 'Poems of 1912–13' section of *Satires of Circumstance* and serves as an introduction to the new kind of elegy developed in those poems. We know the picnic took place on 19 August from a drawing that Hardy made of Emma searching for the tumbler and dated. They were on their way 'to sketch at Boscastle Harbour', as Hardy notes at the top right of his drawing, sketching *en plein air* being another highly respectable art form that they enjoyed sharing during their courtship and, to a certain extent, in the course of their marriage.[3] Hardy's frankly admiring drawing depicts Emma with her hand in the stream, her cascading locks obscuring her face, her whole being absorbed in her search for the dropped tumbler,

---

[3] Sir George Douglas, for instance, describes a 'delightful wrangle' that developed while Emma was at work on a sketch during their stay on his estate at Kelso in Scotland in September 1891: 'On an off day, for I didn't want to work my guests too hard, Mrs Hardy attempted a sketch of the house from a rising ground near at hand, and I well remember the delightful wrangle between husband and wife that ensued. "Now you'd better let me touch in the perspective", said the quondam architect; or again, grasping the sketch-book, "Let me put in the trees, and the gable and balustrade will come in almost of themselves". But though Hardy was by much the better draughtsman, and in fact wanted to do the whole picture himself, his good lady had confidence in her own handiwork' (from 'Thomas Hardy: Some Recollections and Reflections' (1928), reprinted in THR, 84).

which becomes, in the 'real love-rhyme' that the poem offers to Hardy's drawing, a 'drinking-glass', then a 'vessel', then a 'chalice'.

The backward-looking temporal layering dramatized in the poem is increased further by a footnote in the *Life* acknowledging that the poem was inspired by Hardy's reading of *Some Recollections* (L 74). In other words, the reminiscences put by her ventriloquizing husband into the mouth of the recently deceased Emma are a means of converting for him, rather than for her, their picnic mishap of over four decades earlier into a recurring series of recoveries of lost time:

> 'Whenever I plunge my arm, like this,
> In a basin of water, I never miss
> The sweet sharp sense of a fugitive day
> Fetched back from its thickening shroud of gray.
>> Hence the only prime
>> And real love-rhyme
>> That I know by heart,
>> And that leaves no smart,
> Is the purl of a little valley fall
> About three spans wide and two spans tall
> Over a table of solid rock,
> And into a scoop of the self-same block;
> The purl of a runlet that never ceases
> In stir of kingdoms, in wars, in peaces;
> With a hollow boiling voice it speaks
> And has spoken since hills were turfless peaks.'   (CP 335–6)

Symmetries here abound, perhaps primarily in the way that the poem's own rhymes match the rhyming of the arm plunged into the waterfall with the arm plunged into the basin in a moment of synchrony that manages to elide the steady obliteration of the passing years, here given a funereal tinge in the image of the 'thickening shroud of gray'. The poem's overall paradox, which is why it serves so well as a prologue to the 'Poems of 1912–13', is that it is the loss of the drinking glass that preserves it in memory, and indeed invests it with a sacred aura. It comes to seem like a religious symbol of their love at its purest, a relic sequestered forever from the quotidian, although it is the everyday action of putting her arm into a basin of cold water that triggers the memory. 'And why,' enquires Emma's friend or acquaintance,

does plunging your arm in a bowl
Full of spring water, bring throbs to your soul?'

'Well, under the fall, in a crease of the stone,
Though where precisely none ever has known,
Jammed darkly, nothing to show how prized,
And by now with its smoothness opalized,
  Is a drinking-glass:
  For, down that pass
  My lover and I
  Walked under a sky
Of blue with a leaf-wove awning of green,
In the burn of August, to paint the scene,
And we placed our basket of fruit and wine
By the runlet's rim, where we sat to dine;
And when we had drunk from the glass together,
Arched by the oak-copse from the weather,
I held the vessel to rinse in the fall,
Where it slipped, and sank, and was past recall,
Though we stooped and plumbed the little abyss
With long bared arms. There the glass still is.
And, as said, if I thrust my arm below
Cold water in basin or bowl, a throe
From the past awakens a sense of that time,
And the glass we used, and the cascade's rhyme.
The basin seems the pool, and its edge
The hard smooth face of the brook-side ledge,
And the leafy pattern of china-ware
The hanging plants that were bathing there.

'By night, by day, when it shines or lours,
There lies intact that chalice of ours,
And its presence adds to the rhyme of love
Persistently sung by the fall above.
No lip has touched it since his and mine
In turns therefrom sipped lovers' wine.' (CP 336–7)

The rhyming extends to the mutuality established by the courting couple
drinking 'lovers' wine' in turn from the same 'chalice'—which, in retrospect

at any rate, can be viewed as their love's holy grail—and then by their both plunging their arms into the pool in search of it. To be in love, Roland Barthes reflected in *A Lover's Discourse*, is to be in 'the crucible of meaning'[4] and from their 'opalized' drinking glass radiate correspondences connecting not only past and present, or the feel of cold water then and now, but the edge of the basin with the 'brook-side ledge', and even the plants hanging over the pool with the leafy pattern of chinaware above the basin. Furthermore, it transforms the 'hollow boiling voice' of the stream itself into a sung 'rhyme of love', illustrating again the Ovidian mode deployed in so many of Hardy's poems about his courtship in Cornwall. And, as is so often the case in poems about containers, from Keats's 'Ode on a Grecian Urn' to Wallace Stevens's 'Anecdote of the Jar' or 'The Poems of Our Climate', the most telling correspondence of all is that developed between the poem itself and the lovers' shared drinking vessel, which, though submerged 'past recall', is yet preserved as the source of the poem's intricate thematic and imagistic patterning and its insistently rhyming couplets.

Hardy is himself absent, it is worth noting, from the supposed present of the poem, that is the conversation between Emma and her interlocutor, although one can of course sense him, with 'bared arm', plumbing a personal abyss in the wake of Emma's death, in search of some redemptive 'chalice' in which to enshrine his happy memories of their courtship, and thus preserve them from contamination by the misery that followed. It accordingly lacks the strains of self-recrimination and despair that surface in the 'Poems of 1912–13', or the mournful brooding of other lyrics about their sketching expeditions of August 1870, such as 'Why Did I Sketch?' or 'The Figure in the Scene'. In the latter poem Hardy's drawing is blotted by raindrops (the good weather having broken) that end up 'engrained' on the paper, just as Emma's image ends up 'engrained', or so the poem claims, on the cragged slope on which he drew her:

> Yet her rainy form is the Genius still of the spot,
>   Immutable, yea,
> Though the place now knows her no more, and has
>   known her not
>   Ever since that day.   (CP 476)

---

[4] Roland Barthes, *A Lover's Discourse*, trans. Richard Howard (New York: Hill and Wang, 1978), 67.

As the dropped wineglass of 'Under the Waterfall' survives in a metamorphosed state, 'opalized' by the water coursing around it, so Emma emerges as the immutable 'Genius' of the shore only once she has been stained by rainfall, rendered as opaque and unreachable as the precious chalice of 'Under the Waterfall', enveloped in the 'gauze / Of moisture, hooded, only her outline shown'.

While Mrs Smith may have been convinced that Elfride would have ended up an old maid had her son not been summoned to draw up plans for the restoration of Endelstow Church, the original of Hardy's heroine, possibly in collusion with her sister and brother-in-law, felt it important to establish that there was local competition for her hand. Much play was evidently made during Hardy's visits to St Juliot rectory of other possible suitors, and he himself appears to have been convinced by, or at least ready to entertain the notion that he had rivals to see off. In *Some Recollections* Emma excludes from her general condemnation of the Cornish working classes one who

> stands out [saliently] amongst them with worth of character and deep devotion though rather dumb of expression, a man gentle of nature, musical, christlike in guilelessness, handsome of face and figure, David-like farming his own land: he never married, and told after I had left of his disappointment, and [of his] attraction on first seeing me on the stairs. (SR 59) [Emma is here referring to the welcome party arranged for Caddell Holder and his bride by their parishioners at which the 'foremost young farmer' (SR 47) made a speech, while Emma looked on from the rectory stairs.]

This David-like figure was probably John Jose (MM 113), but no evidence has emerged to suggest that he was seriously courting Emma. Imaginatively, however, Hardy was compulsively drawn to the dynamics of male rivalry, and poems such as 'The Face at the Casement' and 'The Young Churchwarden' introduce analogous elements of rivalry to his poetic narrative of his own wooing. The manuscript of the latter includes the subheading 'At an Evening Service, August 14, 1870', that is five days before the episode of the lost tumbler. Hardy and Emma attended evensong at Lesnewth Church on that Sunday. Unlike 'Under the Waterfall', 'The Young Churchwarden' filters the moment recalled from the distant past through the embittering lenses of disappointment and then loss:

When he lit the candles there,
And the light fell on his hand,
And it trembled as he scanned
Her and me, his vanquished air
Hinted that his dream was done,
And I saw he had begun
            To understand.

When Love's viol was unstrung,
Sore I wished the hand that shook
Had been mine that shared her book
While that evening hymn was sung,
His the victor's, as he lit
Candles where he had bidden us sit
            With vanquished look.

Now her dust lies listless there,
His afar from tending hand,
What avails the victory scanned?
Does he smile from upper air:
'Ah, my friend, your dream is done;
And 'tis *you* who have begun
            To understand!'   (CP 457)

The final stanza uses in the same order the same rhyme words as the first, thereby linking the courtship moment of triumph with the churchyard moment of defeat. The repetition mimes the neat satirical twists that the poem performs, as the triumphant suitor has the tables turned on him twice: first by his miserable marriage—the unstringing of 'Love's viol'— which makes him wish that he, rather than the churchwarden, had been 'vanquished'; then by the further revenge of her death, which unstrings him in new and unexpected ways. As so often in Hardy, he can only begin to 'understand' because it is too late for that understanding to change anything.

The lineaments of disaster ironically traced in 'The Young Churchwarden', as in analogous poems such as 'The Prophetess' and 'By the Runic Stone' that also open with a vignette from his Cornish romance and then jump cut to tragedy, wistfully reverse or undermine the triumphant note of many of the poems inspired by Hardy's stays in the rectory. Little is revealed in the *Life* about the two visits that he made to St Juliot in the second year of his courtship, 1871. On his journey home from the first of these, which ran from late May to early June, he recalls browsing through the Smith and Son's surplus catalogue in their shop at Exeter station, and discovering that *Desperate Remedies*, published only two and a half months earlier, had already been remaindered, with all three volumes available for a mere two shillings and sixpence. He bitterly concluded that a hostile review in the *Spectator*—the one that he read on a stile overlooking a eweleaze near Higher Bockhampton which made him wish 'he were dead' (L 507)—had 'snuffed out the book' (L 87).

A similarly extreme degree of sensitivity is on display in 'Love the Monopolist', one of the few courtship poems dated to an incident of 1871. It describes bidding farewell to Emma at Launceston station. As the young lover's train pulls out, he is disconcerted to see the 'airy slim blue form' of Emma turn around and gaily greet some friends instead of watching his train disappear into the distance:

> 'O do not chat with others there,'
>   I brood. 'They are not I.
> O strain your thoughts as if they were
>   Gold bands between us; eye
> All neighbour scenes as so much blankness
>   Till I again am by!   (CP 479)

Hardy's early poetry, as he acknowledged in the *Life*, was strongly influenced by John Donne (L 51), and he is here adapting an image from 'A Valediction Forbidding Mourning', which fancifully imagines the distance between the lovers not as a 'breach, but an expansion, / Like gold to airy thinness beat'.[5] Its companion poem, within Hardy's own poetic oeuvre, is 'The Minute Before Meeting' (also dated to 1871, and the only sonnet that Hardy ever wrote about Emma), which makes use of the Elizabethan-style poetic idiom of his early love poetry to register the trials of a Victorian long engagement. Arriving, in this poem, is as fraught with anxiety and disappointment as departing is in 'Love the Monopolist':

> And knowing that what is now about to be
> Will all *have been* in O, so short a space!

---

[5] John Donne, *The Complete English Poems*, ed. A. J. Smith (Harmondsworth: Penguin, 1986), 84 (ll. 23–4).

> I read beyond it my despondency
> When more dividing months shall take its place,
> Thereby denying to this hour of grace
> A full-up measure of felicity.   (CP 236)[6]

These two poems both dramatize and anatomize Hardy's tendency to see 'the *other side* of common emotions' (L 59), to return to the aspect of his poetry discussed in Chapter 2, that is his interest in the flux of feeling 'before & after the usually chief incident' (PM 54), as well as his propensity, to quote Thomas Carlyle on Jean Paul Richter, 'to change a laughing face into a sad one.'[7] Both, further, suggest the cost of such a habit when it comes to transitions in and out of the presence of the beloved. Donne surely appealed to the young Hardy for his ability to fuse extravagance and irony, and something of Donne's compulsion to monopolize through self-mocking exaggeration inflects the last stanzas of 'Love the Monopolist':

> 'A troubled soughing in the breeze
>   And the sky overhead
> Let yourself feel; and shadeful trees,
>   Ripe corn, and apples red,
> Read as things barren and distasteful
>   While we are separated!
>
> 'When I come back uncloak your gloom,
>   And let in lovely day;
> Then the long dark as of the tomb
>   Can well be thrust away
> With sweet things I shall have to practise,
>   And you will have to say!'   (CP 479–80)

Undoubtedly central to the 'felicity' that Hardy derived from Emma's company and correspondence were the 'sweet things' that she had to say about his authorial ambitions. By the summer of 1871 he had been havering for five or six years between architecture and literature, and he would not commit himself irrevocably to the latter until July the following year. He had

---

[6] See Marion Thain, 'The Poetics of Touch', *Victorian Poetry*, 51, 2 (2013), 137–9, for an insightful exposition of this poem's conjugations of time and space.

[7] Thomas Carlyle, 'Jean Paul Friedrich Richter', *Critical and Miscellaneous Essays*, Vol. 1 (London: Chapman and Hall, 1888), 13.

lost, he learned from William Tinsley, the publisher of *Desperate Remedies*, only £15 of the £75 that he had been obliged to stake on the first of his novels to make it into print, and although he reported himself in the *Life* much gratified to discover he was only this amount out of pocket, it could hardly be construed as a promising debut. One gets the impression that doubting Thomas, at least in his exchanges with Emma, was all for abandoning his hope of making a career as an author, while she remained 'Unchilled by damps of doubt', as he puts it in his frankest tribute to her support, 'A Woman's Trust', included in *Late Lyrics*:

> If he should live a thousand years
> He'd find it not again
> That scorn of him by men
> Could less disturb a woman's trust
> In him as a steadfast star which must
> Rise scathless from the nether spheres:
> If he should live a thousand years
> He'd find it not again.
>
> She waited like a little child,
> Unchilled by damps of doubt,
> While from her eyes looked out
> A confidence sublime as Spring's
> When stressed by Winter's loiterings.
> Thus, howsoever the wicked wiled,
> She waited like a little child
> Unchilled by damps of doubt.   (CP 682–3)

He often appended, during this period of acute uncertainty, dates to pertinent lines from Shakespeare as a way of recording his state of mind. 'July 1871' is inserted beside Ross's attempt to comfort Lady Macduff (just before she is murdered) in *Macbeth*: 'Things at their worst will cease, or else climb upward / To what they were before' (L 88). This suggests Hardy felt that he was approaching either the nadir or the turn in his fortunes. The following month he dispatched *Under the Greenwood Tree* to Alexander Macmillan and during his October stay in St Juliot received back a letter that must have left the expectant pair dismally deflated: 'There is really much charming writing in it,' Macmillan began promisingly, only to dash immediately whatever hopes he had raised: 'But I think the public will find the tale very slight and rather unexciting. The first 50 or 60 pages too are really rather tedious and should at least be shortened by about one half.[8] There followed a tepidly expressed offer to reconsider the matter in the spring, but Hardy interpreted the letter to mean yet another rejection.

At this point Emma's 'simple faith' in her suitor proved crucial, for Hardy—or so he later told the playwright and novelist Eden Phillpotts—resigned the matter entirely to her. Phillpotts lived near Torquay in Emma's beloved Devon, and he hosted Hardy and Florence there in mid-October 1917. During one of their walks the view from a limestone bluff of the bay between Torquay and Berry Head rekindled in Hardy—how one hopes that Florence missed this particular excursion!—memories of his courtship of Emma on the Cornish coast. 'There', Phillpotts reflects, 'he had met his fate and lost his heart; and now, half a century later, those days of bygone happiness could still warm his soul and bring a glimmer of contentment through the grey ambience of old age.' Phillpotts continues:

As we stood looking out upon the sea, Hardy related—very cheerfully and with keen interest—the story of a crucial challenge that faced him upon marriage, when his own future course of action still demanded decision. The problem lay between two professions, and it remained for him to determine whether he would devote his life to the business of Letters, as the more attractive yet more hazardous career, or cleave to architecture for the security it promised, while practising poetry and fiction as an occupation for leisure and an addition to less vital activities. It seems fantastic that one so rich in great endowments should have felt any shadow of doubt upon such a question, but the extreme modesty of his self-estimate had made him consider decision a matter of utmost difficulty. Then he told me how he had solved the problem by shifting its final solution upon the shoulders of his future wife. To Emma Gifford he left the great decision, and looking back he indicated his sense of everlasting gratitude to her. He seemed to feel his future had rested in her hands, and that only by a brave exercise of her faith in him had she fulfilled his destiny. All that happened afterwards of tragedy and grief was swept away when he fixed his thoughts on that tremendous fact. One cannot put any definite words into the mouth of the dead unless they were recorded when spoken, but I well remember his animation at this recital and his use of one adjective.

[8] Charles Morgan, *The House of Macmillan (1843–1943)* (London: Macmillan, 1943), 99.

He declared that it was a 'fine' thing that his first wife had done, and clearly he held it in precious memory as the turning-point of his career: a stimulus to make life worth living where stimuli had always been few.   (THR 54–5)

The *Life* makes it clear that Emma's letters urged him to persevere with his writing in gloriously peremptory terms (it was 'her desire that he should adhere to authorship, which she felt sure would be his true vocation' (L 89)), whereas his family seemed to have been neutral, at best, on which profession he should adopt. She 'believed in him', as the last stanza of 'A Woman's Trust' asserts twice, while acknowledging that her staunch faith in him as 'a steadfast star' would by no means guarantee her lasting happiness:

> Through cruel years and crueller
> > Thus she believed in him
> > And his aurore, so dim;
> That, after fenweeds, flowers would blow;
> And above all things did she show
> Her faith in his good faith with her;
> Through cruel years and crueller
> > Thus she believed in him!   (CP 683)

St Juliot Church was reopened on 11 April 1872. The architect who had drawn up the plans for its restoration was, for reasons unknown, not able to be present at this 'brilliant occasion' (SR 57), but the statement of receipts and expenditure reveals that he had donated ten shillings of his own money towards the total costs of around £1,240. Miss Gifford contributed the same amount, but also raised eight shillings and ten pence from the sale of sketches. Her brother, her uncle, and her sister also made modest donations but her father's name is conspicuously absent from this list.

Some three and a half months later, Hardy found himself on the banks of the Rubicon of his professional life. *Under the Greenwood Tree* was issued by the early Hardy's publisher-of-last-resort, Tinsley—this time without a subvention—in June 1872, and although sales were modest it found favour with several reviewers. Pleased with his discovery, Tinsley offered Hardy £200 for the right to serialize his next novel (provisionally entitled *A Winning Tongue Had He*) in *Tinsley's Magazine*, followed by publication in three volumes. Hardy had by this time moved back to London and found work with the architect Roger T. Smith, who specialized in designs for new schools—and whose surname Hardy would soon borrow for his youthful architect protagonist. The letter that Hardy sent to Tinsley on 27 July agreeing to his terms committed him to delivering an instalment a month; and although some Victorian novelists, such as the ferociously industrious Anthony Trollope, managed to combine a day job with the writing of three-decker fictions, for Hardy this proved the decisive fork in the road. By the time that he boarded an Irish Mail Packet Company vessel bound for Plymouth at London Bridge on 7 August—a journey that would also find its way into *A Pair of Blue Eyes*—Hardy had dispatched to Tinsley the first five chapters with the instruction that two proofs were to be sent to the author 'Care of John Gifford, Esq. Kirland House, nr. Bodmin' (RP 11). He had finally chosen 'Between Literature and Architecture', to borrow the title of chapter 4 of the *Life*, and planned to reveal himself as a promising young novelist to his future father-in-law.

We will never know the exact nature of Hardy's encounter with John Attersoll Gifford, if it ever occurred, but his decision to have his proofs sent to Kirland House surely indicates that Emma had not fully apprised her fiancé of his future father-in-law's mental instability. Gifford had in fact only recently been released from his third residence at the Cornwall County Asylum, and his reception order for this admission, which took place in October 1871, suggests that he was prone to the most extreme delusions of grandeur: 'Says he hears voices as of a man and woman disputing together—says he hears a voice speaking to him telling [him] he is the Lord Jesus Christ...Great incoherency of speech; and great restlessness of manners. Says he cannot be mad, as he is only so in particular states of the wind! Has many delusions.'[9] The *Life* and *Some Recollections* are both stubbornly silent on the attitude of Emma's parents to her suitor, although Hardy does allow himself the clearly mendacious assertion that the happy pair received 'much encouragement from all parties concerned' (L 77). And yet, vitiating Hardy's instinctive secrecy was a compulsion to use his poetry to disclose the most wounding and private of experiences, to the point that he can sometimes resemble the kind of master criminal who cannot bear to allow his schemes to go undetected. Why else would he choose the very same form and metre for 'I Rose and Went to Rou'tor Town' as he deployed for 'When I Set Out for Lyonnesse'? Or embed, as in some cryptogram begging to be solved, in 'Rou'tor' a reference to Rough Tor, a granite ridge eight miles north of

[9] Quoted in Andrew Norman, *Thomas Hardy: Behind the Mask* (Stroud: The History Press, 2011), 151.

Bodmin? The poem is spoken by Emma ('*She, alone*' it is subtitled), and again pays tribute to her staunchness in the face of family disapproval:

> I rose and went to Rou'tor Town
>> With gaiety and good heart,
>> And ardour for the start,
> That morning ere the moon was down
> That lit me off to Rou'tor Town
>> With gaiety and good heart.
>
> When sojourn soon at Rou'tor Town
>> Wrote sorrows on my face,
>> I strove that none should trace
> The pale and gray, once pink and brown,
> When sojourn soon at Rou'tor Town
>> Wrote sorrows on my face.
>
> The evil wrought at Rou'tor Town
>> On him I'd loved so true
>> I cannot tell anew:
> But nought can quench, but nought can drown
> The evil wrought at Rou'tor Town
>> On him I'd loved so true!   (CP 517)

'What is the "evil wrought at Rou'tor Town"?' Vere Collins demanded in their discussion of Hardy's moments of poetic obscurity. 'Slander, or something of that sort…' Hardy responded, before deftly shifting the subject, by enquiring, 'Do you think the price of books is likely to go down?'[10] It is not known if Hardy ever crossed the threshold of Kirland House, and certainly this poem implies that it was Emma who made the case for their proposed union. If he had hoped that the arrival of authorial proofs from a London publisher might sway opinion in his favour, then that gambit miserably failed.

This fifth visit to Cornwall, at over a month, was Hardy's longest stay in the 'Delectable Duchy' (L 76) and his first as a freelance writer. In mid-August Roger T. Smith wrote to convey the news that his practice had been successful in their application to build various London board schools and to ask if 'more liberal terms' (L 94) might lure Hardy back. By now at work on the second

---

[10] Vere H. Collins, *Talks with Thomas Hardy at Max Gate 1920–1922* (London: Duckworth, 1928), 26.

instalment of his fictional Smith's romance and buttressed by Emma's 'confidence sublime' (CP 683) in her man of destiny, he turned down the offer, and, aside from a few later dabblings, his career as an architect was over.

These five weeks in Cornwall were spent partly at St Juliot and partly at St Benet's Abbey, Lanivet, the residence of Emma's friends Jane and Captain Charles Serjeant. It was in the course of a walk in this region, possibly from Kirland House to St Benet's Abbey after their failed attempt to win her parents' approval of their marriage, that Emma draped herself on a stunted handpost, as recounted in 'Near Lanivet, 1872':

> There was a stunted handpost just on the crest,
> > Only a few feet high:
> She was tired, and we stopped in the twilight-time for her rest,
> > At the crossways close thereby.
>
> She leant back, being so weary, against its stem,
> > And laid her arms on its own,
> Each open palm stretched out to each end of them,
> > Her sad face sideways thrown.
>
> Her white-clothed form at this dim-lit cease of day
> > Made her look as one crucified
> In my gaze at her from the midst of the dusty way,
> > And hurriedly 'Don't,' I cried.
>
> I do not think she heard. Loosing thence she said,
> > As she stepped forth ready to go,
> 'I am rested now.—Something strange came into my head;
> > I wish I had not leant so!'
>
> And wordless we moved onward down from the hill
> > In the west cloud's murked obscure,
> And looking back we could see the handpost still
> > In the solitude of the moor.
>
> 'It struck her too,' I thought, for as if afraid
> > She heavily breathed as we trailed;
> Till she said, 'I did not think how 'twould look in the shade,
> > When I leant there like one nailed.'
>
> I, lightly: 'There's nothing in it. For *you*, anyhow!'
> > —'O I know there is not,' said she...

> 'Yet I wonder ... If no one is bodily crucified now,
>   In spirit one may be!'

> And we dragged on and on, while we seemed to see
>   In the running of Time's far glass
> Her crucified, as she had wondered if she might be
>   Some day.—Alas, alas!   (CP 436)

'Near Lanivet, 1872' is one of a group of poems that Hardy composed about his courtship that conclude with a sorrowful 'Alas, alas!' or its equivalent. Like 'Where Three Roads Joined' and 'Self-Unconscious', it reveals how future excruciation is latent in the scene or incident, and broods on the introduction of 'wormwood' (as Hardy terms it in 'Where Three Roads Joined' (CP 588)) into the seeming paradise of the Cornish landscape. All are poems of place as emphatically as 'Beeny Cliff' or 'At Castle Boterel'. The unsettling complexity of these poems derives from the implication that it is more than embittered hindsight that infuses them with an aura of ghastly disillusionment: something at once uncanny and compulsive is at work, presenting clues to the poet that he is either unable to interpret or to act upon. In this they refract not just Hardy's habitual awareness of life's propensity to throw up satires of circumstance, but his helplessness in the face of the grimmer workings of the Spirit Sinister, as he calls it in *The Dynasts*. 'O it would have been good', he reflects ruefully in 'Self-Conscious' (which takes place, we are told, 'Near Bossiney')

> Could he then have stood
> At a clear-eyed distance, and conned the whole,
>   But now such vision
>   Is mere derision,
> Nor soothes his body nor saves his soul.   (CP 332)

Hardy felt 'Near Lanivet, 1872' was 'among the best [poems] I have written' (CL VI 96), and in a letter of 11 February 1919 to Harold Child, who had just reviewed *Moments of Vision* (where 'Near Lanivet' first appeared), he reflected:

> One poem that I thought critics might select (not for its supposed excellence but for the strange incident which produced it, & really happened) was 'Near Lanivet'; but *nobody* did. It is curious how often writers are thus mistaken in what they think will strike readers. The explanation is, of

course, that the author judges from the actual event, which he has seen &
been impressed by: & the critic from the description only, which may not
convey the event as it was.   (CL V 295)

The 'actual event' was one of those that haunted Hardy for nearly half a century before it emerged as a poem, his memory 'exhuming it' (with the help
of 'an old note' as he wrote, and then deleted, at its conclusion on the manuscript) 'as fresh as when interred' (L 408). His assumption that because the
story it relates 'really happened', the poem is therefore bound to be interesting to a reader or reviewer reveals much about the literalism of his imagination. It cannot be known if it was parental intransigence that was the
catalyst for this charged and iconographical moment of extreme crisis at the
crossroads, but certainly the poem mobilizes all the most powerful Hardyan
signifiers of looming tragedy, including the intermingling of pagan and
Christian motifs of human sacrifice: the stunted handpost, for instance,
looks forward to (or recalls, since the poem was written later) the sinister
stone pillar known as 'Cross-in-Hand' on which Alec—who tells her it is a
Holy Cross—makes Tess swear that she will never again tempt him, and
which she later learns marks the punishment site of a 'malefactor' who had
his hand nailed to it, and is indeed buried beneath it, having, it is rumoured,
'sold his soul to the devil' (T 332). The couple's 'wordless' 'dragg[ing] on and
on' along the 'dusty way' beneath the 'west cloud's murked obscure' in the
'dim-lit cease of day' summons up any number of silent and unhappy Hardy
wayfarers, and what they do eventually say to each other in desultory bursts
recalls the dreadful collusion in each other's fears that makes the inter-
changes of such as Jude and Sue so harrowing. Further, the visual tableau it
presents of Emma nailed on a cross occurs at a temporal as well as an actual
crossroads, for the site and incident emerge as a kind of decisive Golgotha
of romance, one that they both look back on ('And looking back we could
see the handpost still / In the solitude of the moor') and forward from, in
'the running of Time's far glass', making it feel as if Emma's spiritual cruci-
fixion is already imaginatively under way.

As gruesome, if more far-fetched, is 'Where Three Roads Joined', which
envisions its crossroads subject to nightly haunting by the returning spirits
of the doomed lovers. The manuscript includes the deleted subtitle 'Near
Tresparrett Posts, Cornwall', which is about a mile and a half north-east of
St Juliot. The 'spectre-beridden' site of disaster is itself imagined as grieving
for the unlucky couple who, though 'in bliss for a spell', inexplicably 'let it
roll / Away from them down a plumbless well' (CP 588). Like 'Near Lanivet',

it deploys the symbolism of the Bible as a means of conveying the scope of the unnamed catastrophe, 'wormwood' being a reference to Revelation 8:10–11: 'And the third angel sounded, and there fell a great star from heaven, burning as it were a lamp, and it fell upon the third part of the rivers, and upon the fountains of waters; And the name of the star is called Wormwood: and the third part of the waters became wormwood; and many men died of the waters, because they were made bitter.' Hardy's return to the fatal, haunted crossroads avoids disclosing what actually happened there, but reveals his spirit world at its most nightmarish and unforgiving, making the poem read like a scene from Dante's *Inferno*:

> While the phasm of him who fared starts up,
> And of her who was waiting sobs from near
> As they haunt there and drink the wormwood cup
> They filled for themselves when their sky was clear.   (CP 588)

If the Emma crucified in the gloom of 'Near Lanivet' is the antithesis of the 'girl of grace' who irradiates so many of Hardy's recreations of their courtship in romantic Lyonnesse, this 'wormwood cup' is the lurid counterpart of the sacred tumbler of 'Under the Waterfall' from which they once, in turn, sipped lovers' wine.

Hardy's two final trips to see Emma took place at either end of 1873. The first was 'a flying visit' (L 94) to the rectory in early January, during which he drew up the final tally of the costs for the restoration of St Juliot Church for Caddell Holder's approval and signature. But by Christmas of that year Emma had moved out, her testy relationship with her sister having frayed the nerves of both, and was living either in Launceston or Plymouth.[11] These visits were much shorter than his previous sojourns in Cornwall, although 'The Seven Times' suggests that the sixth trip was decisive in forwarding their plans to wed ('I reached a tryst before my journey's end came, / And found her there' (CP 688)). It was during the summer of 1873, however, that Hardy and Emma enjoyed the first of many holidays together, staying—in separate accommodations of course—from 22 June to 2 July in Bath, and making excursions to local beauty spots such as

[11] F. B. Pinion argues for the former ('Hardy's Visits to Cornwall', 193), Michael Millgate for the latter (MM 145).

Tintern Abbey, 'where we repeated some of Wordsworth's lines thereon' (L 96). Poetry, clearly, was still proving a source of mutual enjoyment. The only lyric inspired by this leg of their courtship, 'Midnight on Beechen, 187–' (Beechen being a cliff overlooking Bath), records a nocturnal walk taken by Hardy in which he savours first the sleeping city below and then his beloved asleep within it, Emma here gallantly figured as 'one, all testify, / To match the maddest dream's desire' (CP 769).

A more ominous poem dramatizing an incident from towards the end of their four-year engagement is 'The Change', two stanzas of which depict Emma's arrival in London, probably in the late summer of 1874 in preparation for their marriage in September, although it is possible that this poem records a trip that she made to the capital at some earlier date. In *Some Recollections* she recalls:

> And I went as country cousin to my brother in London, and was duly astonished, which gave him even more pleasure than it did me. I was rather bewildered with the size and lengths and distances, and very much embarrassed at going in an omnibus, which seemed a very undignified method of getting about.   (SR 60)

The brother in question was Walter Gifford, who lived in Maida Vale, but 'The Change' suggests that it was her fiancé who met her at Paddington Station, which was a mere stone's throw from where he was then living at 4 Celbridge Place:

> In a tedious trampling crowd yet later—
>   Who shall bare the years, the years!—
> In a tedious trampling crowd yet later,
>   When silvery singings were dumb;
> In a crowd uncaring what time might fate her,
> Mid murks of night I stood to await her,
> And the twanging of iron wheels gave out the signal that
>   she was come.
>
> She said with a travel-tired smile—
>   Who shall lift the years O!—
> She said with a travel-tired smile,
>   Half scared by scene so strange;
> She said, outworn by mile on mile,

> The blurred lamps wanning her face the while,
> 'O Love, I am here; I am with you!' . . . Ah, that there should
>   have come a change!   (CP 455)

Aside from the sleeping Emma in Bath, and following the chronological narrative of her life as it is developed in Hardy's poetry, this is the first vision of Emma transplanted from 'the craggy nook' (CP 637) in which he found her. It is one of the rare glimpses that we get in Hardy's poetic oeuvre of Emma in London, a city which, as the passage above from *Some Recollections* indicates, she found far from accommodating. 'The Change' does moving justice to her loyalty and bravery ('O Love, I am here; I am with you!') but the dot-dot-dots that follow convey much foreboding, and Hardy's imagery in these stanzas presents her as fundamentally as out of place as Elfride found herself on her disastrous trips to London, first in her aborted attempt to elope with Stephen, and then to plead with Knight for forgiveness. The 'change' lamented by Hardy would take all manner of forms, but the first involved changing her name, as she did that autumn. And despite the many '*unhappy happenings*' (SR 61) that this gave rise to, she yet celebrated the day when she came to recount it in the memoir that she composed in her attic isolation not long before her death:

The day we were married was a perfect September day—the 17th, 1874— not brilliant sunshine, but wearing a soft, sunny luminousness; just as it should be.   (SR 60)

THE RIFT

5

A Preface without Any Book

On 19 February 1896, some three and a half months after the publication of
Jude the Obscure, Hardy wrote to Emma from the Saville Club in London.
Like so many of his surviving letters to her from the thirty-eight years of
their marriage, it is affectionate, solicitous, informative, undemonstrative,
offering an account of his activities in the metropolis as well as a brief
snapshot of a recently attended social event. I give it in full as a typical
example of the style, tone, and length of the many bulletins that he
dispatched to his wife whenever they were apart:

> My Dear Em:
> Postcard received. I am going back to Max Gate this afternoon; & intend
> to run up again from next Saturday to Monday—to meet a manager [Hardy
> was in the middle of negotiations over a stage version of *Tess of the
> d'Urbervilles*]. As there is no reason for me to stay on through the week
> I thought this the best plan. I went to Mrs Crackanthorpe's masked ball
> with Lady J. & Madeleine last night. It was the most amusing experience
> I have lately had. I did not recognize people I knew very [*illegible*]: & a
> lady took *me* down to supper (being leap year) whom to this moment I have
> not been clear about. They were sorry you could not come. Lady J. says it
> *may* be shingles that you have had, as that goes in a circle round the body.
> The Miss Thornhills return to Brighton in 2 or 3 weeks. Don't have a cheap
> lodging, as I will willingly pay the difference between the prices. Next
> Monday I cd of course run down if you wish to see me about anything.
> > Yours
> > T.
> Lady J. says you can stay there any time by letting her know—except when
> the room is occupied by a previous comer.   (CL II 112)

Emma had fallen victim to a skin disease and was recuperating on the
Sussex coast—hence the reference to Lady Jeune's diagnosis of shingles and
the details about the Miss Thornhills in Brighton. Since none of Emma's

Woman Much Missed: Thomas Hardy, Emma Hardy, and Poetry. Mark Ford, Oxford University Press.
© Mark Ford 2023. DOI: 10.1093/oso/9780192886804.003.0006

letters to Hardy escaped destruction, it is not known if or how she replied to this mundane report of his doings in the capital, but we do know that three days later she wrote from Worthing to Hardy's sister Mary. Again, I give the letter in full:

Miss Hardy,

I dare you, or any one to spread evil reports of me—such as that I have been unkind to your brother, (which you actually said to my face,) or that I have 'errors' in my mind, (which you have also said to me,) and I hear that you repeat to others.

Your brother has been outrageously unkind to me—which is *entirely your* fault: ever since I have been his wife you have done all you can to make division between us; also, you have set your family against me, though neither you nor they can truly say that I have ever been anything but, just, considerate, & kind towards you all, notwithstanding frequent low insults.

As you are in the habit of saying of people whom you dislike that they are 'mad' you should, & may well, fear, least the same be said of you; what you mete out to others shall be meted to you again; & I have, heard you say it myself, of people. I defy you ever to say such a thing of me or for you, or any one, to say that I have done anything that can be called unreasonable, or wrong, or mad, or *even unkind*! And it is a wicked, spiteful & most malicious habit of yours.

Now—what right have you to assert that I have been no 'help' to my husband? That statement, false & injurious, as it is, you have constantly repeated without warrant or knowledge of the matter.

How would you like to have your life made difficult for you by anyone saying, for instance, that you are a very unsuitable person to have the instruction of young people?

You have ever been my causeless enemy—causeless, except that I stand in the way of your evil ambition to be on the same level with your brother by trampling upon me. If you did not know, & pander to his many weaknesses, & have secured him on your side by your crafty ways, you could not have done me the irreparable mischief you have. And doubtless you are elated that you have spoilt my life as you love power of any kind, but you have spoilt your brother's & your own punishment must inevitably follow—for God's promises are true forever.

St Juliot Church 1870 – Before restoration

1. St Juliot Church before restoration in 1870

2. Emma, Helen, and the Reverend Caddell Holder at St Juliot Rectory in 1870

Antient North Door - St Juliot Church - Cornwall -
(accidentally destroyed)
J. Hardy. del. 1870.

3. Drawing by Hardy of the North Door of St Juliot Church

4. Drawing by Emma of Hardy hoisting a flag (18 August 1870)

5. Drawing by Hardy of Emma searching for the lost tumbler (19 August 1870)

6. Drawing by Hardy of Beeny Cliff in the rain (22 August 1870)

Mrs. Thomas Hardy

Whose husband wrote *Far From the Madding Crowd*

7. The wife of the novelist

Emma

8. Emma Hardy reading

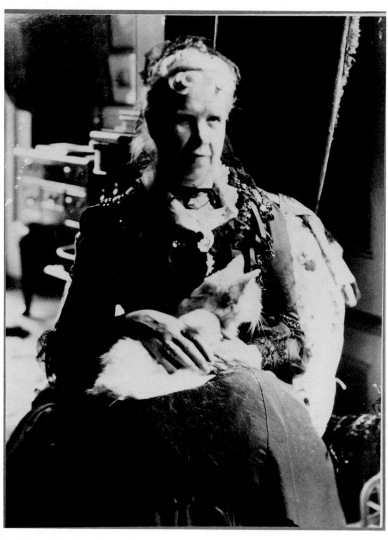

9. Emma Hardy in her mid-sixties

10. Emma Hardy and Florence Dugdale on the beach at Worthing in August 1911

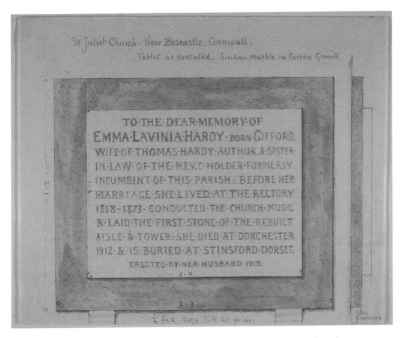

11. Hardy's design for the memorial tablet erected in St Juliot Church

Imaginary View of Tintagel Castle.
at the Time of the Tragedy.

T. H.
May 1923.

[Frontispiece to "The Famous Tragedy of the Queen of Cornwall."]

12. Drawing by Hardy of an imaginary Tintagel used as the frontispiece for *The Famous Tragedy of the Queen of Cornwall* (1923)

You are a witch-like creature quite equal to any amount of evil-wishing & speaking—I can imagine you, & your mother & sister on your native heath raising a storm on a Walpurgis night.

You have done irreparable harm but now your power is at an end.

E.

If you will acknowledge your evil pride & spite & change your ways I am capable of forgiving you though I cannot forget or trust your nature but I can understand your desire to be considered cleverer than I which you may be I allow.

Doubtless you will send this onto your brother but it will not affect me, if you do as he will know from me that I have written thus to you—which I consider a duty to myself.   (LEFH 7–8)

Mary (who was a year younger than her brother) was at this point head-mistress of Bell Street junior girls' school in Dorchester. Clearly, she took seriously Emma's threat of publicly questioning her suitability to undertake 'the instruction of young people', for this letter was deposited with the Hardys' solicitor, Arthur Henry Lock, which is why it survives. Had the 'rift' between Emma and Hardy's family ever resulted in a court case, it would no doubt have been used in evidence.

As mentioned in the Prologue, it was Jemima Hardy's peculiar wish that, instead of marrying, her four children should live together as sibling pairs: Thomas with Mary, and Kate with Henry (born 1851 and 1856 respectively). Hardy was well aware that Emma would not be received into his close-knit family with open arms, which is perhaps why none of his relations were present in St Peter's Church on 17 September 1874. One wonders if they even knew the marriage was happening that day. Hardy's letter to his brother Henry from Brighton the day after is terse in the extreme:

I write a line to tell you all at home that the wedding took place yesterday, & that we are got as far as this on our way to Normandy & Paris. There were only Emma & I, her uncle who married us, & her brother, my landlady's daughter signed the book as one witness.   (CL I 31)

And, as if additional proof were needed, he advised Henry to look out for an advertisement that would appear in the *Dorset County Chronicle* the following week. There the Hardys would have learnt that the 'son of Mr. T. Hardy, of Bockhampton' had married the 'younger daughter of J. A. Gifford Esq. of Kirland, Cornwall'.

Despite the difference in class signified by the honorifics here deployed (Mr T. Hardy, J. A. Gifford Esq.) it is not easy to determine whether it was the Giffords or the Hardys who were more displeased with the connubial link forged between their households. And surely a major catalyst for the heroic mythologizing of their Cornish romance performed in Hardy's poetic recreations of it after Emma's death was memory of the sheer courage required to ignore their families' opposition and, like Tristram and Iseult or Romeo and Juliet, commit all to each other. It is striking to note that in March 1884, some eight months after the return of the native to Dorchester, Hardy toyed with the idea of writing a novel to be called *Time against Two*, 'in which the antagonism of the parents of a Romeo and Juliet *does* succeed in separating the couple and stamping out their love,—alas, a more probable development than the other!' (L 171).

While it was plain there was no point in hoping that Emma's alcoholic and paranoid father might soften his disapproval of the 'low-born churl' his daughter had married 'for praise or blame', for 'bale or else for bliss', as Hardy rephrases the wedding service in 'She Revisits Alone the Church of Her Marriage' (CP 638), there was some reason to think that amicable relations might be established with Hardy's siblings, and possibly even with his formidable mother. In July 1875 Emma wrote to Jemima suggesting a rendezvous in Bournemouth, where the peripatetic couple were staying for a few days, only to receive back a cutting rebuff: 'Mother is much obliged to you for your kind invitation,' wrote Kate on Jemima's behalf, 'but she is so very busy just now that she cannot possibly come.' Dire warnings follow: 'Mother says you are not to get into the sea or go boating at Bth [i.e. Bournemouth] because she is afraid you will both be drowned or come to some untimely end' (MM 163). Her son's new wife and disaster appear firmly linked in Jemima's imagination here. Some two months later, however, and perhaps in an attempt to build bridges, Mary and Kate joined their brother and Emma for a fortnight's stay in Swanage, where Hardy and Emma had rented a cottage above the town overlooking the sea. Emma's diary from this period records what sounds like a successful picnic on 13 September at Corfe Castle, a visit to which would feature in a forthcoming instalment of *The Hand of Ethelberta*, and Emma's accusation in her Walpurgis-night letter to Mary that 'ever since I have been his wife you have done all you can to make division between us' evidently elided possibly extended periods of cordial, or at least unhostile, relations with Hardy's siblings, particularly with Kate.

Nevertheless, before exploring Hardy's poetic responses to the conflicts that beset the marriage, it is worth dwelling on the difficulties inherent in Emma's situation. Although she remained in contact with her sister Helen and her brother Walter, as well as with Walter's children Gordon and Lilian, most of Emma's married life was spent in Hardy's native region, and on his terms. By all accounts Jemima never accepted her as a suitable wife for her son, and Emma's withering account of the miseries of marriage in a letter of 20 August 1899 to Elspeth Grahame, who had recently married Kenneth Grahame of *Wind in the Willows* fame, pointedly refers to the difficulties presented by a husband's meddling relatives:

Interference from others is greatly to be feared—members of either family too often are the cause of estrangement. A woman does not object to be ruled by her husband, so much as she does by a relative at his back,—a man seldom cares to control such matters when in his power, & let's things glide, or throws his balance on the wrong side which is simply a terrible state of affairs, & may affect unfavourably herself in the end.   (LEFH 15)

By returning to Dorchester in the summer of 1883 Hardy ensured that for the rest of his marriage he would be torn between the competing interests of his wife and his family. Battle lines would end up starkly, if inexplicitly, drawn. Although it was Hardy's father and brother who undertook the construction of Max Gate, his parents and siblings were not included in guest lists for garden parties and only rarely entertained there; and while Hardy would visit the Higher Bockhampton family home on a weekly basis, and take guests to meet his parents too, he would not be accompanied on these visits by his wife. 'Keeping separate', Emma advised poor Elspeth Grahame, was the best 'plan' in times of marital crisis, and when it came to relations between Emma and her in-laws, this, in the end, became Hardy's *modus operandi* too.

Certainly, as her violent outburst against Mary in her letter from Worthing shows, Emma was prone to lurid depictions of the Hardy clan, and indeed of her 'outrageously unkind' husband too, as Florence, for instance, discovered when staying at Max Gate in 1910: 'Mrs Hardy', she wrote on 19 November to Edward Clodd, seems to be queerer than ever. She has just asked me whether I have noticed how extremely like *Crippen* [who would be executed for the murder of his wife four days later] Mr TH. is, in personal appearance. She added darkly that she would not be surprised to find herself in the cellar one morning. All this in deadly seriousness.   (LEFH 68)

Further, Emma came to construe Hardy's views on marriage, as dramatized in *Jude the Obscure* in particular, as an explicit personal attack, indeed almost as a literary marital betrayal. The dramatist Alfred Sutro recalls a typically awkward lunch at Max Gate shortly after the novel's publication: 'I was loud', he recalls,

> in my praises of that work. Mrs Hardy was far from sharing my enthusiasm. It was the first novel of his, she told me, that he had published without first letting her read the manuscript: had she read it, she added firmly, it would *not* have been published, or at least, not without considerable emendations... Hardy said nothing, and did not lift his eyes from the plate.
>
> (IR 50)

While Ford Madox Ford's account in *Mightier than the Sword* (1938) of Emma beseeching Dr Richard Garnett, the keeper of printed books at the British Museum, to undertake to convince Hardy to burn the manuscript of *Jude* has long been exposed as pure invention, Ford's imaginary anecdote undoubtedly captures Emma's dismay at the bleakness and—as she saw it— atheistic tendencies of Hardy's final novel. The sense of shared literary enterprise that had proved so uplifting and unifying during the early years of their courtship, and continued, if in diminished forms, up until the composition of *Tess of the d'Urbervilles* in 1889–90, reached its dispiriting nadir in the rupture occasioned by a narrative itself obsessed with rupture, with the disappointment of ideals, with betrayal and marital unhappiness.

Paradoxically, Emma's increasing impatience with her husband's failings during the last decades of their marriage can frequently make her sound in letters like Hardy himself at his most remorselessly unillusioned. Her advice to the newly wed Elspeth Grahame on the best way of approaching married life makes a potent case for stemming 'strain and ache' (CP 886) by expecting as little as possible:

> Keeping separate a good deal is a wise plan in crises—and being both free—& *expecting little* neither gratitude, nor attentions, love, nor *justice*,

nor *anything* you may set your heart on. Love interest—adoration, & all
that kind of thing is usually a *failure*—complete—some one comes by &
upsets your pail of milk in the end. If he belongs to the public in any way,
years of devotion count for nothing. Influence can seldom be retained as
years go by, & *hundreds* of wives go through a phase of disillusion,—it is
really a pity to have any ideals in the first place.   (LEFH 15)

The Black Diaries must have contained much along these lines. And as
Hardy's poems often seem compelled to secrete private disclosures even as
they respond to a landscape or recreate a striking tableau or encounter, so
Emma's state of mind irresistibly makes itself felt in her correspondence,
whatever the topic. In November 1903 Louise MacCarthy wrote requesting
advice regarding her son Desmond's decision to embark on a literary career.
Emma uses her reply to expatiate on the manifold miseries of being the wife
of a writer and, less directly, on her troubles with Hardy's mother and sisters:

> To those who *marry* authors, & ask my advice, I say, 'Do not help—him—so
> much as to extinguish your own life—but go on with former pursuits'.
>   I fear I am prejudiced, against authors—living ones!—they too often
> wear out other's lives with their dyspeptic moanings if unsuccessful—and
> if they become eminent they throw their aider over their parapets to enemies
> below, & revenge themselves for any objections to this treatment by
> stabbings with their pen!   (LEFH 26)

Here Emma sees her husband as a literary Crippen vindictively 'stabbing'
her with his pen on a daily basis. And her ongoing feud with Jemima seems
also to have been triggered by this epistolary contemplation of her unhappy
lot as the wife of a famous but ungrateful novelist all too willing to sacrifice
her to her 'enemies'. Exactly who these 'enemies' are emerges clearly in the
following paragraph: 'certainly it is true that clever men have generally had
an early spur from their mothers. For my part, I have suffered much, &
greatly from the ignorant interference of others (of the peasant class)'
(LEFH 27).

Emma's frequent trumpeting to all and sundry of her superior class status
to the Hardys, normally through reference to her uncle Edwin Hamilton
Gifford, who had been appointed Archdeacon of London in 1884, no doubt
played its part in her ostracism by her 'peasant' in-laws. That the antipathy
between Hardy's wife and family was mutual is most clearly evidenced by
Christine Wood Homer (1883–1975), whose parents were well-to-do and

long-standing friends of the Hardys and were often invited to tea *en famille* at Max Gate. In her pamphlet 'Thomas Hardy and His Two Wives' (1964) Wood Homer reflects:

> Thomas Hardy was a devoted son, and during her life he visited his mother every week on Sunday. He was very fond, too, of his two sisters, Mary and Katherine (or Kate as she was always called). It had been a burdensome grief to him that the first Mrs Hardy had not cared for any of his family.   (IR 49)

Even as a child Wood Homer and her siblings picked up on one of the causes of this rift: their private nickname for the first Mrs Hardy was 'Lady Emma' (IR 48).

Wood Homer records rather liking Lady Emma, for all her 'obvious defects', but other visitors were less tolerant: 'Most unfortunately', George Gissing wrote in a letter of 22 September 1895 in the wake of a weekend at Max Gate, Hardy 'has a very foolish wife—a woman of higher birth than his own [clearly he had been apprised by his hostess of her familial connection to the archdeacon], who looks down upon him and is utterly discontented' (IR 50). Hardy's penchant, so fully exemplified in the *Life*, for recounting in detail his and Emma's movements in fashionable London social circles deeply disappointed the visiting devotee of social realism, although, as Michael Millgate suggests, this may well have been one of Hardy's strategies for making Emma feel included in the conversation (MM 338). 'A strange unsettlement appears in him; probably the result of his long associations with such a paltry woman', is Gissing's summary judgement on the Hardy ménage. And 'discontent' was also discerned by A. C. Benson, who included in his diary a somewhat brutal account of lunch with the Hardys and Edmund Gosse at Max Gate on 5 September 1912, that is, some two and a half months before Emma's death:

> It was intensely interesting, but it gave me rather a melancholy impression; the poor house, uncomfortable and rather pretentious, in its close planta-tion, airless and dark, like a house wrapped up and put away in a box, the crazy and fantastic wife, the stolid niece [Lilian Gifford] didn't seem the right background for the old rhapsodist, in the evening of his days. It gave me a sense of something intolerable the thought of his having to live day and night with the absurd, inconsequent, huffy, rambling old lady.

They don't get on together at all. She confided to Gosse once that they were always squabbling. 'I beat him!' she said. Gosse said that it was very improper, so she added, 'only with the *Times* rolled up.' Today she told Gosse that he was more difficult to live with than ever, so inflated with his greatness that he wouldn't let her have a motor, and would accept no honours except what he could keep to himself. This referred to the O.M. [Order of Merit] and the fact that he had refused a knighthood. The marriage was thought a misalliance for her, when he was poor and undistinguished, and she continues to resent it.

He is not agreeable to her either, but his patience must be incredibly tried. She is so queer, and yet has to be treated as rational, while she is full, I imagine, of suspicions and jealousies and affronts which must be half insane. She must be a singular partner for a man interested in a feminine temperament; and they neither of them seemed at all content… (IR 106)

Hardy's most direct response to animadversions of this kind can be found in the poem 'You Were the Sort that Men Forget', where he gallantly asserts that '[y]our slighted weakness / Adds to the strength of my regret!' (CP 434). There is no overlooking, however, the overall tone of ruefulness that governs his poetic recollections of the social awkwardness of the (now dead) woman whom this poem addresses:

> You'd not the art—you never had
>   For good or bad—
> To make men see how sweet your meaning,
>   Which, visible, had charmed them glad.
>
> You would, by words inept let fall,
>   Offend them all,
> Even if they saw your warm devotion
>   Would hold your life's blood at their call.

The gaucheness wistfully anatomized here is of a piece with Emma's disconcertingly abrupt decision-making as described in the elegy 'Without Ceremony', which recalls how she would 'career / Off anywhere—say to town' (CP 343) without bothering to inform her puzzled spouse. Both poems record how easy it was to 'miss' Emma, how hard it was to follow her unpredictable movements as well as to do justice to the 'sweet…meaning' animating her equally errant conversational style.

It was, of course, her very artlessness which first appealed to Hardy, and which never staled in his memory: 'It was that strange freshness you carried / Into a soul / Whereon no thought of yours tarried / Two moments at all,' as he put it in 'Without, Not Within Her' (CP 647). The last stanza of this poem suggests that Hardy was profoundly troubled by his own Knight-like propensities to quell precisely the 'breathless vivid innocence',[1] to quote from Larkin's review of *Some Recollections*, that so fascinated him. Like poems such as 'Quid Hic Agis?' or 'Where Three Roads Joined', 'Without, Not Within Her' makes use of heightened biblical language to convey the catastrophic effects of this compulsion:

> And out from his spirit flew death,
>   And bale, and ban,
> Like the corn-chaff under the breath
>   Of the winnowing fan.

Whatever the practical considerations that motivated Hardy's move back to Dorchester in 1883, one of the effects was to subject Emma's 'strange freshness' to the 'winnowing fan' of his family's dislike. In futile defiance of the limited role on offer to her as the unwanted and expensive helpmeet of the triumphant son and brother, she exaggerated her role in the composition of his novels to any who would listen, and even composed a short story of her own, now lost, called 'The Inspirer', about a wife who inspires her husband's fiction (MM 452). That Emma, in her more paranoid moments, saw the Hardy clan as a whole as fundamentally committed to denying her even a limited share of her husband's glory is clear from a letter sent to Clement Shorter, editor of the magazine the *Sphere*, where one of her poems, 'Spring Song', had appeared in 1900. In April 1908 she attempted to persuade him to include a photograph of her along with those of Max Gate and of the garden's cemetery for cats that Shorter planned to use for a feature. She then had second thoughts:

> I think the photo must be returned—as I fear that T.H.: will not like it added to his affairs he has an *obsession* that I must be kept out of them lest the dimmest ray shoud alight upon me of his supreme story— '*This to please his family*,' chiefly. He is like no other man—nor himself as '*was*.'   (LEFH 38)

----

[1] Philip Larkin, 'Wanted: Good Hardy Critic', in *Required Writing* (London: Faber & Faber, 1983), 143.

The Hardy poem that most vividly dramatizes Emma's insistence to Elspeth Grahame on the importance of being less deceived even when just wed is 'Honeymoon Time at an Inn', included in *Moments of Vision*. The Hardys spent the first four nights of their marriage at D. Morton's Family and Commercial Hotel in Brighton, and the first entries of Emma's first diary, which runs from their wedding day to September 1875, somewhat uncannily focus on eyes in a manner that looks forward to Hardy's poem: 'All fish close their eyes whilst sleeping' (EHD 21), she notes (erroneously) after their visit to the Brighton aquarium on the Saturday, and the next day: 'Seals' eyes flash extraordinarily as they flounder over in the water' (EHD 22). In Hardy's ominous poetic recreation of a wedding night as disastrous as that of Tess and Angel, the moon is figured as a misshaped Cyclopean eye peering into the bridal chamber, and the pier glass that inauspiciously crashes to the floor directs its 'shattered gaze' at the distraught couple, who in turn stare with 'large-pupilled vision' at the 'many-eyed' fragments at their feet. 'Vision' or 'eyeing', 'Honeymoon Time at an Inn' relentlessly demonstrates, initiates kaleidoscopic catastrophe:

> At the shiver of morning, a little before the false dawn,
> > The moon was at the window-square,
> > Deedily brooding in deformed decay—
> > The curve hewn off her cheek as by an adze;
> At the shiver of morning a little before the false dawn
> > So the moon looked in there.
>
> Her speechless eyeing reached across the chamber,
> > Where lay two souls opprest,
> > One a white lady sighing, 'Why am I sad!'
> > To him who sighed back, 'Sad, my Love, am I!'
> And speechlessly the old moon conned the chamber,
> > And these two reft of rest.
>
> While their large-pupilled vision swept the scene there,
> > Nought seeming imminent,
> > Something fell sheer, and crashed, and from the floor
> > Lay glittering at the pair with a shattered gaze,
> While their large-pupilled vision swept the scene there,
> > And the many-eyed thing outleant.

> With a start they saw that it was an old-time pier-glass
>   Which had stood on the mantel near,
>   Its silvering blemished,—yes, as if worn away
>   By the eyes of the countless dead who had smirked at it
> Ere these two ever knew that old-time pier-glass
>   And its vague and vacant leer.

> As he looked, his bride like a moth skimmed forth, and
>   kneeling
>   Quick, with quivering sighs,
>   Gathered the pieces under the moon's sly ray,
>   Unwitting as an automaton what she did;
> Till he entreated, hasting to where she was kneeling,
>   'Let it stay where it lies!'   (CP 514–15)

The complex interchange of gazes between the moon, the couple, and the mirror is itself mirrored by Hardy's intricately patterned verse form, with its sinister repetition or quasi-repetition of each stanza's opening line by its fifth, its delayed rhyming of lines two and six. And moon and mirror are as alive as the poem's husband and bride: the former broods, looks, eyes, cons, casts a 'sly ray', while the Argus-like 'many-eyed' latter is 'outleant' (a word also applied to the century's corpse in 'The Darkling Thrush'), and its blemishes figured as recording the smirking eyes of the honeymooners' 'countless dead' predecessors. More unnerving still, these smirking eyes are compounded and projected into the horrified eyes of the couple by the pier glass's 'vague and vacant leer'.

Consciously or not, this grotesque scenario cannot help but read as an inversion of traditional celebrations of the wedding night, one paralleled in poetry perhaps only by T. S. Eliot's equally ghastly hymeneal 'Ode' ('When the bridegroom smoothed his hair / There was blood upon the bed').[2] The concept of seeing the beloved, under the aegis of matrimony, with unprecedented fullness is refracted into the multiple angles of vision the poem dramatizes: the waning moon, itself depicted as slightly wounded as if by an adze, casts a probing yet silent and pitiless light on the unhappy pair, each immured in a listless sadness. Hardy's coinage, 'large-pupilled', catches precisely their defencelessness in the face of whatever has driven them apart. Further—although it may seem tactless to suggest this—the shattered

---

[2] T. S. Eliot, *The Poems of T. S. Eliot*, Vol. 1, eds. Christopher Ricks and Jim McCue (London: Faber & Faber, 2015), 280 (ll. 9–10).

pier glass inevitably summons up the failure of the couple to fulfil the rites of marriage on their wedding night. No transformation of their unmentioned, and possibly fully clothed, bodies takes place; it is to their suffering souls and vulnerable eyes that the poem attends. As is so often the case with Hardy's doomed innocents, his 'Etherealists' or 'Flutterhearts' or 'Emotionalists', to quote from the list of potential titles set out in his *Poetical Matter* notebook (PM 20), it is surely their repulsion at the commonplace nature of sex which undoes them: what the leer of the mirror forces them to confront is that 'countless' others have had sex in this room on this bed, reflected in this mirror, before them, and this they cannot bear.

The dialogue in which they engage after the mirror's fall echoes that of the unhappy couple of 'Near Lanivet, 1872'. She succumbs at once to the implications of the bad omen, while he offers cheerless and unconvincing words of comfort:

> 'Long years of sorrow this means!' breathed the lady
>> As they retired. 'Alas!'
> And she lifted one pale hand across her eyes.
> 'Don't trouble Love; it's nothing,' the bridegroom said.
> 'Long years of sorrow for us!' murmured the lady,
>> 'Or ever this evil pass!'

Their looming division can be tracked in Hardy's subtle use of differing words of utterance: in stanza two both are presented as sighing, but after the pier glass has shattered, while he becomes explicitly vocal ('he entreatied...the bridegroom said'), her voice dies away ('quivering sighs...breathed the lady...murmured the lady'). Like Tess in her trance after the murder of Alec, she behaves like 'an automaton', while he wanly attempts to assume control. And as if the poem were on his side and also eager to downplay the significance of what has transpired in such excruciating yet fascinating detail, Hardy cuts in the last two stanzas to his cosmic spirit world, where such occurrences, however appalling, merely illustrate the way things are:

> And the Spirits Ironic laughed behind the wainscot,
>> And the Spirits of Pity sighed.
> 'It's good,' said the Spirits Ironic, 'to tickle their minds
> With a portent of their wedlock's aftergrinds.'
> And the Spirits of Pity sighed behind the wainscot,
>> 'It's a portent we cannot abide!

> 'More, what shall happen to prove the truth of the portent?'
>   —'Oh; in brief, they will fade till old,
> And their loves grow numbed ere death, by the cark of care.'
>   —'But nought see we that asks for portents there?—
> 'Tis the lot of all.'—'Well, no less true is a portent
>   That it fits all mortal mould.'

Hardy's finely honed and generalizing irony in these last two stanzas is pitted against the specificity with which he depicts the honeymoon night. If their misery derived from their sense of singularity, the wide-angled vistas opened by this jump cut allow us to see how their travails, however distinctive or peculiar they may make them feel, are themselves run of the mill. The 'aftergrinds' of marriage reduce all to numbness, as Emma, a quarter of a century after her own honeymoon, so vehemently counselled Elspeth Grahame.

'Am I a <u>strange-looking</u> person—or merely picturesque in this hat,' Emma mused in her disjointed record of the week that the newlyweds spent in Paris:

> Women sometimes laugh a short laugh as they pass. Men stare—some stand—some look back or turn, look over their shoulders—look curiously inquisitively—some <admiringly> tenderly without my being mistaken— they <u>do</u> in a French manner
>   As it is remarkable I note it—
>   Children gape too—   (EHD 40)

It was her first time abroad, and her diary presents an intriguing collage of scenes and vignettes garnered from the streets and cafés and tourist sights of Rouen and the French capital. Whether it was her hat, her trousseau outfits, or her unabashed interest in the *quartiers* she explored, she clearly cut something of a dash; and as she looked about her, 'curiously inquisitively', she noticed that Parisian men, women, and children returned the compliment. It was her more soberly dressed and habitually reserved husband's first time in Europe too, but nothing survives of his impressions beyond the chapters set in Rouen in *The Hand of Ethelberta*, although later travels to Switzerland and Italy would inspire various 'Poems of Pilgrimage', as he titled them, which resemble no other British poet's responses to these countries. Notwithstanding relatively frequent subsequent trips across the Channel, and his life-long obsession with the Napoleonic wars that would eventually result in *The Dynasts*, France barely features in Hardy's eight collections of poetry.

In *The Older Hardy* Robert Gittings described *Some Recollections* as revealing 'distinct flashes of real poetic observation and expression',[3] and the same can be said of Emma's four travel diaries. Indeed, the texts that they most resemble are Hardy's own collections of jottings, particularly his *Poetical Matter* notebook. One can imagine many of the anecdotes and tableaux and snatches of conversation set down by Emma as furnishing matter for a Hardy poem, and reading her diaries and his notebooks side by side can feel almost like participating in a lively stream of ideas, reflections, and memories made by a couple who relish each other's quirky ability to discover the intersection of the unusual and the everyday—in other words 'the *other side* of common emotions'. Emma's surviving four diaries were written out in two tiny pocket notebooks and mainly recount aspects of their travels on the continent together. These diaries' compressed accumulation of details and vivid images ('Soeurs de l'Hospice Hats like bats' wings or cats' ears' (EHD 27)), their swift transitions and frequent use of dashes, effectively immerse the receptive reader in Emma's free-flowing conscious-ness as it processes the whirling pageant of abroad or hits off characters glimpsed while on the move. The following depiction of the woman sharing her cabin on the steamboat back to England at the end of their two weeks in France could easily have been penned by her husband:

> The lady on the highest berth in the Steamboat on our return voyage—opposite me—had firm flesh & complexion which <u>can</u> only belong to <u>high-fed</u> & comfortably-living people. The combination grand. In her chemise she was a perfect Juno. Flesh, <u>tinted</u>—neither dark nor yellow white—perfect flesh & form—   (EHD 55)

Certain entries also deftly recreate the speech rhythms of those she encounters and suggest a gift for fusing character and narrative only fitfully in evidence in her novella *The Maid on the Shore*. Consider this quasi-dramatic mono-logue, clearly transcribed *in medias res*, also from their return voyage across the Channel:

[3] Robert Gittings, *The Older Hardy* (Harmondsworth: Penguin, 1978), 198.

One lady has just come in—& is chatting so much—she has awoke all the other ladies—She is speaking of her travels—has been journeying for a week past—She says she had a champagne dinner—& has just been eating as much bread & butter as she can see—& drinking brandy as much as she can get down—A lady asks her if she is not tired—She replies no she feels as lively as a <u>moth!</u> It appears so—for she continues in a buzzing way about her travels—Been within 10,000 feet of Mont Blanc's summit. The guide fell through a crevasse & a Mr. Marshall fell upon him. A very stout man—his head struck the guide & with the blow killed himself—the guide wedged in at the lowest & narrow part of the crevasse for 4 hours—

Her husband she refers to incessantly much to the amusement of my two chatty vis-à-vis above me—towards my feet

She thinks it does not matter about lost trains, or losing times etc—for after travelling abroad you get into a '<u>preciosa</u>' sort of life—   (EHD 51–3)

Emma's staccato shorthand brilliantly captures this voluble lady, with her distinctive turns of phrase ('as lively as a <u>moth</u>...a "<u>preciosa</u>" sort of life'), and her tumbling narrative, at once gruesome and comic, of alpine disaster.

Although poetry and romance were so closely interknit for the young Hardy, he also understood that the fulfilment of romance, marriage, with all its consequent financial burdens, entailed suppressing his poetic '*tendencies*' and committing himself to writing fiction that sold. In the course of the peripatetic nine years between their return from their honeymoon and the move to Dorchester in 1883, Hardy composed five novels that were all extremely different from each other, and show him struggling to prove himself both a 'good hand at a serial' (L 102), as he famously put it in a letter discussing editorial changes suggested by Leslie Stephen to *Far from the Madding Crowd*, and able to gratify the complex vocational and imaginative impulses that finally drove him to abandon architecture for literature back in 1872. During these nine years the Hardys lived in Surbiton, in Westbourne Grove, in Swanage, in Yeovil, in Sturminster Newton, in Tooting, and in Wimborne Minster. 'Going back to England,' Emma dolefully observed in her diary on the last day of their tour of Holland, the Rhine, and the Black Forest in mid-June 1876, 'where we have no home & no chosen county' (EHD 103). Hardy would himself date the origins of the rift that would drive them so disastrously apart to their residence at 1 Arundel Terrace in Tooting (1878–81), 'where they seemed to begin to feel that "there had past away a glory from the earth".[4] 'And it was in this house', Hardy adds, some-what elliptically, 'that their troubles began' (L 128). A stark and dispiriting intimation of these troubles, however, had occurred some three and a half years earlier during their brief stay in Bournemouth in the summer of 1875, to be precise on 15 July, St Swithin's day.

If it rains on St Swithin's day, according to legend, it will keep raining for the next forty days, but if it is fair the next forty days will be fair too. On that particular St Swithin's day, it poured down:

> *We Sat at the Window*
> *(Bournemouth, 1875)*
>
> We sat at the window looking out,
> And the rain came down like silken strings
> That Swithin's day. Each gutter and spout
> Babbled unchecked in the busy way
>   Of witless things:
> Nothing to read, nothing to see
> Seemed in that room for her and me
>   On Swithin's day.
>
> We were irked by the scene, by our own selves; yes,
> For I did not know, nor did she infer
> How much there was to read and guess
> By her in me, and to see and crown
>   By me in her.
> Wasted were two souls in their prime,
> And great was the waste, that July time
>   When the rain came down.   (CP 428–9)

Hardy's ability to create haunting tableaux of disaffected lovers, each immured in different but equally unassailable forms of subjectivity, had first revealed itself in 'Neutral Tones' of 1867. In both poems, the firm anchoring of the scene in time and place ('We stood by a pond that winter's day' (CP 12)) proves crucial to the evocation of emotional paralysis and the dispiriting onset of private misery that accompanies the failed encounter; and both

---

[4] He is here quoting from the second stanza of Wordsworth's 'Ode: Intimations of Immortality', which concludes: 'But yet I know, wher'er I go, / That there hath past away a glory from the earth' (*Selected Poems*, ed. John O. Hayden (London: Penguin, 1994), 140 (ll. 17–18)).

couples find their unhappiness echoed and mocked by the 'witless' workings of indifferent nature as they impinge on their consciousness: the dismal fallen ash leaves and the 'God-curst sun' in the earlier poem, the torrential rain in the later. 'Misprision' (CP 303), 'misconceit', 'misvision' (CP 355–6), and 'misapprehension' were among the terms applied by Hardy to domestic exchanges that worsened matters between husband and wife, as well as to the fatally misguided interpretations of each other's states of mind or emotions that resulted. 'Misapprehension' he glossed in a highly revealing diary entry of 6 January 1886:

> Misapprehension. The shrinking soul thinks its weak place is going to be laid bare, and shows its thought by a suddenly clipped manner. The other shrinking soul thinks the clipped manner of the first to be the result of its own weakness in some way, not of its strength, and shows its fear also by its constrained air! So they withdraw from each other and misunderstand.
>
> (L 183)[5]

In terms of the chronological narrative of Hardy's relations with Emma as it is developed in his poems, 'We Sat at the Window', although not published until 1917, marks the first instance after their honeymoon of the kind of 'misprision' or 'misapprehension' that would come to afflict their marriage. Perhaps most striking is the shift in register from 'irked' to 'wasted', which, as in the diary entry, captures the escalation of a petty annoyance into a damaging and irremediable failure. She is unable to 'read and guess', he to 'see and crown'; meanwhile, the rain babbles 'unchecked', its 'silken strings' metaphorically pinning them down like Gulliver by the Lilliputians, and—it being St Swithin's day—subliminally activating their shared propensity to give credence to evil omens. As in 'Neutral Tones', Hardy does full justice to the banality of the scene remembered, while also, in retrospect, and as if adopting the role of a Greek chorus, attempting to imbue the dreary hours with a significance they plainly lacked—'Wasted were two souls in their prime'. This resonant line, like the image of the 'God-curst' sun in the earlier poem, shows Hardy seeking to elevate boredom and disappointment onto the more dignified plane of the tragically missed opportunity, but extracting only cold comfort from the process.

----

[5] The poem 'Had You Wept' (CP 380) presents a situation in many ways similar to that diagnosed in this diary entry.

Since nearly all the poems that Hardy wrote about Emma were composed after her death, the tale they tell is balanced between recrimination, remorse, and the recovery of lost time. Cherished moments of mutuality are juxtaposed with occasions when husband and wife found themselves out of tune with each other, to borrow the musical analogy deployed in 'The Rift':

> 'Twas just at gnat and cobweb-time,
> When yellow begins to show in the leaf,
> That your old gamut changed its chime
> From those true tones—of span so brief!—
> That met my beats of joy, of grief,
>   As rhyme meets rhyme.   (CP 623)

One of the most striking 'rhyming' memories that Hardy converted into a poem derived from their time in Swanage, where they spent eight months in West End Cottage, from 15 July 1875 until March 1876, having travelled there from Bournemouth by steamer on the afternoon of the wet day lamented in 'We Sat at the Window'. Hardy was mainly occupied with the closing instalments of *The Hand of Ethelberta*, whose heroine is herself a poet, although a much less romantic one than Ella Marchmill. Ethelberta's 'Metres by Me' consists mainly of 'soft and marvellously musical rhymes, of a nature known as *vers de société*. Their romance elements are ludic rather than heartfelt, offering 'a series of playful defences of the supposed strategy of womankind in fascination, courtship, and marriage'.[6] Only the Wyatt-like lyric 'Cancelled Words' escapes the archly teasing tone of the rest of the volume. Ethelberta, like her creator, must turn to prose and her skilfully managed gifts in the art of storytelling to support those depending on her.

Although un-Elizabethan in diction, 'Once at Swanage' is as charged as 'Cancelled Words' and can be construed as conveying both the danger and the exhilaration involved in Hardy's defiance of his mother's taboo on her children marrying. Its lurid, witchy imagery, and recreation of the violent surging of the sea, serve, from this perspective, to dramatize the energies required to overcome his family's resistance to Emma and propel him decisively into her orbit. Both the supernatural and the maritime become vectors for the forces impelling them towards each other; and, as in so many of Hardy's coming-together poems, such as 'The Wind's Prophecy' or

---

[6] *The Hand of Ethelberta*, ed. Tim Dolin (London: Penguin, 1996), 26.

'A Man Was Drawing Near to Me', agency is suspended by a mixture of the magical and the elemental.

> The spray sprang up across the cusps of the moon,
>   And all its light loomed green
>   As a witch-flame's weirdsome sheen
> At the minute of an incantation scene;
> And it greened our gaze—that night at demilune.
>
> Roaring high and roaring low was the sea
>   Behind the headland shores:
>   It symboled the slamming of doors,
> Or a regiment hurrying over hollow floors...
> And there we two stood, hands clasped; I and she!   (CP 783–4)

The turbulent Channel (which had rendered both seasick on their honeymoon voyages across it) here assumes the vitality and unpredictability that Hardy habitually associated with the Atlantic off the Cornish coast. Some twenty-five miles from Higher Bockhampton, Swanage was the first of the Dorset locations with which they would experiment before settling in Dorchester and was where they hosted Mary and Kate in September 1875. Whether the poem's title signals the unique momentousness of the occasion—that of finding themselves rapt and united witnesses to the romantic sublime, even undergoing a kind of pagan connubial rite—or the distance between the remembering poet and the long-ago incident is not clear, but in either case the title frames in time and place what might otherwise read as a high symbolist poem by such as Baudelaire. And the poem clearly lodged in the mind of Hardy's admirer and successor Philip Larkin, himself something of an occasional high symbolist, who borrowed its imagery for his depiction of the sea in 'Absences'—'Fast-running floors, collapsing into hollows, / Tower suddenly, spray-haired'.[7] Hardy's 'slamming of doors' and 'regiment hurrying over hollow floors' are not easy to parse: has the sea in turmoil triggered and then overcome a memory of a domestic row? is it inciting cosmic visions of the sort that one gets in 'The Souls of the Slain', in which those killed in the Boer War are imagined returning over the Bill of Portland to their native soil? Such imaginative vistas, at once discordant and vatic in the mode of a poem like Coleridge's 'Kubla Khan', are in turn gloriously trumped by the

---

[7] Philip Larkin, *Collected Poems*, ed. Anthony Thwaite (London: Faber & Faber, 1988), 49.

poem's emphatic and celebratory concluding line: 'And there we two stood, hands clasped; I and she!'

Another stirring Swanage memory surfaces in the first part of the diptych, 'Days to Recollect', which contrasts an early autumn walk towards Saint Alban's Head from 1875 with Emma's death day thirty-seven years later. It is only on reading the poem's second stanza and realizing that the person addressed with such homely familiarity in the first ('Do you recall / That day in Fall...Or must I remind you?') is now dead, that the ironies latent in Hardy's serial questioning and detailed remembering become apparent:

> Do you recall
> That day in Fall
> When we walked towards Saint Alban's Head,
> On thistledown that summer had shed,
> Or must I remind you?
> Winged thistle-seeds which hitherto
> Had lain as none were there, or few,
> But rose at the brush of your petticoat-seam
> (As ghosts might rise of the recent dead),
> And sailed on the breeze in a nebulous stream
> Like a comet's tail behind you:
> You don't recall
> That day in Fall?   (CP 811)

Emma here excites from her husband the sort of curious attention bestowed on her by Parisians during their honeymoon. Overriding the evangelical views that she held during the later years of their marriage, Hardy reconfigures her, as in his Cornish elegies, as a minor pagan deity, trailed by thistle seeds that her petticoat has brushed, and which he compares to the ghosts of those who have just died, as if she were unconsciously initiating them into their afterlives. In contrast to the *sturm und drang* of 'Once at Swanage', this delicately limned tableau exhibits Hardy's imaginative ability to recreate with exquisite finesse interactions with nature that occur in the gentlest and subtlest of ways, as well as his fascination with the contact between airborne seeds and women's clothes.[8]

---

[8] One might compare the scene in *The Mayor of Casterbridge* in which Donald Farfrae blows wheat husks off Elizabeth-Jane's 'back hair, and her side hair, and her neck, and the crown of her bonnet, and the fur of her victorine, Elizabeth saying, "Oh thank you," at every puff' (*The Mayor of Casterbridge*, ed. Dale Kramer (Oxford: Oxford University Press, 2004), 89).

That Hardy is himself addressing a ghost perhaps explains the richly textured access granted to the remembered walk from Swanage:

> Then do you remember
> That sad November
> When you left me never to see me more,
> And looked quite other than theretofore,
> As if it could not *be* you?

The estranging otherness of Emma's corpse, grimly emphasized by the italics on *be*, yet fails to deter Hardy from seeking to explore further memories, both of her and with her, to recollect the 'joys, hopes, fears' that they shared together during their marriage, and the poem concludes with the inevitable but somewhat mind-dizzying request that she remember her own death—'Say you remember / That sad November!'

In retrospect Hardy came to consider the twenty months (from July 1876 to March 1878) that the couple spent in Riverside Villa in Sturminster Newton as the high point of their marriage. This assessment came with a characteristic Hardy proviso best summed up by the last lines of 'The Self-Unseeing': 'Everything glowed with a gleam; / Yet we were looking away!' (CP 167). In the *Life* he noted: 'It was their first house and, though small, probably that in which they spent their happiest days. Several poems commemorate their term there of nearly two years' (L 115). 'Overlooking the River Stour', 'The Musical Box', 'On Sturminster Foot-Bridge' (a trio collected back to back in *Moments of Vision*), and 'A Two-Year's Idyll' share the notion that the couple's happiness in their rented semi-detached villa perched above Blackmore Vale was somehow dependent on their inability to grasp or appreciate it. The *Moments of Vision* poems are all elegantly mimetic of the way the ironic dynamics of double consciousness play out in Hardy's conjugations of the past. His wholly intent absorption in the particulars of the scene depicted in the first three stanzas of 'Overlooking the River Stour', for instance, turns out to have been primarily a means of 'looking away':

> And never I turned my head, alack,
> While these things met my gaze
> Through the pane's drop-drenched glaze,
> To see the more behind my back...

> O never I turned, but let, alack,
>> These less things hold my gaze!   (CP 482)

Emma is a shadowy presence at his 'back' on the rainy day remembered here, and yet is also the poem's focal—and vanishing—point; without her it couldn't have come into existence, for Hardy's brilliant recreation of the flight of the looping swallows ('Like little crossbows animate') and moorhens 'planing up shavings of crystal spray' and sodden mead dripping in 'monotonous green' are made, by this last stanza, into complex, devious means of avoiding paying attention to 'the more' behind him.

It is in these Sturminster-based poems that Hardy comes closest to figuring Emma as a version of 'the angel in the house' made popular by Coventry Patmore. At the conclusion of 'On Sturminster Footbridge' she is pictured as fulfilling the Victorian ideal of the young wife on whom her husband, wherever and however late he roams, may reliably depend, his domestic comfort in an increasingly complicated world: 'And beneath the roof is she who in the dark world shows / As a lattice-gleam when midnight moans' (CP 484). She is a metaphorical beacon of light in 'The Musical Box' too, remembered as 'white-muslined' on the porch of their house, patiently awaiting 'with high-expectant heart' the return of her husband, whom she greets happily when he eventually arrives, again late at night and amid wheeling bats—'She laughed a hailing as she scanned / Me in the gloom' (CP 483). The tinkling musical box seems a further indicator of domestic comfort, but the poem's premise is that a spirit accompanies 'the mindless lyre' with a song that urges the poet to enjoy to the full these happy hours, since they are numbered.

>> Lifelong to be
> I thought it. That there watched hard by
> A spirit who sang to the indoor tune,
> 'O make the most of what is nigh!'
> I did not hear in my dull soul-swoon—
>> I did not see.

As in 'Overlooking the River Stour' and 'On Sturminster Foot-Bridge' (of whose onomatopoeic sound effects Hardy seems to have been especially proud),[9] the expertise displayed in the prosody and rhyme is in collusion, so to

---

[9] He twice mentions in the *Life* a review that denigrated this poem's 'music', comparing it to that made by a 'milk-cart' (L 324), whereas, as he thought was obvious, the lines were attempting to 'convey by their rhythm the impression of a clucking of ripples into riverside holes when blown upon by an up-stream wind' (L 422).

speak, with the accurate registering of detail by the poet, as he goes about his business of describing 'Stourside Mill, where broad / Stream-lilies throng', or the 'Swart bats, whose wings, be-webbed and tanned, / Whirred like the wheels of ancient clocks'. The irony again is that this seemingly professional and purposeful accumulation of observations is revealed at the poem's conclusion to be its opposite, a 'dull soul-swoon' that prevents him from hearing or seeing the thing that most needed noticing.

It is only in his chapter in the *Life* describing their time in Riverside Villa that the possibility of Emma's becoming a mother ever surfaces. A pregnancy did in fact occur in the house, which gave rise to the reference. In June 1877 the Hardys discovered that their servant Jane Phillips, whom they 'liked very much' (L 118) and who has been seen by some as a prototype for Tess, had been secretly meeting at night with her 'young man', both in the villa and in its outhouse. Reprimanded by Emma when caught in the act of stealing back in from the garden one night, Jane absconded. Some six weeks later Hardy made this melancholy entry in his diary: 'We hear that Jane, our late servant is soon to have a baby. Yet never a sign of one is there for us' (L 119). Like Tess's Sorrow, Jane's baby died in infancy after a home baptism.

It is likely the musical box had been acquired by the Hardys while on a shopping spree in Bristol during which they purchased '£100 worth of mid-Victorian furniture in two hours' (L 115). Some weeks earlier they had attended an auction at which they successfully bid for 'a door-scraper and a book-case, with which two articles they laid the foundation of household goods and effects'. These Pooterish triumphs suggest an attempt on their part to set up as a bourgeois couple possibly planning to start a family of their own, while also enjoying, as far as possible, amicable relations with both their families of origin: Emma's diary records a visit to Riverside Villa by her brothers Walter and Willie in late October 1876 (EHD 103), and that Christmas was spent with Hardy's family in Higher Bockhampton (L 116). In addition, the Hardys called on and dined with various suitable 'leading Sturminster families' (MM 172)—the Youngs, the Dashwoods, the Warrys, Dr Leach…These happy forays into elegant provincial society were, it is perhaps worth pointing out, in stark contrast to the landscapes and characters that Hardy was exploring each day in his study, where he was at work on the most archetypal and elemental of his novels, *The Return of the Native*.

Sturminster Newton, with its population of around 1,500, its favourable situation amid the lush farmland of the Vale of Blackmore, or the Vale of the Little Dairies as it is called in *Tess*, seemed to offer a happy medium between the Hardys' shared social aspirations and his complex imaginative needs as a writer. Yet deeming, as he put it in the *Life*, that 'the practical side of his vocation of novelist demanded that he should have his head-quarters in or near London' (L 121), Hardy opted not to renew the lease on Riverside Villa. In the first week of February 1878 they entrained for the capital in search of a suitable property to rent and on 22 March moved into a large family house at 1 Arundel Terrace, Trinity Road, Tooting. Their 'Two-Years' Idyll' was over:

> Yes; such it was;
> Just those two seasons unsought,
> Sweeping like summertide wind on our ways;
> Moving, as straws,
> Hearts quick as ours in those days;
> Going like wind, too, and rated as nought
> Save as the prelude to plays
> Soon to come—larger, life-fraught:
> Yes; such it was.
>
> 'Nought' it was called,
> Even by ourselves—that which springs
> Out of the years for all flesh, first or last,
> Commonplace, scrawled
> Dully on days that go past.
> Yet, all the while, it upbore us like wings
> Even in hours overcast:
> Aye, though this best thing of things,
> 'Nought' it was called!
>
> What seems it now?
> Lost: such beginning was all;
> Nothing came after: romance straight forsook
> Quickly somehow
> Life when we sped from our nook,
> Primed for new scenes with designs smart and tall...
> —A preface without any book,
> A trumpet uplipped, but no call;
> That seems it now.   (CP 628–9)

6

Divisions Dire and Wry

There is no evidence to suggest that Emma felt either at the time or subsequently the same way as her husband about their sojourn in Sturminster Newton. While the note of self-reproach in poems such as 'Overlooking the River Stour' and 'The Musical Box' is more muted than in Hardy's 1912–13 elegies for Emma, it seems clear that even when hymning their 'happiest time', as he calls it in the *Life* (L 122), he was aware of an incipient tendency to neglect her. A great deal of Emma's married life was spent alone indoors, and a poignant poem entitled 'Lonely Days' included in *Late Lyrics and Earlier* opens by brooding over her housebound solitude.

> Lonely her fate was,
> Environed from sight
> In the house where the gate was
> Past finding at night.
> None there to share it,
> No one to tell:
> Long she'd to bear it,
> And bore it well.
>
> Elsewhere just so she
> Spent many a day;
> Wishing to go she
> Continued to stay.
> And people without
> Basked warm in the air,
> But none sought her out,
> Or knew she was there.
> Even birthdays were passed so,
> Sunny and shady:
> Years did it last so
> For this sad lady.
> Never declaring it,

Woman Much Missed: Thomas Hardy, Emma Hardy, and Poetry. Mark Ford, Oxford University Press.
© Mark Ford 2023. DOI: 10.1093/oso/9780192886804.003.0007

> No one to tell,
> Still she kept bearing it—
> Bore it well.   (CP 652–3)

An endnote to the poem reveals that it was '*Versified from a Diary*'. Like 'During Wind and Rain', 'Lonely Days' exemplifies Hardy's poetic ability to inhabit vicariously Emma's experience, or in this case non-experience, as well as his tendency to encode into his 'dramatic or impersonative' (CP 84) lyrics personal references, such as his repeated failure to commemorate her birthday each year (including her final one three days before she died), or the surreptitious allusion in the third line to Max Gate. Even when escaped from the gloom of her lonely days there to some unnamed 'elsewhere', Emma is figured as a dithering and unwanted recluse, blithely ignored by all those who 'basked warm in the air'. From the early 1890s on, the enormous success of *Tess of the d'Urbervilles* made Hardy into something of a social lion at the various gala events that he attended in London during the Season, despite his shyness and reserve. His consort, however, was by no means embraced by fashionable metropolitan circles. All too typical of the responses she inspired was the quip made by the politician and journalist T. P. O'Connor at a reception at Stafford House, as recalled by the American writer Gertrude Atherton in her memoir *Adventures of a Novelist*:

> Hardy drifted by, looking as little interested in his surroundings as usual. In his wake was an excessively plain, dowdy, high-stomached woman with her hair drawn back in a tight little knot, and a severe cast of countenance. 'Mrs Hardy,' said T.P. 'Now you may understand the pessimistic nature of the poor devil's work.'   (IR 26)

It seems that even the much-vaunted uncle who became Archdeacon of London kept a wary distance from Emma during their annual sojourns in the capital, and the Jeune family, in whose house on Harley Street Hardy frequently stayed—and whose spare bedroom, he suggested in the letter of 19 February 1896 quoted earlier, might be at her disposal—were united in their dislike: 'We all hated her' is how the daughter Dorothy once put it (MM 251).

The final section of 'Lonely Days' derives from an entry that must have recorded Emma's dismay on returning alone to Plymouth for her father's funeral in 1890 and discovering the city so changed from her recollections of it:

The days grew chillier,
And then she went
To a city, familiar
In years forespent,
When she walked gaily
Far to and fro,
But now, moving frailly,
Could nowhere go.
The cheerful colour
Of houses she'd known
Had died to a duller
And dingier tone.
Streets were now noisy
Where once had rolled
A few quiet coaches,
Or citizens strolled.
Through the party-wall
Of the memoried spot
They danced at a ball
Who recalled her not.
Tramlines lay crossing
Once gravelled slopes,
Metal rods clanked,
And electric ropes.
So she endured it all,
Thin, thinner wrought,
Until time cured it all,
And she knew nought.

Formally and thematically, this poem is itself committed to thinness, to miming the erosion of life to chilliness and frailty, the fading of colour to the dull and the dingy; and with the introduction of the new trams and tramlines it is as if Hardy is presenting modernity and entropy in sinister collusion, finally draining the lonely lady of all resistance to the trajectory outlined for her of obsolescence and oblivion. At once bleak and sorrowing, 'Lonely Days' salvages little from the attenuated life it depicts in such compressed, indeed brutally straitened, terms.[1]

---

[1] Because Hardy burnt Emma's diaries after reading them, we will never know how typical of them was the defeated, melancholy tone conveyed by 'Lonely Days'. It is to be hoped that

Hardy was also adept at converting his own sense of desertion, misery, and loneliness into poetry, some of which Emma must have read. 'In Tenebris', for instance, originally titled 'De Profundis', dates from 1895–6 and was collected in *Poems of the Past and the Present* of 1901. Its first section in particular registers a devastation that, while it undoubtedly reflects the hurt and outrage provoked in Hardy by the attacks levelled at *Jude the Obscure*, also suggests a more existential crisis. Like 'Lonely Days', it finds new ways of conjugating unhappiness and isolation, while also insisting that the despair it delineates is unremitting and beyond amelioration. Indeed, 'In Tenebris I' offers a poetic equivalent to the overall mood of Hardy's final novel and similarly makes one wonder, to borrow Edmund Gosse's famous query in his review of *Jude the Obscure* for *Cosmopolis*, precisely 'what has Providence done to Mr Hardy that he should rise up in the arable land of Wessex and shake his fist at his Creator?'[2]

> Wintertime nighs;
> But my bereavement-pain
> It cannot bring again:
> Twice no one dies.
>
> Flower-petals flee;
> But, since it once hath been,
> No more that severing scene
> Can harrow me.
>
> Birds faint in dread:
> I shall not lose old strength
> In the lone frost's black length:
> Strength long since fled!
>
> Leaves freeze to dun;
> But friends can not turn cold
> This season as of old
> For him with none.
>
> Tempests may scath;
> But love can not make smart

Emma also recorded personal triumphs, such as her spirited assault on the three street thieves attempting to steal a painting from Hardy on the Via di Aracoeli in Rome in 1887 (L 196), or the impressive distances that she covered on her bicycle (nicknamed The Grasshopper) both in England and on the Continent during the mid-1890s.

[2] *Thomas Hardy: The Critical Heritage*, ed. R. G. Cox (London: Routledge, 1970), 269.

> Again this year his heart
>> Who no heart hath.
>
>> Black is night's cope;
> But death will not appal
> One who, past doubtings all,
>> Waits in unhope.   (CP 167)

In poetry in English of the nineteenth century, only the rigorous negations of James Thomson rival Hardy's in dramatizing states of 'unhope'.[3] The abba rhyme scheme deployed in these bitterly truncated quatrains mockingly summons up that great mid-Victorian compendium of grief and melancholy, *In Memoriam*, in section V of which Tennyson argues that 'for the unquiet heart and brain, / A use in measured language lies; / The sad mechanic exercise, / Like dull narcotics, numbing pain'.[4] Hardy's stunted dimeters and jarring trimeters are the opposite of soothing and reveal again how much he learned from the experiments of John Donne. 'In Tenebris I' accumulates its conceits of dispossession or 'bereavement-pain' much in the manner of 'A Nocturnal upon St Lucy's Day', as if driven to seek out and define what Donne calls 'a quintessence even from nothingness, / From dull privations, and lean emptiness'.[5] As in Donne, nature becomes wholly allegorical, enabling him to shrink the world to a stylized simulacrum of his depression—and no heroically carolling thrush will interrupt this particular 'full look at the Worst', to quote from 'In Tenebris II' (CP 168).

At once outspoken and doleful, 'In Tenebris I' conceals the exact nature of the 'severing scene' that so harrows the poet. Division marks Hardy's relationships, or at least his poetic accounts of them, not only with Emma, but with Florence Henniker and Florence Dugdale, indeed with all the desired women who feature in his poetic oeuvre, from Lizbie Browne to Helen Paterson to Agnes Grove to Rosamund Tomson. His various infatuations with society women undoubtedly played their part in deepening the rift that opened up between husband and wife around the time the 'In Tenebris' poems were composed, and which would eventually lead to Emma's retreat, towards the end of the decade, to her attic rooms above his study in Max

---

[3] In his short monograph on Hardy first published in 1942, Edmund Blunden observes of the 'In Tenebris' poems that 'they are, as nearly as anything can be, Hardy's parallel to James Thomson's *City of Dreadful Night*' (*Thomas Hardy* (London: Macmillan, 1954), 96).

[4] Alfred Lord Tennyson, *A Selected Edition*, ed. Christopher Ricks (Harlow: Longman, 1989), 349 (ll. 5–8).

[5] John Donne, *The Complete English Poems*, ed. A. J. Smith (Harmondsworth: Penguin, 1986), 72 (ll. 15–16).

Gate. '& at fifty,' as she noted to Elspeth Grahame in her cautionary letter of 1899, 'a man's feelings too often take a new course altogether. Eastern ideas of matrimony secretly pervade his thoughts, & he wearies of the most perfect, & suitable wife chosen in his earlier life' (LEFH 15). Hardy's mid-life crisis, if it can be called such, perhaps inspired some of the fantasies of illicit relations so resented by Emma, but it also resulted in a retreat of a different but perhaps analogous kind to that chosen by his wife. 'The misrepresentations of the last two or three years', as he put it in chapter 24 of the *Life*, musing on the attacks inspired by *Jude*,

> turned out ultimately to be the best thing that could have happened; for they well-nigh compelled him, in his own judgment at any rate, if he wished to retain any shadow of self-respect, to abandon at once a form of literary art he had long intended to abandon at some indefinite time, and resume openly that form of it which he had just been able to keep alive from his early years, half in secrecy... (L 309)

He would no longer compose novels 'as near to poetry in their subject as the conditions would allow', but would write and publish only poetry itself. For over two decades Emma had been involved, in varying ways, with Hardy's career as a writer of fiction, but—apart from unwittingly furnishing details and material for many of his most successful poems— she would play no part at all in his private or professional life as a writer of verse.

As mentioned in the previous chapter, Hardy suggested in the *Life* that it was during their residence in Tooting 'that their troubles began' (L 128). Further, he adduces the poem 'A January Night', subtitled '1879', in relation to the onset of these difficulties. 'A January Night' certainly condenses a haunting and pervasive sense of unease into its three rhymed quatrains, all ending abruptly in a dimeter final line. Like 'Honeymoon Time at an Inn', it reveals primitive superstition undermining the confidence of a couple made vulnerable for reasons that are never disclosed, but who here seem exposed to some supernatural hostility activated by a death and the subsequent funeral preparations taking place in a nearby house:

> The rain smites more and more,
> The east wind snarls and sneezes;

> Through the joints of the quivering door
> > The water wheezes.
>
> The tip of each ivy-shoot
> Writhes on its neighbour's face;
> There is some hid dread afoot
> > That we cannot trace.
>
> Is it the spirit astray
> Of the man at the house below
> Whose coffin they took in to-day?
> > We do not know.   (CP 466)

The anxious couple, feeling themselves stalked by some 'hid dread afoot', are in this instance united by their shared apprehension, but as in all Hardy's explicitly personal poems of premonition, such as 'Near Lanivet, 1872' or 'Self-Unconscious' or 'The Interloper' or 'At a Fashionable Dinner' or 'At the Piano', our foreknowledge that the instinctual fears unleashed will prove true, that some kind of curse, possibly related to his belief in Emma's inherited insanity, will destabilize their relationship and prise them apart, lurks in the ominous atmosphere created.

On 1 January that year Hardy set down a striking 'New Year's Thought':

> A perception of the FAILURE of THINGS to be what they are meant to be, lends them, in place of the intended interest, a new and greater interest of an unintended kind.   (L 127)

A theory, derived from experience, of disappointment and division, and of their role in his imaginative processes, seems latent in this notion. And it is a notion that perhaps helps explain the peculiar equanimity with which in his autobiography he assesses the various vexed and crucial decisions that determined the direction of his life; as when, reflecting on Horace Moule's unwelcome advice that he give up studying Greek literature in 1859—advice which, in a flight of fancy, he then goes on to suggest was all that prevented him from becoming a don at Cambridge—he merely observes: 'But this was not to be, and it was possibly better so' (L 38). A similar stoicism inflects his ruminations on the wisdom of moving into the purpose-built Max Gate, where his marriage would deteriorate beyond repair, but where he would also compose his greatest novels—as well as numerous poems dramatizing that deterioration:

This removal to the county-town [i.e. Dorchester], and later to a spot a little outside it [Max Gate is on the south-eastern fringes of the town], was a step they often regretted having taken; but the bracing air brought them health and renewed vigour, and in the long run it proved not ill-advised.

(L 167)[6]

For those attuned to Hardy's frequent recourse to periphrases, 'not ill-advised' is a good example of how they serve to enact his lukewarm or Laodicean habits of mind and emotion. Emma, on the other hand, could be as bracingly vigorous as the Dorset air when identifying the main source of that regret as far as she was concerned: in 1895 she told Edward Clodd, who transferred the remark to his diary: 'A man who has humble relations shouldn't live in the place where he was brought up' (MM 326).

After protracted negotiations, the plot of land on which Max Gate was built had been acquired from the Duchy of Cornwall in June of 1883, a few weeks before Hardy and Emma moved from Wimborne Minster, the last of the Dorset towns some twenty miles from Higher Bockhampton where they temporarily settled, to Shire-Hall Place, in the centre of Dorchester. Hardy had, however, embarked on his search for a suitable site for a permanent home back in the spring of 1880. On 20 April that year he wrote to his brother Henry, who had joined his father in the family building trade, about 'the plot of land we want to get in Dorchester' (CL I 73), having learned from the family's lawyer, Arthur Henry Lock, of the conditions under which portions of land were put up for sale by the Duchy. To whom exactly, one cannot help wondering, does Hardy's 'we' refer? The search for the land was undertaken by Hardy and his brother, and it seems more than likely that the 'troubles' experienced in Tooting were in part the result of Hardy's openly declared resolution to return, like Clym Yeobright, to his native region. '[T]here lay hidden', Hardy observes of another of his fictional idealists, Angel Clare, 'a hard logical deposit, like a vein of metal in a soft loam, which turned the edge of everything that attempted to traverse it' (T 260–1). Emma would increasingly be confronted by a similar 'vein of metal' in her

---

[6] One can precisely follow him in the act of reaching for this equilibrium in his diary entry for 31 December 1885, by which time they had lived in Max Gate for almost exactly six months: 'This evening, the end of the old year 1885 finds me sadder than many previous New Year's eves have done. Whether building this house at Max Gate was a wise expenditure of energy is one doubt, which, if resolved in the negative, is depressing enough. And there are others. But: "This is the chief thing: Be not perturbed; for all things are according to the nature of the universal." [Marcus Aurelius]' (L 182–3).

husband. It is not known how strenuously she resisted the proposal at the time, but she was certainly not present at the conclave in Higher Bockhampton in mid-September 1880 when the Hardy clan gathered to discuss these plans. The decision then taken to seek out a suitable site, writes Michael Millgate, 'constituted a victory for Jemima, and for Emma a corresponding defeat, one which she never forgave and from which she never fully recovered' (MM 199). The closest Hardy comes to acknowledging their difference of opinion on the matter is in a diary entry of the spring of 1885 made in response to his being 'taken up' by Lady Portsmouth, at whose country seat, Eggesford House in Devon, he had stayed (without Emma) as a houseguest in March of that year: 'Lady P.', he reflects, 'wants us to come to Devonshire and live near them. She says they would find a house for us. Cannot think why we live in benighted Dorset. Em would go willingly, as it is her native county; but alas, my house in Dorchester is nearly finished' (L 177).

Max Gate is, in the main, the setting for Hardy's poetic recreations of episodes in the breakdown of their relationship. In 'The Spell of the Rose' the construction of the house and the planting of the garden are developed into a fabular encapsulation of their twenty-seven years together there. This elegy reworks a conceit initially developed in 'Heiress and Architect', composed back in 1867 while Hardy was working in Arthur Blomfield's architectural practice in Adelphi Terrace. In this early poem about an heiress's plans for the design of an ideal dwelling, male and female values and sensibilities are revealed to be disastrously at odds. And 'The Spell of the Rose' recalls an even earlier Hardy text as well, the Dickensian squib 'How I Built Myself a House', published in *Chambers Journal* in 1865 and his first ever appearance in print. 'How I Built Myself a House' depicts the trials and tribulations of a harassed family man overseeing the plans and erection of a villa in the outer suburbs of London, and is Hardy's first attempt to exploit his knowledge of architecture in a commercial fiction. 'The Spell of the Rose' also deploys a recognizable mid-Victorian genre, translating the domestic conflicts and awkward silences involved in 'keeping separate' in Max Gate into medievalism of the kind popularized by Tennyson and Swinburne and the Pre-Raphaelites. Spoken by Emma's ghost, it opens by recalling Hardy's peremptory decision to build his love a house. While it is bars on the nursery windows that are suddenly discovered to be unaccountably missing at the conclusion of the early story, in the poem something more fundamental has been omitted:

'I mean to build a hall anon,
  And shape two turrets there,
  And a broad newelled stair,
And a cool well for crystal water;
  Yes; I will build a hall anon,
  Plant roses love shall feed upon,
   And apple-trees and pear.'

He set to build the manor-hall,
  And shaped the turrets there,
  And the broad newelled stair,
And the cool well for crystal water;
  He built for me that manor-hall,
  And planted many trees withal,
   But no rose anywhere.

And as he planted never a rose
  That bears the flower of love,
  Though other flowers throve
Some heart-bane moved our souls to sever
  Since he had planted never a rose;
  And misconceits raised horrid shows,
   And agonies came thereof.

'I'll mend these miseries,' then said I,
  And so, at dead of night,
  I went and, screened from sight,
That nought should keep our souls in severance,
  I set a rose-bush. 'This,' said I,
  'May end divisions dire and wry,
   And long-drawn days of blight.'   (CP 355)

The second of the two turrets mentioned in the first stanza was in fact added about a decade later, but Emma's ghost is accurate in her recollection of Hardy's involvement in every detail of the construction of their 'manor-hall': he drew up the plans, hired his brother and father to build it, was 'constantly overlooking operations' (L 508), and determined every feature, from the large carefully placed windows with their sills of Portland stone to the 'small square hall, floored with dark polished wood' to the attic bedrooms for the maids. The original edition of the *Life* quotes extensively from an admiring but unnamed visitor of 1886 who describes Max Gate, as seen from the Wareham Road, as 'an unpretending red-brick structure of moderate size, somewhat quaintly built'. In time, however, its unpretending quaintness became obscured from passing or prying eyes by Hardy's recreation of the arboreal defences surrounding the cottage at Higher Bockhampton, at least as depicted in 'Domicilium': 'Some two or three thousand small trees, mostly Austrian pines, were planted around the house by Hardy himself, and in later years these grew so thickly that the house was almost entirely screened from the road, and finally appeared, in summer, as if at the bottom of a dark green well of trees' (L 509). In this Max Gate came to resemble an enlarged version of the 'spray-roofed house' that the young Hardy ingeniously fashioned from 'green rafters' as recounted in 'Childhood among the Ferns' (CP 864).[7]

The garden enclosed by Hardy's palisade of trees was pre-eminently Emma's domain, and she did indeed plant a rose there shortly before she died. 'As it is an exceptionally mild afternoon,' he wrote to Florence Henniker on 28 December 1918, 'I have been gardening a little, & had to tie up a rosebush planted by Emma a month or two before her death: it has grown luxuriantly, & she would be pleased if she could know & that I care for it' (CL V 287). This reveals him, six years on from her death,

---

[7] These trees are also referred to in 'Everything Comes', another poem about the failure of Max Gate to become a satisfactory 'bower' for Emma. It recreates the openness of the plot on which Max Gate was built as well as the rawness of the garden in their early years there, before the Austrian pines had grown sufficiently to serve 'as a screen' from the road:

> 'The house is bleak and cold
> > Built so new for me!
> All the winds upon the wold
> > Search it through for me;
> No screening trees abound,
> And the curious eyes around,
> > Keep on view for me.'
>
> 'My Love, I am planting trees
> > As a screen for you
> Both from winds, and eyes that tease
> > And peer in for you.
> Only wait till they have grown,
> No such bower will be known
> > As I mean for you.'
>
> 'Then I will bear it, Love,
> > And will wait,' she said.
> —So, with years, there grew a grove.
> > 'Skill how great!' she said.
> 'As you wished, Dear?'—'Yes, I see!
> But—I'm dying; and for me
> > 'Tis too late,' she said.   (CP 508)

still attempting to atone for his negligence, both in the garden and by recounting his care of her rose in this letter. It is only in the last two stanzas of 'The Spell of the Rose' that it becomes clear that the poem is spoken from beyond the grave:

> But I was called from earth— yea, called
>   Before my rose-bush grew;
>   And would that now I knew
> What feels he of the tree I planted,
>   And whether, after I was called
>   To be a ghost, he, as of old,
>   Gave me his heart anew!
>
> Perhaps now blooms that queen of trees
>   I set but saw not grow,
>   And he, beside its glow—
> Eyes couched of the mis-vision that blurred me—
>   Ay, there beside that queen of trees
>   He sees me as I was, though sees
>   Too late to tell me so!   (CP 355–6)

'Eyes couched of the mis-vision that blurred me' is instantly recognizable as the kind of line that only Hardy could write: couching is a primitive form of cataract surgery, and a dismayingly literal term to apply to the release of the poet from his misinterpretations of the wife he is elegizing. It introduces into the poem's allegorical formulations that most vulnerable of organs, the eye, which, in 'Honeymoon Time at an Inn', had proved defenceless against the intrusions of the ancient mocking moon, and the leering, then shattered, 'many-eyed' mirror, both of which, to the couple's distress, had seen it all before. 'The Spell of the Rose' seems an attempt to recover some of the innocence the honeymooners lost that night, and its archaic compounds, such as 'manor-hall' or 'heart-bane', exude a quaintness in keeping with Hardy's original vision of the 'quaintly built' house with its turrets, broad newelled stair, and 'cool well for crystal water' (all water used at Max Gate had to be pumped by resentful servants each morning from this well to the roof tank). The regal bearing Emma might assume when presiding over Max Gate garden parties, or when addressing his family, or in his imagination as Iseult the Fair, Queen of Cornwall, is adumbrated in this imaginary sighting of her beside the fittingly emblematic rose bush: transplanted to the poem, the flowering 'queen of trees' is intended as a belated compensation for Emma's 'long-drawn days of blight'.

The garden at Max Gate features in many of Hardy's poetic commemorations of Emma. 'The Tree and the Lady', for instance, is spoken by Emma's favourite of the many trees planted by Hardy. Now that she is dead, it is depicted musing on all it has done for her: shading her in summer, attracting songbirds to sing in its branches for her, tempting her to set a chair in May under its 'new bravery / Of greenth' (CP 531). Like 'The Spell of the Rose', the poem acknowledges the embittered relations that led to Emma's isolation by having the tree reflect, 'Much did I treasure her / During those days she had nothing to pleasure her; / Mutely she used me as friend'. Whether true or not, this image of arboreal sympathy certainly tallies with Hardy's own extreme affection for his trees, which his gardener was instructed not to prune for fear of 'wounding' them (MM 244). And Emma's enjoyment of her shrubs and flowerbeds could, at least on the evidence of A. C. Benson, be equally extreme: in the course of a tour of the garden during his visit with Gosse of September 1912 she became so absorbed in pinching the pods of yellow balsam that she began executing 'little jumps' and uttering 'elfin shrieks of pleasure' (MM 443).

In 'The Ivy-Wife' of *Wessex Poems*, which so distressed Emma, ash tree and ivy end up destroying each other: 'Soon he, / Being bark-bound, flagged, snapped, fell outright, / And in his fall felled me!', it grimly concludes (CP 57). Another lament for lost marital happiness published while Emma was alive is 'Shut Out That Moon', included in *Time's Laughingstocks* of 1909, and dated 1904. It pivots on the contrast between inside and outside, between the romantic garden at night and the banality of artificially lighted rooms indoors:

> Close up the casement, draw the blind,
>   Shut out that stealing moon,
> She wears too much the guise she wore
>   Before our lutes were strewn
> With years-deep dust, and names we read
>   On a white stone were hewn.
>
> Step not forth on the dew-dashed lawn
>   To view the Lady's Chair,

Immense Orion's glittering form,
    The Less and Greater Bear:
Stay in; to such sights we were drawn
    When faded ones were fair.

Brush not the bough for midnight scents
    That come forth lingeringly,
And wake the same sweet sentiments
    They breathed to you and me
When living seemed a laugh, and love
    All it was said to be.

Within the common lamp-lit room
    Prison my eyes and thought;
Let dingy details crudely loom,
    Mechanic speech be wrought:
Too fragrant was Life's early bloom,
    Too tart the fruit it brought!   (CP 216)

Hardy composed many generic laments for the passing of time, and never tired of hymning lost joys from 'the other side' of some unnamed but decisive divide. The steady erosion of the years is here shown conspiring with 'lamp-lit' bourgeois modernity to deprive the poem's 'you and me' of all romantic impetus. It was not until Emma had died that Hardy would be able to promulgate the myth of exceptionalism that could raise them to the legendary status of a Tristram and Iseult; without that myth, they are just another couple who have outlived the clichés of love (however consummately deployed), inevitably succumbing to the 'common', the 'dingy', and the 'mechanic'. What is perhaps surprising is Hardy's surprise at this turn of events; or, to put it another way, if poetry and memory combined to enable him to recover the romance of 'Life's early bloom', even if only by way of contrast with the 'common lamp-lit room' in which a disaffected or warring couple, both aged sixty-four, spend their evenings together, how might such disjunctions or divisions be managed?

That he was himself taken aback by the extent to which Emma's death transformed her into an irresistible muse-figure is surely implied by his description in his autobiography of his poetic output of 1912–13:

Many poems were written by Hardy at the end of the previous year and the early part of this—more than he had ever written before in the same space of time—as can be seen by referring to their subjects, as well as to the dates attached to them. To adopt Walpole's words concerning Gray, Hardy was 'in flower' in these days, and, like Gray's, his flower was sad-coloured.   (L 389)

The gulf separating Emma's spectre from Hardy on the many occasions on which she returns to haunt him can be seen as a final embodiment of the divisions that separated them in the later years of their marriage. The conditions vary: sometimes she can be seen and not heard, and sometimes heard but not seen. Whatever the nature of the visitation, each is interpreted by Hardy as either promising or refusing to mend the breach that they failed to mend in life, or as a disconcerting mixture of both. The spectral apparition of Emma in the garden at Max Gate in the third stanza of 'The Going', for instance, offers no comfort at all:

> Why do you make me leave the house
> And think for a breath it is you I see
> At the end of the alley of bending boughs
> Where so often at dusk you used to be;
>   Till in darkening dankness
>   The yawning blankness
> Of the perspective sickens me!   (CP 338)

Emma's instability here parodies the fascination that her unpredictable movements had for him during their courtship: as then, he has surrendered to her whims or injunctions, but to no avail, as the momentary glimpse of her proves a ghastly mirage. The tone of quotidian complaint implicit in this stanza's opening line gives way to images of possible romance in the next three—a shadowy female figure at dusk and in the distance is frequently pregnant with erotic potential in Hardy—only to collapse into vertiginous emptiness. This in turn triggers a compensatory memory of their happy courtship, of Emma riding Fanny on 'beetling Beeny Crest' while 'Life unrolled us its very best', only to be succeeded, in accordance with the poem's oscillating dynamics, by broodings on their estrangement:[8]

---

[8] For an excellent discussion of the ways in which the poem's prosody is mimetic of these oscillations, see John Hughes's 'Metre and Mourning: "The Going" and Poems of 1912–13', The Hardy Review, 17, 1 (Spring 2015), 28–36, and collected in Hughes's The Expression of Things: Themes in Thomas Hardy's Fiction and Poetry (Brighton: Sussex Academic Press, 2018), 143–66.

Why, then, latterly did we not speak,
Did we not think of those days long dead,
And ere your vanishing strive to seek
That time's renewal? We might have said,
    'In this bright spring weather
    We'll visit together
Those places that once we visited.'   (CP 339)

The disjunctions between now and then dramatized in 'Shut Out That Moon' have here become both fiendishly ironic and multilayered: why, before your death, 'did we not speak' (during that period when we weren't speaking to each other) of days themselves 'long dead', but that might somehow have been resuscitated—as they were, in imagination at least, in the poem's recalling of Hardy and Emma on Beeny Cliff? In a stanza so saturated in regret and impossibility, the echo of Tennyson's 'Ulysses' at the end of the third line ('To strive, to seek, to find, and not to yield')[9] only heightens the pathos of what they 'might have said' in the would-be-jaunty final lines, whose rhymes (weather/together, said/visited) gesture towards an innocence and naivety savagely at odds with the swirling fantasia and disconnections of bereavement enacted by the poem.

It is no wonder that in 'The Shadow on the Stone', a poem begun at the same time as the 1912–13 elegies but not completed until 1916, Hardy cannily avoids the distress of confronting Emma's ghost when he suspects she is lurking behind his back, having returned to Max Gate to undertake a stint of gardening. In an inventive reconfiguration of the myth of Orpheus, on this occasion the poet refuses to turn his head for fear of experiencing the dispersal of her illusory presence that so dismays him in 'The Going':

        Yet I wanted to look and see
        That nobody stood at the back of me;
    But I thought once more: 'Nay, I'll not unvision
        A shape which, somehow, there may be.'
    So I went on softly from the glade,
    And left her behind me throwing her shade,
    As she were indeed an apparition—
    My head unturned lest my dream should fade.   (CP 530)

---

[9] Tennyson, *Selected Edition*, 145 (l. 70).

It was, of course, precisely Hardy's refusal to turn his head to look at Emma that was presented, in 'Overlooking the River Stour', as initiating their 'troubles'. In the curious double bind of this particular non-encounter in the garden at Max Gate, to try to 'vision' Emma's ghost would in practice be to 'unvision' her in the manner that he so often did when she was alive.

Hardy's ability to 'unvision' or blank or exclude Emma in the later years of their marriage was witnessed by numerous visitors. The best-known occasion was on the presentation to Hardy by W. B. Yeats and Henry Newbolt of a gold medal on behalf of the Royal Society of Literature, on 2 June 1912, Hardy's seventy-second birthday. Newbolt left a bemused account in his autobiography of 1942 of the peculiarities of their reception at Max Gate:

> The dinner lives in my memory beyond all others unusual and anxious. Mr and Mrs Hardy faced one another the longer way of the table: Yeats and I sat rather too well spaced at the two sides: we could hold no private communication with each other. I had the feeling that I was about to play a card game which I did not know. Hardy, an exquisitely remote figure, with the air of a nervous stranger, asked me a hundred questions about my impressions of the architecture of Rome and Venice, from which cities I had just returned. Through this conversation I could hear and see Mrs Hardy giving Yeats much curious information about two very fine cats, who sat to right and left of her plate on the table itself. In this situation Yeats looked like an Eastern Magician overpowered by a Northern Witch—and I too felt myself spellbound by the famous pair of Blue Eyes, which surpassed all that I had ever seen. We were no longer in the world of our waking lives...
>
> At last Hardy rose from his seat and looked towards his wife: she made no movement, and he walked to the door. She was still silent and unmoved: he invited her to leave us for a few minutes, for a ceremony which in accordance with his wish was to be performed without witnesses. She at once remonstrated, and Yeats and I begged that she should not be asked to leave us. But Hardy insisted and she made no further appeal but gathered up her cats and her train with perfect simplicity and left the room.   (IR 99–100)

Newbolt and Yeats then made their official perorations in praise of the recipient, and Hardy replied by reading out a pre-prepared speech of his own to the bewildered deputation of two. No reason was proffered for his insistence that Emma leave the room against her wishes, although Emma no doubt interpreted it as evidence of her husband's '*obsession*', as she had put it in her letter to Clement Shorter some four years earlier, that not even 'the dimmest ray shoud light upon me of his supreme story' (LEFH 38).

Many Hardy poems reflect remorsefully on occasions when he spurned her attempts to broker a truce. The destruction of both his and her diaries means it is not possible to date the incidents to which these poems refer, but there is no doubting the anguish with which he recalls her efforts to end the marital impasse they had reached:

> *The Peace-Offering*
>
> It was but a little thing,
> Yet I knew it meant to me
> Ease from what had given a sting
> To the very birdsinging
> > Latterly.
>
> But I would not welcome it;
> And for all I then declined
> O the regrettings infinite
> When the night-processions flit
> > Through the mind!   (CP 464)

Knowing, not-knowing, half-knowing, pretending not to know, and coming to full knowledge too late are fundamental to the drama presented in these self-excoriating poems. In this they refract in the realm of the personal or confessional lyric the narrative arc of so many of Hardy's fictions. Angel, to take the most obvious example, rejects all of Tess's attempts to palliate the effects of her momentous disclosure, and is similarly seized with 'regrettings infinite'. Characters such as Angel or Knight or Henchard or Pierston illustrate Hardy's lifelong fascination with male egotism in all its self-destructive perversity; and in poems like 'The Peace-Offering', 'Lost Love', and 'Penance' Hardy revisits this theme, with the gruesome added twist that their male speaker or protagonist is revealed as guilty of exactly the compulsive behaviour and inflexibility that his novels so remorselessly diagnose. In 'Penance' Hardy recalls Emma's forlorn stints at the piano, brusquely ignored at the time by her unyielding husband:

'Why do you sit, O pale thin man,
        At the end of the room
By that harpsichord, built on the quaint old plan?
        —It is cold as a tomb,
And there's not a spark within the grate;
        And the jingling wires
        Are as vain desires
        That have lagged too late.'

'Why do I? Alas, far times ago
        A woman lyred here
In the evenfall; one who fain did so
        From year to year;
And, in loneliness bending wistfully,
        Would wake each note
        In sick sad rote,
        None to listen or see!   (CP 630–1)

The archaic language and use of a ballad-style format initially work to frame and distance the dreadful memory of Emma vainly attempting to rekindle her husband's interest by playing the songs that had so enraptured him during their courtship. A literary descendant of Keats's ailing knight, alone and palely loitering, or Coleridge's ancient mariner, this 'pale thin man', marooned in his tomb-like room with an old-fashioned harpsichord, illustrates Hardy's willingness to apply the salient tropes of romantic medievalism to his own condition in the wake of Emma's death. His training in gothic architecture was, no doubt, a crucial factor in the freedom that he assumed as a poet to layer past and present, to transpose onto the now unused piano in the drawing room at Max Gate the macabre image with which this poem concludes:

'I would not join. I would not stay,
        But drew away,
Though the winter fire beamed brightly...Aye!
        I do to-day
What I would not then; and the chill old keys,
        Like a skull's brown teeth
        Loose in their sheath,
        Freeze my touch; yes, freeze.'   (CP 631)

Such moments suggest the impact on Hardy of the work of Edgar Allan Poe, who also reached into the past for his scenarios of morbid horror.[10] Emma's death—and the dissolution of her corpse—are often incorporated even into poems that pay tribute to her *living*ness: the tree in 'The Tree and the Lady' declares itself in that poem's final stanza to be 'a skeleton now' (it being winter), and reveals that the lady herself is one too, 'gone, craving warmth' (CP 532). In a similar fashion, the keys of the instrument that once enabled the intimacies so celebrated in poems such as 'To a Lady Playing and Singing in the Morning' and 'The Old Gown' now evoke their opposite, the loose, brown, freezing teeth of a skull.

In the montage of scenes from a marriage that can be assembled from Hardy's *Collected Poems*, the image of Emma performing on the piano while her stubbornly resistant husband pauses to listen, but then refuses to 'balk / His determined walk' (CP 318), is among the most recurrent: 'Now I am dead you sing to me', her ghost expostulates in 'The Upbraiding', 'The songs we used to know, / But while I lived you had no wish / Or care for doing so' (CP 532). He even sallied off to town and so missed what proved to be her deliberately staged finale to their shared musical life together:

> 'I am playing my oldest tunes,' declared she,
>   'All the old tunes I know,—
> Those I learnt ever so long ago.'
> —Why she should think just then she'd play them
>   Silence cloaks like snow.
>
> When I returned from the town at nightfall
>   Notes continued to pour
> As when I had left two hours before:
> 'It's the very last time,' she said in closing;
>   'From now I play no more.'
>
>   ('The Last Performance', CP 487)

A 'few morns onward found her fading', and soon after this poignant revisiting of the past, the poet is left wondering how she knew her death was near.

A much earlier performance witnessed by her husband was also the occasion for one of Hardy's more Poe-like premonitions of disaster, the kind

---

[10] In January 1909 Hardy was invited to attend a commemoration for the centenary of Poe's birth that was held at the University of Virginia. In the letter he sent to the committee declining the invitation he praised the 'fantastic and romantic genius' of Poe (L 370).

dramatized in poems such as 'The Man with a Past' or 'A January Night' or 'The Interloper'. The first stanza of 'At the Piano' recreates the happy harmonies of the musical evenings they so enjoyed during their courtship, but in the second their bliss is interrupted by a mysteriously 'cowled Apparition':

> A Woman was playing,
>   A man looking on;
>   And the mould of her face,
>   And her neck, and her hair,
>   Which the rays fell upon
>   Of the two candles there,
> Sent him mentally straying
>   In some fancy-place
>   Where pain had no trace.
>
> A cowled Apparition
>   Came pushing between;
>   And her notes seemed to sigh;
>   And the lights to burn pale,
>   As a spell numbed the scene.
>   But the maid saw no bale,
> And the man no monition;
>   And Time laughed awry,
>   And the Phantom hid nigh.   (CP 529–30)

It is likely that this Apparition or Phantom is Hardy's melodramatic code word for 'the figure and visage of Madness seeking for a home', to borrow the equally melodramatic phrase used as an epigraph to 'The Interloper' (CP 488). It is not known if Emma ever informed Hardy of her father's numerous admissions to asylums in Plymouth and Bodmin or revealed that other members of the Gifford clan had been diagnosed with related or similar conditions. Hardy had much first-hand experience, however, of Emma's niece Lilian's 'childlike speech and behaviour' (MM 453), for she spent extended periods at Max Gate before her aunt's death, and indeed attempted to settle there permanently after it, until driven from the field by Florence. Lilian suffered a calamitous nervous breakdown in 1919 and was committed in a paranoid state to the London County Council asylum at Claybury in Essex.[11]

---

[11] The medical report made on her admission suggests that, like Emma's father and her older brother, Lilian suffered delusions and was plagued by mysterious voices: 'Patient said she

Medical language does not much enter into Hardy's poetic depictions of the threat of madness hanging over Emma, which draw rather on literary and folkloric traditions of the supernatural: a witch-like 'spell' numbs the 'scene' in 'At the Piano' while the Apparition's cowl links it to any number of gothic visitations in nineteenth-century fiction. The spectre haunting her in 'The Interloper' is equally phantasmagorical, although the poem's penultimate line does perhaps suggest that the poem's sensational imagery can also be viewed as a metaphor for some pernicious disease or condition: 'It is that under which best lives corrode' (CP 489).

Hardy's letters in the wake of Emma's death indicate that it took him wholly by surprise. On the day itself he wrote only to her first cousin, Charles Gifford:

> You will be grieved and shocked to hear that Emma died this morning shortly after nine o'clock. Her illness has been quite a slight one, & she was downstairs at tea on Monday evening. I was with her, fortunately, when she breathed her last. I am too distressed to write more.   (CL IV 237)

To Eva Gosse some two weeks later he confessed:

> I have been full of regrets that I did not at all foresee the possibility of her passing away thus, but merely thought her few days of illness a temporary ailment which I need not be anxious about. Everybody, myself included, supposed her to have a high vitality & the soundest of constitutions.
>
> (CL IV 239)

And in a letter of 17 December to Florence Henniker he gave a full, but still baffled, account of the events leading up to the fatal day, as well as of his immediate responses to it:

> Emma's death was absolutely unexpected by me, the doctor, & everybody, though not sudden, strictly speaking. She was quite well a week before, & (as I fancy) in an unlucky moment determined to motor to some friends

had been very worried lately, chiefly because of a gang of thieves she believed to be about, and against whom she had barred her doors, but she saw them about and could hear their voices which said they were using a microphone and were going to gas her; she showed me her leg which she said showed signs of dropsy (it did not) and said she would rather die than go through such an illness' (quoted by Andrew Norman in *Thomas Hardy: Behind the Mask* (Stroud: The History Press, 2011), 144).

about 6 miles off. During the night following she had a bad attack of indigestion, which I attributed to the jolting of the car. She was never well from that time, though she came down to tea with some callers on the Monday evening before her death on Wednesday morning. I was with her when she passed away. Half an hour earlier she had told the servant that she felt better. Then her bell rang violently, & when we went up she was gasping. In five minutes all was over.

I have reproached myself for not having guessed there might be some internal mischief at work, instead of blindly supposing her robust & sound & likely to live to quite old age. In spite of the differences between us, which it would be affectation to deny, & certain painful delusions she suffered from at times, my life is intensely sad to me now without her. The saddest moments of all are when I go into the garden & to that long straight walk at the top that you know, where she used to walk every evening just before dusk, the cat trotting faithfully behind her; & at times when I almost expect to see her as usual coming in from the flower-beds with a little trowel in her hand.   (CL IV 243)

The breach that was created in Hardy's life by the death of Emma summoned up memories of the breach created in his life by his meeting her. Both days, 7 March 1870 and 27 November 1912, are repeatedly figured as effecting a complete and all-transforming divide between before and after. But while meeting her, as he acknowledged to Eden Phillpotts, proved crucial to his development into a commercially and critically successful novelist, her death proved crucial to his development into the most obsessively productive elegist in English poetry. Feeling 'intensely sad' drove him to transform the 'saddest moments' into verse, as one can see happened to this epistolary account of almost expecting to see Emma at dusk in the garden at Max Gate, which tallies so closely with the third stanza of 'The Going', also dated December 1912.

The 'difference' between before and after is itself the hinge on which many of his grieving poems pivot. 'The Walk' is a good example:

> You did not walk with me
> Of late to the hill-top tree
>   By the gated ways,
>   As in earlier days;
>   You were weak and lame,
>   So you never came,

And I went alone, and I did not mind,
Not thinking of you as left behind.

I walked up there to-day
Just in the former way;
     Surveyed around
     The familiar ground
     By myself again:
     What difference, then?
Only that underlying sense
Of the look of a room on returning thence.   (CP 340)

Emma mentions her 'occasional lameness, suffered from early childhood' in *Some Recollections* (SR 48), yet it is surely inconceivable that Hardy would have referred to it in a poem written before she died. Poetically, the great 'difference' made by her 'vanishing' was the access it granted his imagination to aspects of her life. 'But she is in her grave, and, oh, / The difference to me!' lamented Wordsworth of the enigmatic Lucy in 'She dwelt among the untrodden ways' (included in volume 4 of *The Golden Treasury*).[12] The fall into knowledge through encounters with death so central to the work of many of Hardy's romantic precursors is re-enacted in the emotionally fraught drama between knowing and not-knowing played out in oblique but potent ways in elegies such as 'The Walk'. The stroll taken while Emma was alive to the 'hill-top tree' through 'gated ways' (the sorts of detail that anchor the poem decisively in actuality) is fundamentally different from the same walk taken now that he knows she is dead.[13] In the context of Hardy's repeated evocations in his poetry of 'looking away' (CP 167) or not turning his head (CP 482), the last line of the first stanza, although in its diction quite ordinary, brilliantly sums up the complex processes involved in living with what he called in his letter to Florence Henniker 'the differences between us': 'Not thinking of you as left behind' fuses the attempt to see her absence from his side as understandable and normal, given these 'differences', with the gnawing regret that all too often he *did* leave her behind, or not think of her at all. Further, by dying she has achieved a subtle and unanswerable revenge, having now left *him* behind. The unbearable

---

[12] William Wordsworth, *Selected Poems*, ed. John O. Hayden (London: Penguin, 1994), 78 (ll. 11–12), and GT 251.

[13] See Anne-Lise François, *Open Secrets* (Stanford: Stanford University Press, 2008) for an illuminating discussion of how this poem 'makes permanent and absolute what had seemed a temporary solitude' (180).

absence awaiting him in the room that she has vacated forever in turn prompts one of his most devastating uses of anthropomorphism; he will look at the room and the room will look back at him, both aware that her 'great going' has 'altered all' (CP 338). Traces of Emma's presence no doubt still linger, but her absence is what the room communicates and what he sees.

The first three of the 'Poems of 1912–13' ('The Going', 'Your Last Drive', 'The Walk') address Emma directly as 'you' and show Hardy experimenting with what would become a compulsion, the transformation of her experiences—or his fantasies of her experiences—into poetry.

> Here by the moorway you returned,
> And saw the borough lights ahead
> That lit your face—all undiscerned
> To be in a week the face of the dead,
> And you told of the charm of that haloed view
> That never again would beam on you.   (CP 339)

The 'unlucky' decision to motor off and see some friends six miles away on 25 November is the portal here, allowing the approach to Dorchester by car to be recreated from Emma's perspective. In 'Your Last Drive' Emma is herself caught up in the oscillation between knowing and not-knowing, for it is she who is unable to discern that within a week her face, momentarily lit by streetlamps (another of those anchoring details), will be 'the face of the dead'. In the second stanza she passes Stinsford churchyard, 'Beholding it with a heedless eye / As alien from you, though under its tree / You soon would halt everlastingly'. Shuffled backwards and forwards by the poem over the threshold between life and death, she is at once unknowing or 'heedless' of what awaits her as she is chauffeured home for the last time, and yet propelled by the poem's jump cuts into her transformation into an indifferent corpse. For once underground she will become blissfully oblivious of all marital grievances, as well as of her widower's responses to his loss, at least according to the speech that Hardy imagines her making had she known, as she passed Stinsford churchyard that night, of her imminent demise:

> 'You may miss me then. But I shall not know
> How many times you visit me there,
> Or what your thoughts are, or if you go

There never at all. And I shall not care.
Should you censure me I shall take no heed,
And even your praises no more shall need.'   (CP 340)

Dated, like 'The Going', to December 1912, 'Your Last Drive' reveals Hardy attempting both to inhabit Emma's consciousness as she unwittingly approaches her end and to meld her thoughts with his own habits of mind and beliefs about existence.

That Emma's beliefs were completely at odds with his when it came to envisaging 'the life beyond this present one', as she puts it in the final paragraph of *Some Recollections*, where she trumpets her 'ardent belief in Christianity' and the 'Unseen Power of great benevolence' (SR 61), is most fully proved by the prose texts gathered in *Spaces*, privately published in April 1912. 'The High Delights of Heaven', for instance, depicts the afterlife as a seraphic and unending round of pleasure to be enjoyed even by 'lost pets and martyred ones'—making one wonder if Emma's conversation with Yeats about her two 'very fine cats' touched on the posthumous fates of these cats' numerous predecessors martyred on the nearby railway lines or buried in Max Gate's pet cemetery. The redeemed, she continues, will choir 'inconceivably sweet and wonderful music', probably be equipped with wings for 'ease of locomotion', and be granted 'highest knowledge as known to angels, and special comprehension of the former perplexities about our earthly existence'. Crucially, none will be troubled by 'sadness about those who rejected the great salvation', that is by regrets for the likes of her sceptical husband, undoubtedly a '*non-acceptor*' rather than an '*acceptor*', to use her terms: all thoughts of the miseries awaiting *non-acceptors* will be 'for ever banished from our remembrance— *obliterated*' (PRE 15–16).

If Emma anticipated in death a release from worries about the state of her husband's soul, he used his poetry to imagine for her any number of different sorts of afterlife, from the gruesome humour of 'The Sound of Her' to the spectral visitations recounted in poems such as 'His Visitor' or 'The Haunter', both spoken by her ghost. 'You are past love, praise, indifference, blame' ruefully but even-handedly concludes 'Your Last Drive', yet Emma's unreachability seems only to heighten Hardy's need to 'scan' her 'across the dark space' now separating them (CP 349), to recover traces of her existence. And in the poems recording this compulsion, despite Hardy's rational understanding that Emma is now beyond knowledge, some moment of redemptive understanding is frequently posited as finally healing the 'divisions dire and wry' that afflicted their later years, the 'heart-bane' that moved their 'souls to sever' (CP 355):

> *A Night in November*
> I marked when the weather changed,
> And the panes began to quake,
> And the winds rose up and ranged,
> That night, lying half-awake.
>
> Dead leaves blew into my room,
> And alighted upon my bed,
> And a tree declared to the gloom
> Its sorrow that they were shed.
>
> One leaf of them touched my hand,
> And I thought that it was you
> There stood as you used to stand,
> And saying at last you knew!
>   *(?) 1913*   (CP 586)

AFTERWARDS

7

Dear Ghost

Virgil's *Aeneid* was a book of which Hardy 'never wearied' (L 61). His mother gave him, along with Samuel Johnson's *Rasselas* and Jacques-Henri Bernardin de Saint-Pierre's *Paul and Virginia*, a copy of Dryden's translation into rhyming couplets and triplets when he was just eight (L 21). He began construing the poem in the original when he was sixteen and working as an architect's apprentice in Dorchester. Much of his reading in the years between his leaving school in 1856 and his move to London in 1862 was done either in the office, where his amiable employer, John Hicks, allowed Hardy and his fellow apprentice Henry Bastow to pursue their classical studies when time allowed, or in the early morning before work. He would rise at five o'clock, or four o'clock in summer, in order to devote himself to his studies for three or four hours before setting off from Higher Bockhampton for Dorchester:

> In these circumstances he got through a moderately good number of the usual classical pages—several books of the *Aeneid*, some Horace and Ovid, etc.; and in fact grew so familiar with his authors that in his walks to and from the town he often caught himself soliloquizing in Latin on his various projects.   (L 32)

Hardy could not be called an allusive poet in comparison with such as T. S. Eliot or Ezra Pound or Basil Bunting, but his reading of Latin poets, as well as his deep and ongoing self-education in the technical aspects of Latin prosody, proved a vital influence on aspects of his own poetry. Indeed, although not one to signal his references in the manner of modernist poets, he could get exasperated when reviewers overlooked what seemed to him obvious parallels between his own work and that of classical poets. In a letter of 20 December 1920 to Alfred Noyes (author of 'The Highwayman') he complained:

> This week I have had sent me a review which quotes a poem entitled 'To my father's violin' containing a Virgilian reminiscence of mine of Acheron

Woman Much Missed: Thomas Hardy, Emma Hardy, and Poetry. Mark Ford, Oxford University Press.
© Mark Ford 2023. DOI: 10.1093/oso/9780192886804.003.0008

and the Shades. The pennyaliner who writes it comments: 'Truly this pessimism is insupportable...One marvels that Hardy is not in a madhouse.' Such is English criticism, and I repeat, Why did I ever write a line!

(L 440)[1]

One of his earliest fictional male protagonists, Aeneas Manston of *Desperate Remedies*, is named after Virgil's hero, and this intrepid—and eventually villainous—architect-turned-steward might be read as embodying the more erotically transgressive aspects of Hardy's imagination. Manston's relationship with his mother, Cytherea Aldclyffe, in many ways shadows that of Aeneas with Venus, and the novel includes numerous allusions to the poem, some to the original Latin and some to Dryden's translation.[2] While *Desperate Remedies* is the novel that makes the most explicit use of the *Aeneid*, Virgilian allusions also feature in many of its successors: on her arrival in London Elfride in *A Pair of Blue Eyes* is likened to 'Aeneas at Carthage' (PBE 129) while Jocelyn Pierston, in the second version of *The Well-Beloved*, compares the statues of his past loves in his studio to 'the pictured Trojan women beheld by Aeneas on the walls of Carthage'.[3] It is the last fictional male hero conceived by Hardy, the autodidact Jude, who mirrors most closely his own early experiences of reading the *Aeneid* in the original. Jude plunges, a dictionary on his knees, 'into the simpler passages from Caesar, Virgil or Horace' (JO 26) on his early morning bread round and periodically finds himself 'aroused from the woes of Dido by the stoppage of his cart and the voice of some old woman crying, "Two to-day, baker, and I return this stale one"' (JO 27). The *Aeneid* is among the few books that Jude keeps with him to the bitter end, an 'old, superseded, Delphin' edition of Virgil, 'roughened with stone-dust', figuring among the meagre possessions amidst which he dies (JO 396). In light of Jude's repeated failure to get admitted to Christminster, and Hardy's own wish to apply to Cambridge, how gratifying he must have found the comparison of his work with that of Virgil, as praised by Horace, in the speech made (in Latin) by Oxford University's public orator, A. D. Godley, in the ceremony held on 2 February 1920 in the Sheldonian conferring on one of the few poets of his

---

[1] The complaint is slightly differently phrased in the letter that Hardy actually sent to Noyes. In the *Life* the jibe 'pennyaliner' replaces the straightforward 'reviewer' used in the original (CL VI 54–5).

[2] These occur on pages 157, 187, 213, 334, and 359 of *Desperate Remedies*, ed. Patricia Ingham (Oxford: Oxford University Press, 2003).

[3] *The Pursuit of Well-Beloved and The Well-Beloved*, ed. Patricia Ingham (London: Penguin, 1997), 324.

era not to attend a university an honorary D.Litt.: 'Scilicet ut Virgilio nostro sic huic quoque "mole atque facetum adnuerunt gaudentes rure Camenae"', Godley declared—a passage obligingly translated by Hardy in a footnote: 'Surely as with Virgil, so with him, have the Muses that rejoice in the countryside approved his smoothness and elegance.'[4]

Hardy's epigraph for the 'Poems of 1912–13' section of *Satires of Circumstance* derives from book IV of the *Aeneid*: '*Veteris vestigia flammae*'. 'Sparkles of my former flame' is the first version of this phrase that Hardy would have encountered, in the copy of Dryden's translation given to him by his mother.[5] The words are spoken by Dido to her sister Anna, to whom she is revealing her burgeoning love for Aeneas:

> Anna, fatebor enim, miseri post fata Sychaei
> coniugis et sparsos fraterna caede penatis
> solus hic inflexit sensus animumque labantem
> impulit. agnosco veteris vestigia flammae.   (IV 20–4)[6]

(For I confess, Anna, since the death of my poor husband Sychaeus, whose slaughter by my own brother defiled our household gods, he alone has stirred my feelings and overcome my wavering soul. I feel again the signs of the old flame.)

As has often been pointed out, Hardy was himself, like Dido, in the process of transferring his affections from a dead spouse to a prospective new lover. But while Dido evokes her old love principally as a means of dramatizing her new passion for Aeneas, Hardy—with what degree of deliberation it is not easy to judge—deploys the phrase in a wholly antithetical way, using it to open multiple perspectives on what is now irredeemably lost and accessible only through memories, time and again rejecting even the possibility of a future: 'I seem but a dead man held on end' (CP 339); 'for my sand is sinking, / And I shall traverse old love's domain / Never again' (CP 352); 'To whom to-day is beneaped and stale, / And its urgent clack / But a vapid tale' (CP 353).

When considered in the context of Hardy's elegiac sequence, double meanings or ambiguities radiate in a range of directions from each of Dido's

---

[4] Godley's speech and Hardy's translation are excerpted in chapter 17 of *The Later Years of Thomas Hardy* (reprinted in Florence Hardy, *The Life of Thomas Hardy* (London: Studio Editions, 1994)), 201–2. Since this passage was not present in any of the typescripts prepared while Hardy was alive, it does not feature in the textual notes to Millgate's edition of the *Life*.

[5] *Virgil's Aeneid: Translated by John Dryden*, ed. Frederick M. Keener (London: Penguin Books, 1997) Book 4, (l.31), 89.

[6] All quotations from the *Aeneid* are taken from *The Aeneid of Virgil: Books 1–6*, ed. R. D. Williams (London: Macmillan, 1972). Translations are my own.

three words: *veteris* could be interpreted as ancient or fading or even long-lasting as well as simply former or past or old, while possible translations of *vestigia* include—along with its English derivative, vestiges—footprints or tracks, traces, signs or remnants, as well as—when united with *flammae*—ashes or embers. Further, *flammae* can refer both to the flames of a fire (or a passion) and to the damage that results from those flames, thus implicitly layering both the intensity of first love and its aftermath, rather as the sequence shifts between exhilarating recollections of the couple's courtship in Cornwall to doleful regrets at the miseries of the marriage that ensued.[7] And it is finally worth noting that Hardy had himself loosely translated '*veteris flammae*' when composing the wording of the wreath that he deposited on Emma's grave at her funeral—'From her Lonely Husband, with the Old Affection' (MM 447).[8]

His epigraph also, however, gestures beyond the tale of Dido's love and suicide told in book IV of the *Aeneid* to the meeting between Aeneas and her ghost in his *nekyia* or visit to the underworld in book VI. Virgil's epic hero finds himself addressing Dido's *vestigia* or spectral remains, just as in 'After a Journey' Hardy encounters Emma's ghost on the cliffs above Pentargon Bay (or Pentargan Bay, as he spells it). The crepuscular limbo of Virgil's underworld is transposed to the pre-dawn gloom of the Cornish coast, while Dido's wandering ghost, like that of Emma, emerges fitfully from the shadows, stimulating reminiscence and remorse:

> inter quas Phoenissa recens a vulnere Dido
> errabat silva in magna; quam Troius heros
> ut primum iuxta stetit agnovitque per umbras
> obscuram, qualem primo qui surgere mense
> aut videt aut vidisse putat per nubila lunam,
> demisit lacrimas dulcique adfatus amore est... (VI 450–5)

(Her wound still fresh, Phoenician Dido was wandering among them [underworld ghosts who had died for love] in the great wood. As the Trojan hero stood near her, recognizing her dim figure in the gloom, as early in the month

---

[7] This was first noted by Peter Sacks in *The English Elegy: Studies in the Genre from Spenser to Yeats* (Baltimore: The Johns Hopkins University Press, 1985), 236. For further discussion of the implications of the epigraph, see Tim Armstrong, *Haunted Hardy: Poetry, History, Memory* (Basingstoke: Palgrave, 2000), 134–41. For a more wide-ranging consideration of Hardy's references to Virgil in the sequence, see Anne-Lise François's essay, '"Not Thinking of You as Left Behind": Virgil and the Missing of Love in Hardy's *Poems of 1912–13*' (*ELH* 75 (2008), 63–88).

[8] Hardy had earlier used a version of Virgil's phrase in chapter 6 of *The Return of the Native*: 'The revived embers of an old passion glowed clearly in Wildeve now' (*The Return of the Native*, 65).

one sees, or thinks one has seen, the moon rising through clouds, he shed tears, and addressed her in the tender tones of love.)

'Ah,' Aeneas exclaims in his address to her, 'was it I who caused your death?' ('*funeris heu tibi causa fui?*'). Although Hardy attributes to the phantom Emma a series of imagined laments for the failure of their marriage that faintly echo Aeneas's anguished moment of self-reproach, neither Dido nor Emma is allowed to speak. It is only through variations of *veteris flammae* that they communicate with their estranged lovers, Dido responding with a look of wild, blazing fury ('*ardentem et torva tuentem*' (l. 467)) before turning away, while the more accommodating Emma behaves somewhat in the mode of an *ignis fatuus* or will-o'-the-wisp, her 'rose-flush coming and going' as she leads Hardy on 'To the spots we knew when we haunted here together' (his use of 'haunted' deftly eliding the gap between real and ghost worlds), her now-dimmed flame triggering poignant memories of their courtship years when she was 'all aglow', and not 'the thin ghost that I now fraily follow!' (CP 349).

Hardy's various allusions to Aeneas and Dido operate in a less explicit manner than his references to Tristram and Iseult, but their tenor is similar: Emma and Hardy shared a love that stands comparison not only with that of the most famous doomed lovers of medieval romance, but of classical antiquity too. And indeed it has been argued by such as Donald Davie that Hardy's Virgilian epigraph, if pursued still further, can be seen as positing a connection between Hardy and Emma and the most celebrated Christian lovers in the western canon, Dante and Beatrice. For when Dante finally meets his transfigured early love in canto XXX of the *Purgatorio*, he finds himself borrowing precisely Dido's phrase:

> 'Men che drama
> di sangue m'è rimaso che non tremi:
> conosco i segni dell' antica fiamma.'   (ll. 46–8)[9]

('There is not a drop of blood in my veins that does not throb: I recognize the signs of the old flame.')

---

[9] Dante, *Purgatorio*, trans. and ed. Robin Kirkpatrick (London: Penguin, 2007), 282 (ll. 46–8). See Donald Davie, 'Hardy's Virgilian Purples', *Agenda: Thomas Hardy Special Issue* (1972), 144, rpt. in *The Poet in the Imaginary Museum* (Manchester: Carcanet, 1977), 225–6. Hardy also alludes to this climactic moment in *The Divine Comedy* in chapter 8 of *Desperate Remedies*. This reference occurs in the narrator's discussion of the letter that Cytherea Graye sends her lover Edward Springrove after discovering that he is betrothed to Adelaide Hinton: 'Like Beatrice accusing Dante from her chariot, try as she might to play the superior being who contemned such mere eye-sensuousness, she betrayed at every point a pretty woman's jealousy of a rival, and covertly gave her old lover hints for excusing himself at each fresh indictment' (DR 134).

The allusion's significance is heightened by the fact that this is the moment at which the pagan Virgil (whom Dante thinks he is addressing) disappears from the poem, leaving his charge to the redemptive, if somewhat judgemental, forces of Christian love. For unlike the 'voiceless' ghosts of Dido in the underworld and of Emma in 'After a Journey', Beatrice proceeds to deliver a stinging reprimand to the penitent pilgrim, with the result that his heart melts, flooding his mouth, eyes, and breast with anguish ('*e con angoscia / de la bocca e de li occhi uscì del petto*').[10]

The various spectral appearances of Emma to the sorrowing widower of 'Poems of 1912–13' are similarly initiated by a rebuke, although it is one that cannot be answered or challenged, for it is Emma's death itself that Hardy seems to respond to, in the opening stanzas of the sequence, as a personal affront. As in Dante, this rebuke eventually provokes his quest to share some kind of *vita nuova* with her ghost—or even with her physical remains, for in 'Rain on a Grave' he declares his wish to be 'folded away' with her in her grave, 'Exposed to one weather / We both' (CP 341). His first poetic response, however, combines the inflections of a marital squabble with his awed recognition that her 'great going' has suddenly, shockingly, taken place without his knowledge—although in fact he was at her bedside when she died:

> Why did you give no hint that night
> That quickly after the morrow's dawn,
> And calmly, as if indifferent quite,
> You would close your term here, up and be gone
>   Where I could not follow
>   With wing of swallow
> To gain one glimpse of you ever anon!
>
>   Never to bid good-bye,
>   Or lip me the softest call,
> Or utter a wish for a word, while I
> Saw morning harden upon the wall,
>   Unmoved, unknowing
>   That your great going
> Had place that moment, and altered all.   (CP 338)

---

[10] Dante, *Purgatorio*, 284 (ll. 98–9).

The element of peevishness in his opening question is prolonged by his dwelling in the first three lines of the second stanza on what Emma has (again) failed to do: as was her wont, and as complained about also in 'Without Ceremony', she has not said goodbye properly.[11] Hardy here rather resembles the wife of 'The Slow Nature', who worries about her untidied bedroom and unmade bed when apprised that her husband has been gored to death by a bull: in both cases the breach in manners or etiquette acts as a means of deflecting the ghastly truth. And the momentary flash of lyricism in the rhyme of 'follow' and 'swallow' or wistful hint of the erotic in 'lip me the softest call' ('lip' replacing the 'give' of early printings) also register as waywardly defensive, as a means of dallying 'with false surmise' in the tradition of 'Lycidas', and thus leavening the remorseless imagery of creeping rigor mortis ('indifferent quite…close your term here…harden upon the wall') along with the poem's litany of negatives ('no hint…not follow…Never to bid…unmoved, unknowing').

The focus in the opening stanzas of 'The Going' on the exact 'moment' at which Emma stopped living evidently refracts both the shock of her 'swift fleeing' (one of numerous euphemisms for death deployed in the poem) and the failure of his final attempt to communicate with her: 'Em, Em —don't you know me?' he was overheard by Emma's maid, Dolly Gale, asking her just before she died.[12] Grief and mourning are frequently dramatized in poems collected in Hardy's previous volumes, from 'She at His Funeral' (dated 187–) of *Wessex Poems* to his account of his mother's death in 'After the Last Breath' of *Time's Laughingstocks*, while set pieces such as 'The Dead Quire' or 'The Souls of the Slain' enact in fanciful detail Hardy's compulsive fascination with the world of the posthumous. His elegies for Emma, however, reveal a new kind of figuration of the afterlife, one that oscillates between articulating the absolute impossibility of descending, like Orpheus or Aeneas, into the underworld and thus gaining one final 'glimpse' of her, and moments when, like Dido or Eurydice, her ghost 'shapes' itself to him, a phantom glimpsed or heard (but never both), or imagined speaking, watching over him, returning to Max Gate. 'Slip back, Time!' he commands, helplessly, in 'St Launce's Revisited' (CP 356): poetically compounded of memory and melancholy, and animated by Hardy's obsessive quest to

<hr>

[11] For a searching analysis of the relation between 'The Going' and Coventry Patmore's 'Departure', which also opens with a rebuke, see Eric Griffiths, *The Printed Voice of Victorian Poetry* (Oxford: Oxford University Press, 1989), 211–14. See also Rod Edmond, 'Death Sequences: Patmore, Hardy, and the New Domestic Elegy', *Victorian Poetry*, 19, 2 (1981), 151–65.
[12] CT, xvii.

recover their squandered past, Emma rediviva over and again imparts to the bereaved poet 'a savour that scenes in being lack' (CP 353).

'Dear ghost,' he enquires in 'Your Last Drive', 'did you ever find / The thought "What profit," move me much?' (CP 340). Perhaps the most significant and appealing aspect of Hardy's concept of the afterlife is the release that it offers from notions of 'profit', from assessing one's progress or tactics in life's 'game of sink or swim', as Egbert Mayne, the upwardly mobile hero of 'An Indiscretion in the Life of an Heiress', puts it.[13] 'And I shall not care', Hardy imagines the soon-to-be-dead Emma musing as she is driven past the graveyard in which she will shortly be laid to rest: 'Should you censure me I shall take no heed, / And even your praises no more shall need.' Hardy clearly enjoyed transposing onto his revenants his own deep-seated longing to be free from the relentless processes of judgement, in this respect making them resemble the child ensconced in his 'spray-roofed house' in 'Childhood among the Ferns', determined to preserve his indifference to the 'afar-noised World' (CP 864). Indeed, it is in his depictions of the dead rather than of agricultural labourers in rural Wessex that his writing most strongly evokes classical traditions of the pastoral idyll. In his numerous graveyard poems, buried corpses are often figured as quietly biding their time in cherished privacy, or even relishing their own physical decay:

> These flowers are I, poor Fanny Hurd,
> > Sir or Madam,
> A little girl here sepultured.
> Once I flit-fluttered like a bird
> Above the grass, as now I wave
> In daisy shapes above my grave,
> > All day cheerily,
> > All night eerily!
> ('Voices from Things Growing in a Churchyard', CP 623)

At the conclusion of 'His Visitor', spoken by Emma's ghost, she is presented as preferring 'the roomy silence' of the graveyard, with its 'mute and manifold / Souls of old', to the domestic trappings of Max Gate, especially

---

[13] *An Indiscretion in the Life of an Heiress and Other Stories*, ed. Pamela Dalziel (Oxford: Oxford University Press, 1994), 80.

now that it has been updated by her successor. To what extent the poem ventriloquizes Hardy's own distaste for the 'formal-fashioned border' introduced into the garden, along with the new 'cups and saucers' and 'pictures altered' of the 're-decked dwelling', is not clear, but his attraction to what he called (in the letter of February 1915 to Caleb Saleeby excerpted in the *Life* and quoted in chapter 2) 'spectres, mysterious voices, intuitions, omens, dreams, haunted places, etc, etc' (L 400) can certainly be attributed, at least on one level, to the vistas that they opened beyond the largely bourgeois parameters of his day-to-day existence. The numerous posthumous characters depicted in Hardy's poems, from Fanny Hurd and her graveyard companions to the spectral prostitute of 'The Woman I Met', from Parson Thirdly of 'Channel Firing' to the row of spirits hovering as 'light as upper air' above the garden seat in the poem of that name (CP 567), all buoyantly inhabit a realm in which there is no need to worry about 'profit' or 'praises' or 'censure'. Analogously, it is precisely *because* paying attention to the dead is an inherently profitless activity that Hardy was so committed to it, making sure that all his houseguests at Max Gate paid visits to Stinsford churchyard, and even designing a special implement with which he would scrape off the moss from the gravestones of Emma and of his parents and sister.

In the letter quoted above, one of a series in which Hardy debates with Saleeby the philosophy of Henri Bergson, he confesses that while he doesn't give any credence to the supernatural 'in the old sense of the word', he does 'when writing verse' allow himself to '"believe"' (his quote marks) in such phenomena. The ghostly and the poetic were for Hardy twinned forms of resistance to all that he deplored in the dominant belief systems of his era, even if each offered only a speculative means of evading or suspending the pressures exerted on the individual by social and political realities. His poems featuring revenants or fantasizing about the afterlives of the dead often dramatize particularly compelling or liberating engagements with nature, as in the Darwinian metamorphoses of Fanny Hurd and her fellow corpses in 'Voices from Things Growing in a Churchyard', or in the freedom with which he imagines Emma's 'shade' traversing the landscapes of Dorset and Cornwall, or even in 'I Found Her Out There' migrating 'underground' from Stinsford to the Atlantic coast (CP 343). One of the most striking aspects of Emma's posthumous poetic persona, in other words, is the intense and revitalizing contact with the natural world that she mediates for Hardy, undoing the estrangement between poet and landscape that afflicts all post-Wordsworthian poets—including Wordsworth himself, as in, say, the opening strophes of the 'Immortality Ode'. Indeed, in 'The Haunter' Hardy figures Emma almost as a version of the Dorothy Wordsworth of 'Tintern Abbey', as both muse and companion, uncannily participating in the visits that he makes to sites of natural beauty, to arcane, sacred

> places
> Only dreamers know,
> Where the shy hares print long paces,
> Where the night rooks go... (CP 345)

Despite their closeness (given, with typical literalness, as 'a few feet'), no communication between the severed couple takes place. The conceit of this poem, which involves asking the reader to relay to Hardy all the good deeds that Emma is now invisibly performing on his behalf, reconfigures the gulf that separated them in the later years of their marriage: for he cannot see or hear her, while she can only watch and follow, and eavesdrop on the speeches that he belatedly makes to her during his journeying:

> He does not think that I haunt here nightly:
> How shall I let him know
> That whither his fancy sets him wandering
> I, too, alertly go?—
> Hover and hover a few feet from him
> Just as I used to do,
> But cannot answer the words he lifts me—
> Only listen thereto!
>
> When I could answer he did not say them:
> When I could let him know
> How I would like to join in his journeys
> Seldom he wished to go.
> Now that he goes and wants me with him
> More than he used to do,
> Never he sees my faithful phantom
> Though he speaks thereto.

These 'fancy'-driven, haphazard peregrinations, even if inspired by grief, can also be aligned with those of a nature-worshipper such as Wordsworth, who was happy to declare that should his 'chosen guide / Be nothing better

than a wandering cloud', he could not miss his way.[14] Most travelling in
Hardy is undertaken with a purpose, and has consequences, for good or ill,
but wandering under the aegis of a spectral Emma allows him to share in
the 'profit'-less, 'censure'-less world enjoyed by ghosts, and to recapture
some of the spontaneity and magical access to nature of the first romantics.

At the conclusion of 'His Visitor' Emma's ghost decides that her pre-dawn
haunting of her much-altered former dwelling, with its 'rooms new painted',
was a mistake, and vows 'to return here never'. The dispossession that this
poem ruthlessly itemizes ('The change I notice in my once own quarters!'
(CP 347)) can also, however, be seen as a liberation, a station in the freeing
of Emma from the *vestigia* of her unhappy domestic life. It can be linked
with other of the 1912–13 poems set in Max Gate, such as 'Lament' or 'A
Circular', all of which pivot on the dizzying gap between Emma's role as
mistress of the house, issuing instructions to the servants, performing
approved middle-class leisure activities such as painting or playing the piano,
hosting, 'Bright-hatted and gloved' (CP 344), a garden party, presiding over
a dinner, ordering the new season's dresses as well as 'millinery, / Warranted
up to date' (CP 347), and her radically changed status as either corpse (in
'Lament' and 'A Circular') or ghost in 'His Visitor'. One of the most remarkable
aspects of these elegies is their swivelling between antithetical perspectives
on Emma's afterlife: 'She is shut, she is shut', Hardy somewhat brutally
intones in 'Lament', 'From friendship's spell / In the jailing shell / Of her tiny
cell', whereas in 'His Visitor' and 'The Haunter' her shade is wholly uncon-
strained in its movements, escaping effortlessly through 'the long familiar
door' of Max Gate in the former, accompanying Hardy in the latter on his
ramblings, and even on his antiquarian pilgrimages to 'old aisles where the
past is all to him' (CP 346).

'All to him' rhymes with 'call to him' in 'The Haunter', prefiguring the
opening lines of the poem that comes between these two in the sequence:

> Woman much missed, how you call to me, call to me,
> Saying that now you are not as you were
> When you had changed from the one who was all to me,
> But as at first, when our day was fair.

---

[14] William Wordsworth, *Selected Poems*, ed. John O. Hayden (London: Penguin, 1994), 308
(*The Prelude*, ll. 16–17).

Can it be you that I hear? Let me view you, then,
Standing as when I drew near to the town
Where you would wait for me: yes, as I knew you then,
Even to the original air-blue gown!

Or is it only the breeze, in its listlessness
Travelling across the wet mead to me here,
You being ever dissolved to wan wistlessness,
Heard no more again far or near?

Thus I; faltering forward,
Leaves around me falling,
Wind oozing thin through the thorn from norward,
And the woman calling.   (CP 346)

In his discussion of 'The Voice' in *New Bearings in English Poetry* of 1932,
F. R. Leavis declared it one of the few Hardy poems in which 'oddity
becomes an intensely personal virtue'.[15] It was even odder in manuscript,
initially opening 'O woman weird', as if it were Emma's peculiarity that set
the poem in motion. The other key revision that he made was the substitu-
tion in the *Collected Poems* of 1923 of the 'existlessness' of early printings for
the even more alliterative 'wan wistlessness'—of these Leavis preferred the
former, but it is hard to say which is the odder or weirder. Indeed, deep in
the strata of the poem's many subtexts and precursors surely lurk the most
famous of all literary 'weird' women, the witches of *Macbeth*, who also
vanish into existlessness, as 'what seem'd corporal melted, / As breath into

---

[15] F. R. Leavis, *New Bearings in English Poetry* (Harmondsworth: Penguin, 1979 (first
published 1932)), 48. Leavis's discussion of Hardy is notable for singling out what became
Hardy's two most famous Emma poems, 'The Voice' and 'After a Journey'. Much to Hardy's
distress, contemporary reviewers of *Satires of Circumstance* paid the 'Poems of 1912–13' section of the volume scant attention, although in his short monograph on Hardy of 1916 Harold
Child celebrated these elegies in terms that are likely to baffle the modern reader: 'Perhaps the
pleasantest, the most musically and suggestively beautiful poems that Hardy ever wrote are the
"Poems of 1912–13". They are intimate, they are personal, they are gentle; they come like a
fresh breeze on the fall of a summer evening' (James Gibson and Trevor Johnson, eds., *Thomas
Hardy: Poems* (Basingstoke: Macmillan, 1979), 76). In his reflections on the reception of *Satires
of Circumstance* in the *Life* Hardy complains bitterly about the obtuseness of reviewers, but
acknowledges that the prominence he had given the final 'Satires of Circumstance' section by
using it as the book's title prompted critics to ignore the other sections, even though they 'contained some of the tenderest and least satirical verse that ever came from his pen. The effect of
this misrepresentation upon the poems he most cared for grieved him much; but it could not
be helped. It was another instance of the inability of so many critics to catch any but shrill
notes, remaining oblivious to deeper tones' (L 397).

the wind' (I iii, ll. 81–2).[16] 'The Voice' summons the ghost of Emma in incantatory rhythms (rudely dismissed by Leavis as a 'crude popular lilt') as haunting as those of Shakespeare's weird sisters, and equally deceptive.

The shade of Emma conjured in 'The Voice' again serves to suspend Hardy's habits of defensiveness or irony, opening its speaker to the uninhibited intensities of poems as different from each other as Shelley's 'Ode to the West Wind' and Keats's 'La Belle Dame Sans Merci', as well as to numerous other possible sources. The genealogy of its startling opening line has been traced back by I. A. Richards to that of Horace's *Odes*, II, 14 ('*Eheu fugaces, Postume, Postume*'—'Ah, how they fly by, Postumus, Postumus'), while more recently Susan Stewart has contended that the poem's rhythm echoes that of the dance tune 'Haste to the Wedding', and that elements of its imagery and some of its acoustical effects are borrowed from the popular songs 'Jan O Jan' and 'The Blue Muslin Gown' as well as from Hymn 891in the 1858 edition of *Psalms and Hymns*.[17] Eric Griffiths, on the other hand, argues that the poem develops a profound dialogue with Robert Browning's 'Two in the Campagna', whose Italian imagery it 're-thinks and re-sounds', converting Browning's 'champaign with its endless fleece / Of feathery grasses' into the 'wet mead' in Dorset where the ghostly voice that the poet thinks he hears is agonizingly dispersed.[18] If, then, on this occasion Emma rediviva inspires an 'intensely personal' lyric, it is also one that incorporates all manner of disparate influences. And in a further twist, it is worth noting that the poem's urgency and expressive power derive from its enchanted vision of an Emma stripped of all personal signifiers or 'weird'-ness beyond her intrinsically evanescent 'air-blue gown' (a brilliant revision of the manuscript's original 'hat and gown'). The Em who failed to respond to her husband's pleas on her deathbed has, in a matter of weeks (the poem is dated December 1912), become the generic or archetypal 'woman much missed' whose 'call' evokes not the wife 'who had changed from the one who was all' to him but his summer-outfitted fiancée, waiting for him some forty years earlier on the platform at Launceston station. (It was on his second visit to Cornwall, that of August 1870, that he found Emma 'metamorphosed' from 'the young lady in brown' into 'a young lady in summer blue' (L 81)). And while the

---

[16] All quotations from Shakespeare are from *The Riverside Shakespeare*, ed. G. Blakemore Evans (Boston: Houghton Mifflin, 1997).

[17] I. A. Richards, 'Some Notes on Hardy's Verse Forms', *Victorian Poetry* 17, 1–2 (1979), 6; Susan Stewart, *Poetry and the Fate of the Senses* (Chicago: University of Chicago Press, 2002), 135–8.

[18] Griffiths, *The Printed Voice of Victorian Poetry*, 221–4.

breeze that dissolves her may be listless, or ooze 'thin through the thorn from norward', it yet summons up the dominant trope for poetic inspiration of the romantic era—'O there is blessing in this gentle breeze', for instance, opens *The Prelude*.[19] Therefore, yet again Emma has done 'a fine thing' for which her reward is somewhat dubious, her ghostly call initiating a hypnotically assured poem, but one in whose narrative she is subliminally replaced by poetry itself.

The poignancy of Emma's spectral appearances in Hardy's elegies for her is much heightened by the ways in which the relationship between phantom and survivor remodels the forces that that made them 'miss' each other during their marriage. To an extent she was literally—as well as metaphorically—ousted or supplanted by the very commitment that she had herself fostered to a life of writing. In his speech to Dido in the underworld Aeneas alludes to his divinely ordained destiny as future founder of Rome as an excuse for his sudden desertion of her, and Hardy's Virgilian epigraph might be read as a prompt to analogous musings on how Hardy's literary vocation, particularly after he abandoned novels for poetry, ended up complicating and compromising his attentiveness or sympathy as a husband, especially since it entailed returning to Dorchester and the ambit of his Emma-sceptical family. Hardy's aloneness at the start of the asymmetrical final stanza— 'Thus I'—echoes the solitude in which most of his days were spent in his study, where he was on no account to be disturbed, 'faltering forward' with novel or poem, the 'leaves' of the pages completed that day falling around him. But while implicit in his conjugations of the ghost conceit is a re-angling of the rift that opened up between them, it also allows occasional acknowledgement, as at the end of 'The Voice', of how vital to his imaginative energies Emma was, even during their estrangement or in the years following her death. For after she has disappeared into the wind, to be heard 'no more again far or near', he yet hears 'the woman calling'.

Ghosts, sui generis, are unpredictable, and they generate unpredictability in those they haunt. The shift from its flowing four-beat lines, with their unforgettable and outlandish triple rhyme scheme in lines one and three, to its truncated final stanza, which itself has a single anomalous, stress-heavy third line, makes 'The Voice' the only poem in Hardy's oeuvre that dislocates midstream its underlying 'verse skeleton', to use his own term (L 324).

[19] Wordsworth, *Selected Poems*, 307 (l. 1).

Its asymmetry is of a piece, however, with the asymmetry of 'Poems of 1912–13' as a whole, which reveals his valuing of 'cunning irregularity' and the 'unforeseen' over 'poetic veneer' and 'constructed ornament' (L 323). All twenty-one poems in the sequence as finally constructed are in different stanza patterns and metres, presenting an ever-shifting kaleidoscope of perspectives both on his own grief and on the *vestigia* of Emma that the poems pursue.[20] Insistent verbal echoes, however, such as the 'call to him / all to him' and 'call to me / all to me' rhymes of 'The Haunter' and 'The Voice', impart to the sequence an intricate filigree of cross-references, an internal, if cunningly irregular, patterning that enables the individual poems, in an appropriately gothic way, to haunt each other.

Hardy and his brother Henry set off for Cornwall on Thursday 6 March 1913, a date chosen to commemorate the forty-third anniversary of his meeting Emma on the day after. In the *Life* it is suggested that the estranged couple had in fact decided to return to the region around St Juliot that very year, but given the state of their relations this seems unlikely.[21] In preparation for his pilgrimage Hardy composed 'A Dream or No' (dated February 1913), which, like 'The Voice', reveals him struggling to distinguish between the actual and the phantasmagorical, and readying himself to reconfigure the hallowed locations of their courtship in the disorientating terms dictated by melancholy:

> Does there even a place like Saint-Juliot exist?
> Or a Vallency Valley
> With stream and leafed alley,
> Or Beeny, or Bos with its flounce flinging mist?   (CP 348)

While the *Life* opts to narrate the visit in a dispassionate, neutral tone ('He found the rectory and other scenes with which he had been so familiar changed a little, but not greatly...' (L 389)), a letter to Florence of 9 March indicates a more troubled response:

---

[20] When initially published in *Satires of Circumstance*, 'Poems of 1912–13' consisted of eighteen poems rather than twenty-one. The final three ('The Spell of the Rose', 'St Launce's Revisited', and 'Where the Picnic Was') were transferred from the 'Lyrics and Reveries' section of the volume and added to the sequence in Hardy's *Collected Poems* of 1919.

[21] In a letter of some four years earlier Hardy did, however, float the notion that they might return to Cornwall, although this suggestion was made as part of a campaign to prevent Emma from joining him in London during the summer of 1908 (CL III 324).

The visit to this neighbourhood has been a very painful one to me, & I have said a dozen times I wish I had not come. What possessed me to do it!

(CL IV 260)

In hindsight the trip can be seen as a compulsive rite of mourning for both the 'original' Emma and for the enchanted landscapes of romance now saturated, as by the Atlantic's 'flounce flinging mist', by her death. By metaphorically enacting the epic hero's descent into the underworld, this visit made possible the dozens of poems that Hardy went on to write in which the St Juliot landscape is 'not greatly' changed and yet seems to him utterly transfigured. In 'A Death-Day Recalled', which makes lavish use of the classical pastoral traditions of elegy, Hardy marvels at the failure of Cornish streams and cliffs to commemorate the passing of Emma, remaining 'unheeding, / Listless'. Yet in fact, like the listless breeze of 'The Voice', all are infused with a mythical potency that reverses the poem's negatives:

> Why did not Vallency
>   In his purl deplore
> One whose haunts were whence he
>   Drew his limpid store?
> Why did Bos not thunder,
>   Targan apprehend
> Body and Breath were sunder
>   Of their former friend?   (CP 350)

Transposed to Cornwall, Emma's death day grants poetic access to the elegiac tropes and idioms deployed by such as Theocritus and Virgil and Ovid and Milton. Both Hardy the poet and the landscapes of his Cornish elegies have been catalysed by his bereavement and are now 'in flower' (L 389).

The brothers travelled to and from Devon and Cornwall by train, staying their first and last nights at Plymouth, where Hardy sought out the Gifford graves. Essentially, however, it was a journey taken back through time.

> Hereto I come to view a voiceless ghost;
>   Whither, O whither will its whim now draw me?
> Up the cliff, down, till I'm lonely, lost,
>   And the unseen waters' ejaculations awe me.

Where you will next be there's no knowing,
    Facing round about me everywhere,
        With your nut-coloured hair,
And gray eyes, and rose-flush coming and going.

Yes: I have re-entered your olden haunts at last;
    Through the years, through the dead scenes I have
    tracked you;
What have you now found to say of our past—
    Scanned across the dark space wherein I have lacked you?
Summer gave us sweets, but autumn wrought division?
    Things were not lastly as firstly well
        With us twain, you tell?
But all's closed now, despite Time's derision.   (CP 349)

'The Haunter', whose four stanzas all end 'thereto', imagined Emma's ghost benignly participating in the mourning Hardy's excursions around Dorset, in the hope that her invisible presence would make him realize that, despite her death, 'his path may be worth pursuing, / And to bring peace thereto' (CP 346). The contrasting 'Hereto' with which 'After a Journey' opens signals the decisive crossing the sequence has now made from his territory to hers, and the crepuscular terrain that she uncannily roams is at once shown to be anything but peaceful. 'Whither wilt thou lead me?' asks Hamlet of the ghost of his father on the battlements of troubled Elsinore (I v, l. 1), a question lurking behind the one that the bewildered poet poses as he struggles for bearings on the threshold of his *nekyia*. The firm sense of agency exuded by the poem's first line, as if he had agreed to meet the voiceless ghost at a particular time and place, is fast overcome by sublime 'awe', and the urge to surrender to her 'whim' as definitively as he had on the same cliff forty-three years earlier.

'Thou wouldst not think how ill all's here about my heart: but it is no matter!' This passage was marked by Hardy in his Shakespeare in December of the year that he met Emma as a way of indicating that he 'was far from being in bright spirits' (L 85). It is characteristic of Hardy that even at the age of seventy-two he still felt able to identify with 'young Hamlet', on the evidence at least of the parallels that he develops in 'After a Journey' with the scene in which the prince first confronts the ghost of his father. Initially the apparition is called an 'it', in a touching moment of uncertainty (do ghosts preserve their original gender?), but Hardy quickly falls under her spell and embarks on a direct address to 'you', in this emulating the oscillation between second and third person that occurs throughout Shakespeare's scene: 'It waves me still.—/ Go on, I'll follow thee' (I iv, ll. 78–9). And Horatio's speech warning of the dangers of trusting the elusive spectre of old Hamlet shadows many aspects of Hardy's evocation of his nocturnal coastal encounter with the ghost of Emma:

> What if it tempt you toward the flood, my lord,
> Or to the dreadful summit of the cliff
> That beetles o'er his base into the sea,
> And there assume some other horrible form
> Which might deprive your sovereignty of reason,
> And draw you into madness? Think of it.
> The very place puts toys of desperation,
> Without more motive, into every brain
> That looks so many fadoms to the sea
> And hears it roar beneath.   (I iv, ll. 69–78)

Emma's 'whim' is certainly less menacing than Horatio's 'madness', but both threaten to 'draw' the 'lost' protagonist over the edge of the cliff and into the 'unseen waters' beneath, waters which 'roar' in *Hamlet* and in Hardy utter 'ejaculations' (replacing the perhaps too obtrusively theatrical 'soliloquies' of early printings). '*Hic et ubique?*' exclaims the prince in response to the ghost's mysterious ability to 'shift' its 'ground' (I v, l. 156), while Emma's equally mobile spectre is experienced as at once here and everywhere, its movements beyond 'knowing'. And in accordance with the laws governing ghostly behaviour, both must disappear when nature, in exquisitely phrased lines, is depicted as heralding the approach of dawn:

> The glow-worm shows the matin to be near,
> And gins to pale his uneffectual fire.
> Adieu, adieu, adieu! remember me.   (I v, ll. 89–91)

> Ignorant of what there is flitting here to see,
>   The waked birds preen and the seals flop lazily;
> Soon you will have, Dear, to vanish from me,
>   For the stars close their shutters and the dawn whitens
>   hazily.

'Remember me...': old Hamlet's final injunction sums up the elegiac compulsion underlying Hardy's journey to St Juliot, and the communion with and appeasing of the dead, or rather of the ghostly undead, that is enacted in both play and sequence. The quest for 'expiation'—a term, according to Richard Purdy, that Hardy on occasion applied to his 'Poems of 1912–13' (RP 166)—drives the unfathered young revenge hero and the remorseful widower alike.

The dwarfing perspectives of time and space evoked in the poem's second stanza recall the meditations of Henry Knight in *A Pair of Blue Eyes* as he clings to his tuft of vegetation on the Nameless Cliff and ponders the aeons that have passed since the fossil embedded in the rock before his eyes was alive:

> It was one of the early crustaceans called Trilobites. Separated by millions of years in their lives, Knight and this underling seemed to have met in their place of death...Knight was a fair geologist; and such is the supremacy of habit over occasion, as a pioneer of the thoughts of men, that at this dreadful juncture his mind found time to take in, by a momentary sweep, the varied scenes that had had their day between this creature's epoch and his own. There is no place like a cleft landscape for bringing home such imaginings as these.
>
> Time closed up like a fan before him.   (PB 200 [my ellipsis])

The process whereby Hardy re-enters Emma's 'olden haunts' involves an analogous journey across 'dark space' and back through melancholic 'dead scenes' whose blankness he can traverse only by pursuing her like a hunter. Both 'lacked' and 'tracked', she becomes, as the trilobite does to Knight, an icon of pastness and 'Time's derision', yet also his only possible guide out of the 'cleft landscape' of self-division occasioned by her death. His attempts to 'scan' her into being result in lines that, while not exactly comforting, render their troubles as lyrically inevitable as the passing of the seasons, or infuse them with archaic, elegant cadences: 'Things were not lastly as firstly well / With us twain, you tell'. The compactly eloquent 'Summer gave us sweets, but autumn wrought division' is presented, it is worth pointing out, as emanating as much from Emma's ghost as from Hardy; she too, it is implied, is capable of scanning their past, and of dignifying it with an epitaph at once true and memorable.

The 'verse skeleton' underlying 'After a Journey' is unique in Hardy's oeuvre, but then many of his stanzaic and metrical patterns were used only once.[22] Of the 'Poems of 1912–13', it is undoubtedly the one that most directly assumes the shape and trajectory of a Keatsian ode, and its emotional and narrative arc is especially close to that of Keats's 'Ode to a Nightingale', moving from encounter to enchantment to desertion. The enchantment is richest in its third stanza, which fuses the excitement of Keats's 'Already with thee!' with the prosier rhythms and everyday diction appropriate to a septuagenarian couple revisiting the sites of their courtship:

> I see what you are doing: you are leading me on
>   To the spots we knew when we haunted here together,
> The waterfall, above which the mist-bow shone
>   At the then fair hour in the then fair weather,
> And the cave just under, with a voice still so hollow
>   That it seems to call out to me from forty years ago,
>   When you were all aglow,
> And not the thin ghost that I now fraily follow!

Hardy's recreation of the dynamics of their courtship, her leading and him following, culminates in a ghostly re-enactment of their union, both expressed and sanctified by the landscape: the 'waterfall' with its 'mist-bow' 'above' and 'the cave just under' are here juxtaposed with a dreamy unselfconsciousness only possible for a poet writing without knowledge of Freud. Virgilian precedents further heighten the eros of their cliff-top wanderings, for it is in a cave that Aeneas and Dido, having sought shelter from a storm conjured up by Juno, consummate their love. Hardy's cave is anthropomorphized in classical style and given a voice, whose 'hollow' reverberations allow it to function as an echo chamber momentarily fusing past and present, and which mimic too the peals of thunder as well as the signals emitted by the earth itself in Virgil ('*prima et Tellus et pronuba Iuno / dant signum*' (ll. 166–7: both primal Earth, and Juno, goddess of marriage, gave the sign)). The glow, further, irradiating the Emma of forty years ago picks up the lightning that also commemorates the transition of Aeneas and Dido into lovers, given thus by Dryden:

> Then first the trembling Earth the signal gave;
> And flashing Fires enlighten all the Cave.   (4, ll. 241–2)

---

[22] For an account of its prosody, see Dennis Taylor, *Hardy's Metres and Victorian Prosody* (Oxford: Clarendon Press, 1988), 82–3 and 167–9. Taylor considers it Hardy's 'most metrically interesting poem' (82).

Although the cosmically expansive lament that Virgil orchestrates for his doomed pair is not matched in Hardy's lyric, Emma's shrinking from past glowing womanhood to a 'thin ghost' is like an overlaying of the erotically charged Dido of book IV with the disembodied spectre of the underworld that Aeneas meets in book VI.

This stanza's joyful reuse of the 'weather / together' rhyme, so wistfully deployed in 'The Going', is a telling instance of the familiar necromantic law operative in so much of Hardy's poetry: only when all is 'past amend' can events be summoned up by means of an imaginative *nekyia*, which allows their significance to be fully revealed and long-buried emotions to be retrospectively experienced. No attempt could be made to recreate the happiness of 'then fair hour' and the 'then fair weather' in life, but posthumous Emma and an almost posthumous Hardy—'a dead man held on end' 'fraily' following her—find themselves, after the literal journey made with Henry to St Juliot and the metaphorical one to the past dramatized in the poem, released to wander at will in his version of what Virgil calls '*locos laetos et amoena virecta / fortunatorum nemorum sedesque beatas*' (VI 638–9: the joyful places, delightful glades and happy habitations of the Groves of the Blessed):

> Trust me, I mind not, though Life lours,
>   The bringing me here; nay, bring me here again!
>   I am just the same as when
> Our days were a joy, and our paths through flowers.

Despite the fact that his 'dear ghost' must vanish with the dawn, Emma is here endowed with powers equivalent to those of the Sybil who oversees Aeneas's descent into the underworld, directing him to the golden bough that enables access to the 'Plains of Pleasure' (Dryden, 6, l. 868), to the world of 'afterwards' in which death and romance unite, and where Hardy really is the same, for he is ageless—to the world, that is, of poetry.

Hardy's repeated poetic reincarnations of his 'late, espousèd saint' disconcerted and upset her successor. This jibe occurs in a letter written to Edward Clodd on the day after Hardy and Henry set off for Cornwall on 6 March 1913, and it expresses Florence's bewilderment at Hardy's excessive—as she saw it—response to Emma's death:

> On Thursday he started for Plymouth to find the grave of Mrs H's father (—that amiable gentleman who wrote to him as 'a low-born churl who has

presumed to marry into *my* family.') Today he goes to Cornwall, to St Juliot's Rectory, where he first met his 'late, espousèd saint,' forty-three years ago, this very week.

However, as his youngest sister sensibly observes, 'so long as he doesn't pick up another Gifford down there, no harm will be done'.

His brother is with him, fortunately. It cannot, I think, be good for him to luxuriate in misery to this extent.

He says that he is going down for the sake of the girl he married, & who died more than twenty years ago. His family say *that* girl never existed, but she did exist to him, no doubt.

The strange thing is that this goes on side by side with the reading of those diabolical diaries. I had hoped they were destroyed, but only the other night he produced one from his pocket & read me a passage — written about six weeks before her death —in which she says that her father & *Mr Putnam* (?) were right in their estimate of TH's character: he is…(…various oft' repeated adjectives of abuse…), & '*utterly worthless*'. Of course Mr Putnam, if she means the publisher, could *never* have belittled Mr Hardy to her. It is in this sort of way that the diaries are so poisonous.[23]   (LEFH 78)

Poisonous, perhaps, but also clearly inspiring… A number of these poems, such as 'She Revisits Alone the Church of Her Marriage' or 'Lost Love', are spoken by Emma in the first person, while others commemorate anniversaries or are contemplations of mementoes such as a lock of hair or a miniature.[24] Further, Hardy seems never to have tired of using either their initial meeting or her unexpected demise as a means of dramatizing states of 'before' and 'after':

> The rain imprinted the step's wet shine
> With target-circles that quivered and crossed
> As I was leaving this porch of mine;
> When from within there swelled and paused
>   A song's sweet note;
>   And back I turned, and thought,
>   'Here I'll abide.'

[23] The American publisher George Putnam visited Max Gate in June 1911.
[24] See, for instance, 'Joys of Memory' (CP 437), 'Looking at a Picture on an Anniversary' (CP 533), and 'On a Discovered Curl of Hair' (CP 669).

> The step shines wet beneath the rain,
> Which prints its circles as heretofore;
> I watch them from the porch again,
> But no song-notes within the door
>> Now call to me
>> To shun the dripping lea;
>>> And forth I stride.   ('On the Doorstep', CP 525–6)

Emma's absence pervades Max Gate, from its rained-on doorstep to the bereft tree of 'The Tree and the Lady', from the calendar on his desk set to 7 March to the forlorn mirror of 'The Lament of the Looking-Glass', which he imagines complaining to the curtains:

> 'Why should I trouble again to glass
>> These smileless things hard by,
> Since she I pleasured once, alas,
>> Is now no longer nigh!'   (CP 674)

As Florence was ruefully to discover, *vestigia* of her predecessor lurked everywhere, and are transformed in such poems into the equivalents of a saint's relics, to pick up on her Miltonic allusion. Hardy was acutely sensitive to the impregnation of objects by the spirits of their owners, as expounded in a poem such as 'Old Furniture', in which he insists that he can

> see the hands of the generations
>> That owned each shiny familiar thing
> In play on its knobs and indentations,
>> And with its ancient fashioning
>>> Still dallying...   (CP 485)

Having 'shed her life's sheen' (CP 348) in Max Gate, Emma's 'phasm' (CP 521) still permeates its rooms and garden, and is indeed figured as doing so far into the future. In 'The Strange House', subtitled Max Gate, A.D. 2000, Hardy depicts her haunting its later inhabitants by performing ghostly tunes on a non-existent piano, by appearing as a spectre on the stair, or by stirring the parlour door. The walls of this 'strange house', like a sort of architectural palimpsest, are inscribed with 'weird tales' deriving from this 'queer' couple's romance, and as her fellow 'love-thrall', Hardy too assumes a ghostly afterlife:

> 'The house is old; they've hinted
>> It once held two love-thralls,
> And they may have imprinted
>>> Their dreams on its walls?'   (CP 581)

While the poem's overall conceit is itself abundantly 'weird' and 'queer', and it concludes with the residents of Max Gate in 2000 cheerfully dismissing the 'joy, or despair' of their predecessors, Hardy's imagery in the penultimate stanza brings to the fore the transition from private to public, from 'dreams' to 'imprinted' page, that is enacted in all his elegies for Emma. Fugitive moments of 'joy, or despair' do indeed become permanent once incorporated into the architecture of a poem or projected onto a poem's landscape: 'what they record in colour and cast', he insists of the primaeval rocks bordering the road up from Boscastle in 'At Castle Boterel', 'Is—that we two passed' (CP 352). In this startling assertion, *veteris vestigia flammae* are imagined as embedded, like fossils, into the eternal.

Inherent, then, in Hardy's necromantic poetics is the notion that the poem is itself a means of participating in the afterlife of a 'dear ghost', an afterlife that, however eccentrically figured, can still be traced back to classical or Christian precedents. The misty gloom in which Orpheus and Eurydice ascend to the upper world in *Metamorphoses* book X surely shadows the opening *mise en scène* of 'At Castle Boterel':

> carpitur acclivis per muta silentia trames,
> arduus, obscurus, caligine densus opaca.
> nec procul abfuerunt telluris margine summae;
> hic ne deficeret metuens avidusque videndi
> flexit amans oculos…   (X 53–7)[25]

(They hastened through the utter silence up the steeply sloping, gloomy path, shrouded in thick mist, and were now not far from the border with the upper earth. Then he, fearing that she might be struggling and eager to see her, turned back his loving eyes…)

> As I drive to the junction of lane and highway,
>> And the drizzle bedrenches the waggonette,
> I look behind on the fading byway,

[25] Ovid, *Metamorphoses X*, ed. Lee Fratantuono (London: Bloomsbury, 2014), 20–1.

> And see on its slope, now glistening wet,
>> Distinctly yet...   (CP 351)

While in 'The Shadow on the Stone' the act of turning his head would, he fears, have made Emma's ghost vanish from the garden at Max Gate, on the twilit lane leading up from Boscastle to the 'highway'—here standing in for the upper earth—the Orphic glance behind, like the voice from the cave in 'After a Journey', permits the poem to make its spectacular jump cut to forty-three years earlier:

> Myself and a girlish form benighted
>> In dry March weather. We climb the road
> Beside a chaise. We had just alighted
>> To ease the sturdy pony's load
>>> When he sighed and slowed.
>
> What we did as we climbed, and what we talked of
>> Matters not much, nor to what it led,—
> Something that life will not be balked of
>> Without rude reason till hope is dead,
>>> And feeling fled.
>
> It filled but a minute. But was there ever
>> A time of such quality, since or before,
> In that hill's story? To one mind never,
>> Though it has been climbed, foot-swift, foot-sore,
>>> By thousands more.   (CP 351–2)

Details such as the sturdy pony sighing and slowing and the tender-hearted couple agreeing to alight to ease its load bring to mind the exclamation made by Ezra Pound in a letter of 1937 on the impact of Hardy's career as a novelist on his poetry: 'Now *there* is a clarity. There *is* the harvest of having written 20 novels first.'[26] With trance-like casualness, 'At Castle Boterel' folds into the Orphic myth of the quest for the lost beloved the sorts of quotidian detail that belong to realist fiction, while simultaneously opening time like a fan, to reverse the metaphor applied to Knight's analogous

---

[26] *The Letters of Ezra Pound 1907–1941*, ed. D. D. Paige (London: Faber & Faber, 1950), 294. Pound is somewhat exaggerating—Hardy in fact wrote only fifteen novels, if one includes the unpublished *The Poor Man and the Lady*.

engagement with the 'primaeval' on the Nameless Cliff. Their conversation is pointedly beyond 'profit' ('what we talked of / Matters not much') and yet the 'minute' of their ascent is imbued with a 'quality' so legendary that it transfigures forever the 'hill's story', as the falling in love of Tristram and Iseult transfigured that of nearby Tintagel. Like Orpheus, Hardy here triumphantly asserts his difference from 'foot-swift, foot-sore' common humanity, and proclaims his bardic ability to rescue Emma from the shades of night, and yet does so in terms so beguilingly modest and personal that one loses all perspective on the claims that the poem is making.

Amongst the predecessors of the 'benighted' Hardy and Emma of this poem are not only Orpheus and Eurydice but the various couples in Hardy's own fiction depicted on crepuscular roads and approaching some fateful 'junction' in their lives, such as Henchard and Susan at the beginning of *The Mayor of Casterbridge* or Tess and Angel wandering towards Stonehenge. In 'At Castle Boterel' the onward progress to disaster (so vividly prefigured in 'Near Lanivet, 1872', which is also set on a Cornish road at evening) is suspended, and Emma is allowed to preserve, like a figure in a photograph, her 'girlish form'. They have a pictorial predecessor too, in the couple ascending a path to Clavell Tower as the sun sets in the illustration opposite 'She, to Him I' in *Wessex Poems*, a sonnet concerned, like 'At Castle Boterel', with what can be recovered from 'the toils of Time' (CP 14). This early poem (it is dated 1866) ends with the young woman's plea that, when she is old and has lost her looks, her lover will at least 'grant to old affection's claim / The hand of friendship down Life's sunless hill' (CP 15). Affection of this kind, alas, was in short supply in the years preceding Emma's death, but by both literally and poetically retracing the footsteps of their old love, Hardy strove to keep his 'dear ghost' imaginatively alive, resurrected 'for a breath' (CP 338) from 'the transitory in Earth's long order', until the remorseless contractual terms of elegy return her, like Eurydice, to the gloom:

> And to me, though Time's unflinching rigour,
>   In mindless rote, has ruled from sight
> The substance now, one phantom figure
>   Remains on the slope, as when that night
>   Saw us alight.
>
> I look and see it there, shrinking, shrinking,
>   I look back at it amid the rain
> For the very last time; for my sand is sinking,
>   And I shall traverse old love's domain
>   Never again.   (CP 352)

8

Two Bright-Souled Women

In addition to his elegies for Emma and his parents and his sister and his cousin Tryphena Sparks, and for notables such as Queen Victoria and George Meredith and Swinburne, and for friends such as Horace Moule and Agnes Grove and Sir Frederick Treves and Rosamund Tomson and Arthur Henniker, and for generic figures such as Drummer Hodge or the Mellstock choirmaster, Hardy was fond of composing self-elegies. Characteristic of poems in this genre is 'When Dead', cryptically dedicated 'To —', and collected in *Human Shows* of 1925:

> It will be much better when
>   I am under the bough;
> I shall be more myself, Dear, then,
>   Than I am now.
>
> No sign of querulousness
>   To wear you out
> Shall I show there: strivings and stress
>   Be quite without.
>
> This fleeting life-brief blight
>   Will have gone past
> When I resume my old and right
>   Place in the Vast.
>
> And when you come to me
>   To show you true,
> Doubt not I shall infallibly
>   Be waiting you.   (CP 721)

That the ageing Hardy was far from unconscious of his capacity for 'querulousness' emerges in a letter of Florence's written in August 1920 to Sydney Cockerell, a couple of months after her husband had turned eighty. 'We are reading Jane Austen,' she reported; 'We have read "Persuasion" & "Northanger

Woman Much Missed: Thomas Hardy, Emma Hardy, and Poetry. Mark Ford, Oxford University Press.
© Mark Ford 2023. DOI: 10.1093/oso/9780192886804.003.0009

Abbey", & now are in the midst of "Emma". T.H. is much amused at finding he has *many* characteristics in common with Mr Woodhouse' (LEFH 167).

Hardy's use of the 'To —' dedication, which also occurs before 'In Vision I Roamed' of 1866, compactly dramatizes his conflicting desire to be public and private at once. It inevitably generates speculation: the early poem's suppressed dedicatee is generally supposed to be Eliza Nicholls, linked also to the 'She, to Him' sonnets and to 'Neutral Tones', while Florence, whose occasionally outspoken letters reveal that she had as much 'querulousness' to soothe in Max Gate as Emma Woodhouse had to deal with in Hartfield, is surely the only plausible candidate for the missing name of 'When Dead'.[1] Since he and Florence had been married for over a decade by the time this poem was published, his reticence or coyness can seem somewhat surprising, until one grasps the dilemma that 'When Dead' is subliminally both intimating and evading: that of divided allegiances in the hereafter. In 'the Vast' Emma is already waiting for Hardy, but when he assumes his 'old and right / Place' there, he will 'infallibly' be awaiting the arrival of Florence too. Even in the easy-going and non-judgemental afterworld posited in Hardy's poetry, how will it be possible to manage this posthumous love triangle?

A companion self-elegy, 'His Heart', also evokes death as a source of forgiveness. Probably his most explicitly self-exculpatory poem, and possibly provoked by reading Emma's Black Diaries, it is subtitled 'A Woman's Dream', and uses a quasi-metaphysical conceit to put the case that if only Emma could have divined what Hardy truly felt about her, hostilities and denunciations would have been replaced by remorse:

> At midnight, in the room where he lay dead
> Whom in his life I had never clearly read,
> I thought if I could peer into that citadel
> His heart, I should at last know full and well
>
> What hereto had been known to him alone,
> Despite our long sit-out of years foreflown,
> 'And if,' I said, 'I do this for his memory's sake,
> It would not wound him, even if he could wake.'

---

[1] In *Hardy's Love Poems* (London: Macmillan, 1963) Carl J. Weber suggests that the poem is spoken by Emma to Hardy himself '*before* her death' (75), meaning the dedicatory blank is to be filled by his own name. This seems to me unlikely.

> So I bent over him. He seemed to smile
> With a calm confidence the whole long while
> That I, withdrawing his heart, held it and, bit by bit,
> Perused the unguessed things found written on it.   (CP 461)

Those 'unguessed things' all redound to the dead husband's credit: 'There were his truth, his simple single-mindedness, / Strained, maybe, by time's storms, but there no less.' As the newly made widow pores over the 'quaint vermiculations' engraved on the heart, her eyes are gradually opened to the 'whole sincere symmetric history' of his hidden inner life, and above all to his undying devotion to his spouse:

> There were regrets, at instances wherein he swerved
> (As he conceived) from cherishings I had deserved.
>
> There were old hours all figured down as bliss—
> Those spent with me—(how little had I thought this!)
> There those when, at my absence, whether he slept or waked,
> (Though I knew not 'twas so!) his spirit ached.
>
> There that when we were severed, how day dulled
> Till time joined us anew, was chronicled:
> And arguments and battlings in defence of me
> That heart recorded clearly and ruddily.   (CP 462)

It hardly needs saying that this wife's dream is really the husband's fantasy, and can indeed be read as a passive-aggressive rebuttal of the charges levelled against him by Emma in journals such as the one allegedly titled 'What I Think of My Husband'. How deeply did his spirit ache, one can't help wondering, during the ten days in August 1909 that he spent staying with his 'young friend and assistant' Florence Dugdale as houseguests of Edward Clodd in Aldeburgh (CL IV 35), or during the surreptitious trip that he made with her to Chichester a couple of months later, or to Swinburne's grave on the Isle of Wight in March 1910? How dull was the day on which he met her in the South Kensington Museum 'in the architectural gallery at 4—say by the Trajan column' (CL III 253) in the spring of 1907 shortly after he had taken rooms in Hyde Park Mansions for the Season, but before Emma had joined him? And while 'single-mindedness' was certainly an element in the delicate manoeuvring that resulted in Florence introducing herself to Emma at the Lyceum Club in the summer of 1910, no one could call such machinations 'simple'.

Nearly all the main plots of Hardy's novels are shaped by the dynamics of male rivalry, the only exceptions being *Two on a Tower* and *The Well-Beloved*. Hardy's female protagonists are more often wooed than wooers, but his narratives do on numerous occasions also involve two women pursuing the same man: Cytherea Graye and Adelaide Hinton compete for Edward Springrove in *Desperate Remedies* while Bathsheba Everdene and Fanny Robin both fall under the hypnotic spell of Sergeant Troy in *Far from the Madding Crowd*. Other triangles of this sort include Christopher Julian, Ethelberta, and her sister Picotee in *The Hand of Ethelberta*; Wildeve, Eustacia, and Thomasin in *The Return of the Native*; Farfrae, Elizabeth-Jane, and Lucetta in *The Mayor of Casterbridge*; Giles Winterborne, Grace Melbury, and Marty South in *The Woodlanders*, while Grace, Mrs Charmond, and Suke Damson all tussle over the unworthy Fitzpiers in the same novel; Jude, Arabella, and Sue in *Jude the Obscure*; and Jocelyn Pierston, the first Avice Caro, and Marcia Bencomb in the opening chapters of Hardy's final novel, *The Well-Beloved*.

The shy, pliant, star-struck Florence, plagued by sore throats and prone to bouts of melancholy, clearly resembled minor characters such as Picotee or Marty South more than she did Hardy's leading ladies. Despite her valiant attempts to make an independent living by writing for publications such as the *Sphere*, the *Daily Mail*, and the *Evening Standard* as well as from the composition of short stories for children, she was far from being a New Woman in the mode of Sue Bridehead or Dora Milvain in George Gissing's *New Grub Street* (1891). The year after becoming the second Mrs Hardy she readily agreed with Lady Hoare that women were 'only strong when they realize their weakness & dependence on men' (LEFH 106), and when pressed to participate in a political meeting a few years later claimed to 'wish heartily that women had never been given the vote' (LEFH 151). She did, however, share her future husband's inability to believe in a beneficent deity, and it is also clear that poetry played as important a role in Hardy's courtship of his second wife as it had of his first: among his earliest gifts to Florence were inscribed copies of his own *Wessex Poems* and of Edward Fitzgerald's *The Rubaiyat of Omar Khayyam*, a verse of which she would read to him on his deathbed.[2]

By the time Hardy met Florence in 1905, he had become practised in conducting mild flirtations with younger women who sought his literary

---

[2] Robert Gittings and Jo Manton record that Hardy and Florence exchanged a total of twenty-four pocket volumes of poetry (SMH 30).

advice or patronage. The poems inspired by his various early meetings with his earnest admirer from Enfield, such as 'On the Departure Platform' (first published in *Time's Laughingstocks* of 1909) and 'After the Visit', which appeared (although without its dedication 'To F. E. D.') in the *Spectator* in August 1910, are suffused with poignancy rather than charged with eros, but certain phrases, had either poem come to Emma's attention, might well have confirmed the charge made in her letter to Elspeth Grahame of ten years earlier that her husband was entertaining 'Eastern ideas of matrimony' (LEFH 15): 'We kissed at the barrier', begins the former, which, according to Robert Gittings and Jo Manton, depicts their parting at Liverpool Street Station in April 1907 after a session in the British Library checking references for part III of *The Dynasts* (SMH 31):

> and passing through
> She left me, and moment by moment got
> Smaller and smaller, until to my view
> She was but a spot;
>
> A wee white spot of muslin fluff
> That down the diminishing platform bore
> Through hustling crowds of gentle and rough
> To the carriage door.
>
> Under the lamplight's fitful glowers,
> Behind dark groups from far and near,
> Whose interests were apart from ours,
> She would disappear,
>
> Then show again, till I ceased to see
> That flexible form, that nebulous white;
> And she who was more than my life to me
> Had vanished quite... (CP 221)

The alien crowds into which Florence disappears are an urban equivalent of the dwarfing sea and cliffs and sky against which Emma moves in Hardy's Cornish poems about her. The hectic indifference of a London railway station (a scene similar to the one evoked in the stanzas of 'The Change' in which he recalls meeting Emma at Paddington amid 'a tedious trampling crowd' (CP 455)) here serves to frame and intensify the vulnerability and preciousness of the fragile traveller, whom he watches shrinking to 'a wee white spot of muslin fluff'. Distance, as so often in Hardy, is a catalyst for attraction, but the repeated use of *white* works as a counterbalance, stressing Florence's innocence.

And indeed, whatever appearances may have suggested, it was surely by keeping the relationship innocent as well as 'flexible' and 'nebulous', to use the poem's own terms, that Hardy was able to enjoy further sojourns with her at Clodd's house at Aldeburgh in 1910, 1911, and 1912, seemingly without Emma's knowledge, as well as numerous trysts in London. 'After the Visit', however, which reflects on the call that she made to Max Gate as a long-time admirer of his writing back in August 1905, floats the notion that her presence in his own home was what the 'time-torn man' (CP 136) really longed for:

> Come again to the place
> Where your presence was as a leaf that skims
> Down a drouthy way whose ascent bedims
>   The bloom on the farer's face.
>
> Come again, with the feet
> That were light on the green as a thistledown ball,
> And those mute ministrations to one and to all
>   Beyond a man's saying sweet.   (CP 309)

In an especially neat little irony or satire of circumstance, in the event it would be at Emma's request that Florence found herself attempting to irrigate with her 'mute ministrations' the 'droughty' atmosphere that prevailed at Max Gate. By requisitioning Florence as amanuensis for her own diverse literary enterprises, Emma in fact made possible, for stretches of the second half of 1910, the peculiar ménage à trois that Hardy seems to have desired, and which he would later transmute into the triangulated loves of Sir Tristram, Iseult the Fair, and Iseult the Whitehanded in the verse drama that was his final sustained piece of imaginative writing, *The Famous Tragedy of the Queen of Cornwall*.

Between the turn of the century and her death, Emma made a series of efforts to get her own views and work into print. In August 1899 she published in the *Daily Chronicle* an anonymous letter denouncing as 'a disgrace to civilisation' (LEFH 16) the use of a whip on a Bengal tiger during a circus performance at the Alexandra Palace. And the same paper printed, two years later, her searching diagnosis of the more general evils afflicting society, which were attributed by Emma primarily to failures in education. 'The gaols, asylums, hospitals, workhouses,' she complains,

> are crowded with woeful mortality, accidents, afflictions, illnesses are continually produced by want of care, or stupidity, or lack of interest in others' well-being; sins and sorrows, pain, and anguish follow. Even the well-to-do have continual droppings of jealousies, rivalries, bullyings, and worse—wickedness never known, miseries never spoken of.   (LEFH 24)

The main cause of this sorry state of affairs, she goes on to explain, is the fact that 'the plastic hearts and minds' of the young are consigned to 'ignorant hands'. The relatively wealthy abjectly fail their offspring by employing nursemaids 'of the uncultivated class' while the poor raise their children in still 'greater misery, starved in their bodies, crammed in their minds, morals ignored, religion defied'. Emma's rhetoric throughout this letter is vigorous and impassioned, indeed verges on the Carlylean, while her practical solution is forthrightly delivered—the universal provision of suitably qualified rearers of the young, from cradle to adulthood:

> get instructors as near as you can to the Arnoldian type—that is, get them of a class, high, not for attainments merely, but qualified by excellence of morals, true and simple religion, and good sense…The teaching profession of this high stamp should be everywhere, in towns, cities, country villages, and should have an exalted position.   (LEFH 24–5)[3]

Her focus in this letter on what we now call early years education is at once thoughtful and prescient, and she is careful to balance her unsparing account of the nation's current woes with an exalted vision of its future, should her advice be heeded: 'Lives', she declares in a stirring conclusion, 'would be prolonged blissfully, and in one or two generations nearly every person would in some way or other be *a maker of happiness*' (LEFH 26).

The finale of a letter that appeared in *The Nation* in May 1908 on the suffragette cause is equally resonant. Emma had welcomed the crusade for women's right to vote and readily participated in the mass demonstrations

---

[3] The Arnold referred to here is Thomas, the influential headmaster of Rugby, rather than his son Matthew.

held in London in 1907 and 1908, contributing also to a symposium on the topic published in the March 1907 issue of the magazine *Women at Home*. Composed a year before the espousal of violence by certain activists prompted her to resign her membership of the London Society for Women's Suffrage, her letter to *The Nation* expresses her vehement outrage at the structures and prejudices of patriarchy, while its final image uncannily anticipates exactly the canonization awaiting her after her own death:

> Women have been sacrificed for ages to men. The absurd idea kept up by them, and hitherto humbly accepted by women, that their manhood is a much higher state for a human being than a woman's womanhood, is allied with tyranny and a fearful calculation as to the real capabilities of women, who are abashed and crushed by their treatment, and obliged hitherto to cringe to the idea of the superiority of the male, whose praise has seldom been for a good woman except safely on a tombstone. (LEFH 40–1)

Something of the marital disharmony prevailing in Max Gate seems refracted in this passage. Ironically, Hardy was also 'in favour of woman-suffrage', but for reasons, at least as outlined in a letter of 1906 to Millicent Fawcett, that contravened much that Emma held dear: giving women the vote would act as a catalyst, he hoped, for overturning 'the present pernicious conventions in respect of manners, customs, religion, illegitimacy...' (CL III 238) It would further, in other words, precisely the revolutionary agenda that Emma discerned and abhorred in *Jude the Obscure*.

It is not known on what topic Emma was discoursing to members of the women-only Lyceum Club in the early summer of 1910 when, having lost her place in her script, Florence expeditiously came to the rescue. It seems unlikely that the introduction this made possible was wholly the result of chance. Howsoever it came about, the friendship, once initiated, was swiftly developed, and during June Florence attended several of the Hardys' tea-time 'At Homes' at that year's London residence, 4 Blomfield Court, Maida Vale, and was even accorded the honour of pouring out the tea (MM 430). Clearly her pre-existing relationship to Hardy went either unmentioned or was downplayed. By mid-July Florence is figuring herself and her new friend as a fearless duo, firmly allied in 'the great campaign which lies before us' (LEFH 61). This campaign would indeed prove a challenging one, for their aim was to persuade London editors to publish Emma's writings in various genres. The manuscripts handed over by Emma included *The Maid on the Shore*, the novella set in Cornwall begun nearly four decades earlier ('the more I see of the story,' Florence enthused, 'the more I like it' (LEFH 62)); a series of religious prose effusions such as 'The Acceptors' or 'The Trumpet Call', which unsurprisingly found no takers, although a selection of them eventually appeared in the privately published booklet *Spaces*, issued by F. G. Longman of Cornhill Press, Dorchester in 1912;[4] and a slim manuscript of poems, of which Florence declared, with her fingers no doubt metaphorically crossed behind her back, 'I think we can manage to get that published' (LEFH 67). In the event, this too was privately printed by F. G. Longman, as the pamphlet *Alleys* of 1911.

Alleys consists of fifteen poems, three of which had been published in the *Dorset County Chronicle*, one in the *Sphere*, and one in the *Academy*. They range from blithe snapshots of nature, such as the four-line 'Ripe Summer' ('The meadows lie beneath / The summer sun's hot rays; / O, happy, happy summer, / O golden, golden days' (PRE 4)) to the patriotic 'God Save Our Emperor King', a celebration of the accession of George V spoken in alternate strophes by Great Britain and an India grateful for the mother country's imperial sway. The deftest composition in the pamphlet is the pithy four-line 'The Churchyard', which echoes her husband's penchant for gloom and graveyards:

> Hundreds of times has grief been here,
>> Hundreds of mourners themselves lie here,
> For some no grieved hearts followed their bier,
>> They had outlived all who could shed a tear.   (PRE 7)

One poem mentioned in Florence and Emma's correspondence that was not, alas, included in *Alleys* is the lost 'A Ballad of a Boy', which was sent out for publication by Florence, only to be withdrawn on Emma's instructions. A passage in a letter of 1 December 1910 is the only clue we have to the kind of poem it was. 'On reflection,' Florence writes,

> I see that you are both wise & kind in withdrawing it, if you think it would cause any annoyance. Nevertheless it is so good a poem, & so full of life & originality that I am sorry it cannot be published. Personally I cannot see

---

[4] *Spaces* is made up of four texts: 'The High Delights of Heaven', 'Acceptors and Non-Acceptors', 'The New Element of Fire' (the fire in question being that of Hell), and 'Retrospect' (spoken by Satan, God, Michael, the Holy Spirit, and the erring angels).

in it one line that would identify the boy with Mr Hardy. But of course you know best.   (LEFH 69)

The 'annoyance' it might have caused in all probability relates to the lowly class status of the boy in question, whom Emma clearly feared might be recognized by her husband as a portrait of him as a child. It might have proved interesting to contrast 'A Ballad of a Boy' with Hardy's own ballad-style commemoration of Emma's childhood, 'During Wind and Rain', as well as with his many other poetic figurations of her early life in Plymouth.

Crucial to the enterprise of getting Emma published was the typewriter that Florence had been gifted by the eminent surgeon Sir Thornley Stoker, in whose imposing Dublin residence she had lived for much of 1909, in a somewhat ill-defined role that seems to have been a mixture of companion to his severely ill wife, houseguest, and occasional secretary to Sir Thornley himself. On this typewriter she set about creating fair copies of texts such as 'The Acceptors' and *The Maid on the Shore*. The former vividly anticipates the glorious afterlife awaiting the faithful, from which unbelievers (that is the likes of Florence and of Hardy) would be rigorously excluded. It is to be assumed that Florence avoided disclosing to her new friend her own religious scepticism—indeed in one letter she even echoed Emma's persistent fears of a creeping Roman Catholic 'menace', and went so far as to assert that Asquith, the current prime minister, was 'in league with the R.C.'s' (LEFH 70). Like Emma's other Christian effusions, 'The Acceptors' touchingly conveys her own physical distress at this stage of her life: 'Before every other change after death comes *rest complete*. Muscles, nerves, brain in a state of rest, sweetest of all rests, never had in life...' (PRE 17). The more worldly Florence must have known that it was highly unlikely that a respectable home could be found for a piece in this mode, and yet, after dispatching it to a possible publisher, she reported excitedly, 'I am quite burning with anxiety to know the fate of "The Acceptors"', before laying it on still thicker by declaring that she believed her friend's 'great triumph will be with "The Inspirer"' (LEFH 63). She clearly found typing up the much lengthier *The Maid on the Shore* somewhat irksome; it took her over a week, and balancing her epistolary paeans of praise for this novella's 'vivid & picturesque descriptions of Cornish scenery' was a very particular critical cavil:

> I fancy there are many corrections that must be made. Certain costumes
> are described fully & these—appropriate as they must have been 21 years

ago when the story was written [sic]—would only make the story seem ridiculous now. For instance—'a robe of yellow velvet, golden coins hanging over her brow, & dusky hair floating over her shoulders.'   (LEFH 62)

Many who met Emma towards the end of her life noted her penchant for dressing in an exuberantly youthful manner that harked back to Victorian fashions, and it is perhaps no coincidence that here a similar charge is being levelled at the sartorial style of her female protagonists.

Delighted with her discovery, Emma pressed Florence to stay at Max Gate, which she did from 26 July to 2 August, for most of September, and then again in November. It was during this November visit that Emma pointed out to Florence the resemblance between Hardy and the wife-murderer Dr Crippen, which put her, by inference, into the role of Crippen's mistress, Ethel Clare Le Neve. Florence's letters suggest that she found the Hardys' domestic life at once humorous and pitiable. In her unguarded bulletins both Hardy, depicted solemnly at work on a melancholy elegy for Kitsey, a recently deceased white cat, and the erratic, impulsive Emma are presented as figures of fun. 'The "Max Gate menage"', she reported to Clodd,

always does wear an aspect of comedy to me. Mrs Hardy is good to me, beyond words, & instead of cooling towards me she grows more & more affectionate. I am *intensely* sorry for her, sorry indeed for both.   (LEFH 66)

In the event, it was the decades-old antagonism between Max Gate and Higher Bockhampton that put an end to this comedy. Determined to embed Florence as deeply as possible into his social and familial circles, that autumn Hardy set about introducing her to friends such as Florence Henniker as well as to Mary, Henry, and Kate. The warm reception accorded her by his brother and sisters inevitably opened a new front in the conflict between Hardy's siblings and Emma, who was left fearing that her protégée might be turned against her. Matters erupted on Christmas Day 1910. The fullest account of this row was given by Florence exactly fifteen years afterwards, in a letter to Sydney Cockerell:

Here I sit alone in the drawing room—not quite alone though, for Wessex is here, sulking, because he wants more broadcasting & I have called a halt. My mind goes back to a Christmas Day—1910—when I sat here alone, & vowed that no power on earth would ever induce me to spend another Christmas day at Max Gate. T.H. had gone off to Bockhampton to see his sisters, after a violent quarrel with the first Mrs T.H. because he wanted me to go to see the sisters too, & she said I shouldn't because they would poison my mind against her—and then oh dear oh dear, *what* a scene—and he went off, & she went up to her attic study to write her memoirs till he came back at 8:30. It was the first Christmas of the kind I had ever spent... (LEFH 234)

The only solution to this tug of war was a version of the one adopted by husband and wife: Florence henceforth avoided being caught in further disputes by 'keeping separate' her relations with T. H. and Mrs T. H. Over the next couple of years, she and her eminent admirer were able to enjoy a series of holidays and excursions together, for which Hardy marshalled parties that included Henry and Kate, Florence's sister Constance, and, for a week spent in the Lake District, her father too. Yet Florence also spent 'a delightful fortnight' in Worthing with Emma in August 1911, 'bathing', she reported on a postcard dispatched to Mary, 'once & sometimes twice a day' (LEFH 72), despite her delicate health.[5] A photograph of them on Worthing's stony beach survives, although neither, it must be said, looks particularly gay. Still, in an odd reversal of the trajectory of Hardy's affections, it was not really until after Emma's death that the relationship between the two 'bright-souled women' in his life might be said to have soured. Her last surviving letter to Emma postdates their dreadful Christmas and offers condolences for Emma's various troubles—the departure of a servant, the search for a cook, the death of another Max Gate cat. Emma is urged to compose to the memory of Marky one of her 'delightful poems', 'just as Matthew Arnold did to his canary, & Mrs Browning to Flush' (LEFH 72). If there is a trace of irony in this suggestion, it is wholly deadpan. And the fiction that Emma is about to burst into print is as nobly maintained as ever: 'I suppose you have heard nothing further from the publishers. I have not had a word, but I know their dilatory ways, too well.'

----

[5] Hardy alludes to this holiday in Worthing taken by his first and second wives in the draft that he prepared of the *Life* (383), but in line with her policy of decreasing the presence of Emma where possible, Florence removed the reference when editing *The Later Years of Thomas Hardy* for publication.

'A Poet' is another of Hardy's self-elegies:

> Attentive eyes, fantastic heed,
> Assessing minds, he does not need,
> Nor urgent writs to sup or dine,
> Nor pledges in the rosy wine.
>
> For loud acclaim he does not care
> By the august or rich or fair,
> Nor for smart pilgrims from afar,
> Curious on where his hauntings are.
>
> But soon or later, when you hear
> That he has doffed this wrinkled gear,
> Some evening, at the first star-ray,
> Come to his graveside, pause and say:
>
> 'Whatever his message—glad or grim—
> Two bright-souled women clave to him;'
> Stand and say that while day decays;
> It will be word enough of praise.   (CP 415)[6]

The poem makes use of that most favoured of Hardy scenarios, the graveside meditation, in this case one enjoined on the reader, with the grave being his own. Like 'When Dead' and 'His Heart', or the greatest of his self-elegies, 'Afterwards', it functions as an extended proleptic epitaph, an *apologia pro sua vita* that stresses his ordinariness and lack of ambition. 'A Poet' is dated to July 1914, that is some six months after Hardy and Florence's private wedding in Enfield Parish Church, and a year and eight months after the death of Emma. 'That which mattered most' (CP 310), to adapt the last line of 'After the Visit', had come to be, and, beneath the compliment paid to both dead and living wives, 'A Poet' formalizes the curious rivalry that Hardy, and his poetry, fomented between them. Quite unexpectedly, given her painful first-hand experience of how badly husband and wife got on, poor Florence found herself competing with both the ghost and the memory of Emma at every turn, haunted by the woman whom she had supplanted in

---

[6] In the original printing of 'A Poet' in *Satires of Circumstance* the final verse runs: '"Whatever the message his to tell, / Two thoughtful women loved him well." / Stand and say that amid the dim: / It will be praise enough for him' (CPVE 415).

Hardy's affections while both were alive, but whose *vestigia* remained everywhere, and whose wraith posed an ever-present threat.[7] Even before consenting to marry him she reported finding Hardy's sudden volte-face over Emma bewildering: 'I must say,' she complains in a letter of January 1913 to Clodd,

> the good lady's virtues are beginning to weigh heavily [sic] on my shoulders. I had three pages of them this morning. Chief among the virtues now seems to rank her strict Evangelical views—her religious tendencies, her *humanitarianism* (to cats I suppose he means)...I feel as if I can hardly keep back my true opinion much longer.   (LEFH 77)

Indeed, the triangulation of the poet and of the two women who 'clave' to him appears to have so rooted itself that even Hardy's wooing of Florence involved constant reference to Emma. Time enjoyed with the woman whom he wished to make his second wife needed to be balanced, or atoned for, by ardent tributes to her predecessor, or so another letter to Clodd, written some two months later, implies:

> I have never before realized the depth of his affection, & his goodness & unselfishness as I have done these last three months. All I trust is that I may not, for the rest of his life, have to sit & listen humbly to an account of her virtues & graces.   (LEFH 78)

Ghoulishly, this triangulation extended even to Stinsford churchyard, where, or so Gittings and Manton suggest, he may have made his proposal of marriage (SMH 70). Included in this missive to Clodd is a postcard of Emma's grave heaped with flowers shortly after her burial, and an account of the various family gravestones:

> The flower-covered grave is, of course Mrs Hardy's, the flat tomb beyond, of his father & mother, the two upright stones beyond that, of his

---

[7] Florence's dismay at the disjunction between Hardy's poems about Emma and the antagonism and rancour that she had observed at Max Gate is the subject of a telling diary entry made by Sydney Cockerell on 17 April 1916: 'Went for a short walk with Mrs Hardy who told me what a complete failure TH's first marriage had been and that when the first Mrs Hardy died they were in the midst of a bitter quarrel and even about to separate. All the poems about her are a fiction, but a fiction in which their author has come to believe!' (CT 336–7).

grandparents & great grandparents. There *he* will lie, when the time comes, & a corner, I am told, will be reserved for me.

Whatever tensions alienated Emma from the Hardy clan, as well as from her erstwhile friend and rival for her husband's attentions, would effortlessly dissolve once all were safely buried in Stinsford churchyard. The bride-to-be seems not to have found this an entirely heartening prospect.

Hardy's compulsion to develop a partly posthumous reworking of the ménage à trois attempted in the latter half of 1910 is explicitly dramatized in the wry and unsettling 'The Wistful Lady':

'Love, while you were away there came to me—
    From whence I cannot tell—
A plaintive lady pale and passionless,
Who laid her eyes upon me critically,
And weighed me with a wearing wistfulness,
    As if she knew me well.'

'I saw no lady of that wistful sort
    As I came riding home.
Perhaps she was some dame the Fates constrain
By memories sadder than she can support,
Or by unhappy vacancy of brain,
    To leave her roof and roam?'

'Ah, but she knew me. And before this time
    I have seen her, lending ear
To my light outdoor words, and pondering each,
Her frail white finger swayed in pantomime,
As if she fain would close with me in speech,
    And yet would not come near.

'And once I saw her beckoning with her hand
    As I came into sight
At an upper window. And I at last went out;
But when I reached where she had seemed to stand,
And wandered up and down and searched about,
    I found she had vanished quite.'

Then thought I how my dead Love used to say,
    With a small smile, when she

Was waning wan, that she would hover round
And show herself after her passing day
To any newer Love I might have found,
But show her not to me.   (CP 359)

This poem is placed just after the 'Poems 1912–13' section of *Satires of Circumstance*, several of whose terms and tropes it pointedly echoes or reverses. In 'The Voice' the ghost of Emma evanesces 'to wan wistlessness, / Heard no more again far or near' (CP 346); the first Love's wistful wraith, although equally elusive, here hounds her successor, in the process generating an even more extravagantly alliterative use of the *w* sound: 'And weighed me with a wearing wistfulness, /As if she knew me well.' While Emma's ghost is normally depicted as willing to forgive her errant or inattentive husband, an element of menace accompanies her persistent stalking of his newer Love in this poem. If 'wistlessness' can be glossed as a state of 'nescience', to use another Hardyish term (CP 277/L 152), or unknowing, the wistful lady induces self-consciousness and unease in the clearly shaken woman whom she eyes 'critically', and to whom she beckons with a 'frail white finger' only to disappear. In 'His Visitor' Emma's ghost is similarly critical, eyeing askance the various alterations to Max Gate and its garden undertaken by her successor, but eventually decides to return to Stinsford churchyard and henceforth avoid her former home. 'The Wistful Lady', on the other hand, records a series of hauntings, and its ending suggests that they might be construed as some kind of ongoing curse or revenge. The implication, further, of the concluding stanza is that although the husband would relish a visit from his 'dead Love' after 'her passing day', she will appear only to his second wife, with whom she seems to want to communicate but to whom she will never speak, thus imparting a disturbing and permanent asymmetry to this irresolvable triangle.

In December 1917, shortly after the publication of *Moments of Vision*, which contains over fifty poems commemorating Emma, Florence wrote despairingly to Sydney Cockerell of her personal interpretation of the volume: to her these poems demonstrated that 'T.H.'s second marriage is a most disastrous one & that his sole wish is to find refuge in the grave with her with whom alone he found happiness' (MM 474). It was not, however, so much 'refuge in the grave' with Emma that Hardy longed for in the early years of his marriage with Florence as the opportunity to resuscitate buried memories of his first wife, and of her various relatives too, with his second by his side. Just three months after their wedding he had her join him on a visit to Charles churchyard in Plymouth where he hoped 'to clear up a mystery as to the Gifford vault there' (CL V 30)—a quest that Florence described in a letter to Lady Hoare as 'rather depressing' (SMH 77). In June 1916, this time accompanied by Florence and his sister Kate as well, he returned to Riverside Villa, Sturminster Newton, four decades after he and Emma had settled there: he found it 'much as it had been in the former years' (L 403), and duly composed the various Sturminster Newton poems such as 'Overlooking the River Stour', 'The Musical Box', and 'On Sturminster Footbridge' collected in *Moments of Vision*. And that September he and Florence travelled to the most hallowed site of all, St Juliot, to see the tablet in memory of Emma that he had designed and had erected in the church that brought them together. In a letter to Florence Henniker written shortly before they set off, he explained that his second wife was keen 'to see the place & the cliff scenery, never having been there', while he was himself ready to endure the 'sad' memories that this trip might 'revive' (CL V 176). Accordingly, Florence found herself stepping literally in the *vestigia* of her predecessor, haunting, almost as her proxy, the first Love's sacred Cornish 'haunting-ground', to borrow the title of a poem collected in *Human Shows*, whose second stanza ritualistically itemizes Emma's presence in the landscape:

> Her voice explored this atmosphere,
> Her foot impressed this turf around,
> Her shadow swept this slope and mound,
> Her fingers fondled blossoms here...   (CP 809)

Now her successor could do the same... After tea at St Juliot rectory with the 'very nice Rector & his sister', as she wrote to Cockerell, they 'walked back to Boscastle along the Valency Valley', and the following day rambled around the ruins of Tintagel:

> This morning we explored King Arthur's Castle here, & lay for an hour or so, on the grass, in the sunshine, with sheep nibbling around us, & no other living thing—while cliffs & greenyblue sea & white surf seemed hundreds of feet below. When we came down & saw where we had been my husband declared that it was the last time in his life he was going up there—in such a dangerous place. But we had both enjoyed it, & I hope he has found the germ of an Iseult poem.   (LEFH 119–20)

This Iseult poem would slowly metamorphose into an archaic verse play in which two women of the same name compete for the affections of the minstrel hero. As Florence's letter subliminally suggests, it was the traversing by his second wife of the 'haunting-ground' of his first that so excited Hardy's imagination.

The inspection of his tablet for Emma erected in St Juliot Church resulted in two poems, 'The Marble Tablet' and 'The Monument-Maker', both of which are premised on the difference between the 'cold white look' of the stone and Emma's '*living*'-ness, her 'glance, glide, or smile' (L 76, CP 655). 'It spells not me!' her ghost exclaims in the latter,

> 'Tells nothing about my beauty, wit, or gay time
>> With all those, quick and dead,
>> Of high or lowlihead,
>>> That hovered near,
> Including you, who carve there your devotion;
>> But you felt none, my dear!'
>
> And then she vanished. Checkless sprang my emotion
>> And forced a tear
> At seeing I'd not been truly known by her,
> And never prized!—that my memorial here,
>> To consecrate her sepulchre,
>>> Was scorned, almost,
>>> By her sweet ghost:
> Yet I hoped not quite, in her very innermost!   (CP 707–8)

Emma's imagined complaint directly echoes the one that she had made in her letter to *The Nation* on the suffragette cause, that only on a woman's 'tombstone' was a man able or willing to his express his 'devotion'. The gently bantering tone of this poem's final line might be taken to indicate a new phase in Hardy's mourning, both poetic and actual; the labour of appeasing Emma might be arduous, and meet many a rebuff, but was not hopeless. Less happily, Hardy seems also to have felt that Florence's participation in these rituals was indispensable. Numerous diary entries record pious tributes made jointly on various anniversaries: 'November 27 [1922]. E's death-day, ten years ago. Went with F. and tidied her tomb and carried flowers for her...' (L 452); 'To Stinsford with F. (E. first met 54 years ago)' (L 457).

Florence's co-option into the processes of paying due homage to her pre-decessor is similarly illustrated by Hardy's description of the unfortunate circumstances that marred their attendance at the Sunday morning service held at Tintagel Church on 10 September 1916:

> We sat down in a seat bordering the passage to the transept, but the vicar appalled us by coming to us in his surplice and saying we were in the way of the choir who would have to pass there. He banished us to the back of the transept. However, when he began his sermon we walked out. He thought it was done to be even with him, and looked his indignation; but it was really because we could not see the nave lengthwise, which my wife Emma had sketched in watercolours when she was a young woman before it was 'restored', so that I was interested in noting the changes, as also was F., who was familiar with the sketch. It was saddening enough, though doubtless only a chance, that we were inhospitably received in a church so much visited and appreciated by one we both had known so well.   (L 404)

The rather exaggerated friendship between Emma and Florence insisted upon here also surfaces in his depiction of the two Iseults in *The Famous Tragedy of the Queen of Cornwall*, most notably when Iseult the Fair expresses anguished remorse after Iseult the Whitehanded has appeared unexpectedly in Tintagel in the hope of reclaiming her husband:

> —Th'other Iseult possesses him, indeed;
> And it was I who set it in his soul
> To seek her out!—my namesake, whom I felt
> A kindness for—alas, I know not why!   (FTQC 56)

The 'kindness' that motivated Emma to invite Florence to Max Gate is entangled in such lines in the rivalrous roles that his 'bright-souled women' assumed in Hardy's imagination. And while not exactly a King Mark figure, the officious vicar is similarly disparaged for obstructing yet another attempt to re-experience and commemorate a love that Hardy habitually considered as legendary as that of Tristram and Iseult.

The Famous Tragedy of the Queen of Cornwall, although neither popular nor much discussed, is a startling instance of Hardy's need to find fresh ways of exploring his obsessions, for it reveals him yet again setting out for Lyonnesse and returning with magic in his eyes, but this time in a play observing the unities and with two Iseults to fit into the narrative. A further motivation must have been the prospect of witnessing an actress recreate in person Emma's 'glance, glide, or smile' (CP 655).[8] The potion that Sir Tristram and Iseult the Fair quaff 'witlessly' during their sea voyage from Ireland to Tintagel is the primary instigator of the two triangles that dominate the play's action, Sir Tristram, Iseult the Fair, and King Mark being one, and Sir Tristram, Iseult the Fair, and Iseult the Whitehanded being the other. The evilness of King Mark is succinctly established at the opening of the play when he kicks Tristram's 'brachet' (FTQC 12 (i.e. dog)) but Iseult the Whitehanded is treated by Hardy with sympathy and respect, although it is also made clear throughout that she is not on the same mythical or amatory plane as her namesake. While Queen Iseult is haughty and demanding, her Whitehanded rival is meek and beseeching, although both, as Merlin declares in the Prologue, must suffer for their love:

> And those two
> Fair women—namesakes—well I knew!
> Judge them not harshly in a love
>   Whose hold on them was strong;
> Sorrow therein they tasted of,
>   And deeply, and too long!   (FTQC 6)

While not technically a bigamist as Aeneas Manston of *Desperate Remedies* was, Tristram is effectively divided between the two Iseults, between the romance that made him famous and his less exhilarating obligations as a husband. In the course of their reunion scene, he is pointedly charged by Iseult the Fair with faithlessness and promiscuity: 'A woman's heart has room for one alone,' she complains, 'A man's for two or three!'; to which he somewhat weakly responds, 'Sweet; 'twas but chance!' (FTQC 39).

The play's extended compositional gestation (1916–23) suggests how diffi-cult Hardy found it to develop a suitable style and structure for a verse drama that fuses the conventions of Greek tragedy with native traditions of mum-ming to present a medieval legend fraught with personal significance. The characters all speak the same stylized argot, replete with neologisms, and the

---

[8] Gertrude Bugler, who had already performed Eustacia Vye for the Hardy players, was ini-tially cast in the title role, but in the event a pregnancy prevented her from performing it, thus saving Florence from the ordeal of watching a young living rival for her husband's affec-tions—as she saw it—enacting Hardy's vision of her dead rival, Emma, as both queen and legendary lover.

play offers numerous examples of the sorts of line only Hardy could write: 'Can there be any groundage for his thought'; 'And irk me not while setting to bowse with these'; 'She's glode off like a ghost, with deathy mien' (FTQC 20, 34, 70). It concludes, unsurprisingly, with multiple deaths: King Mark stabs Sir Tristram in the back, and he is stabbed in revenge by Iseult the Fair; she and Tristram's brachet then hurl themselves off an adjoining cliff, their suicides commemorated by the male half of the play's choric commentators:

> Alas, for this wroth day!
> She's leapt the ledge and fallen
>   Into the loud black bay,
> Whose waters, loosed and swollen,
>   Are spirting into spray!
> She's vanished from the world,
> Over the blind rock hurled;
> And the little hound her friend
> Has made with hers its end!   (FTQC 70–1)

As in *The Dynasts*, the somewhat contorted idiom tends to veer between the eccentric and the bathetic. There is no doubting, however, the play's private charge for its Merlin-like creator, who is depicted in Prologue and Epilogue as summoning up 'the ghosts of distant days' (FTQC 77). In a letter thanking Alfred Noyes for a not entirely admiring review in the *Evening News*, Hardy figured *A Famous Tragedy* as a deeply pondered distillation of all that was set in train by his arrival at St Juliot's rectory on the evening of 7 March 1870: 'How kind of you', he wrote to Noyes, 'to take the trouble to write an article on my little play—53 years in contemplation, 800 lines in result, alas!' (CL VI 224).

Much to the relief of Florence, the flood of poems about Emma slowed to a trickle as Hardy neared his end, and the posthumously published *Winter Words* contains only a handful that might be read as relating to his first marriage. The mood of these late poems is captured in 'A Forgotten Miniature', which finds him brooding on a relic that is figured more as a *memento mori* than a means of accessing the past.

> There you are in the dark,
>   Deep in a box

> Nobody ever unlocks,
> Or even turns to mark;
>> —Out of mind stark.   (CP 899)

In contrast to the actual interment of Emma depicted in a poem such as 'Lament', here burial is translated onto a symbolic plane, and the significance generalized:

> Shut in your case for years,
>> Never an eye
> Of the many passing nigh,
> Fixed on their own affairs,
>> Thinks what it nears!

Such a poem makes one aware of the specificity of so many of Hardy's poetic commemorations of Emma, a specificity that runs largely counter to the conventions of elegy deployed in 'Lycidas' or 'Adonais' or *In Memoriam*. Hardy recreates vignettes of Emma in all manner of situations: at a garden party, 'Bright-hatted and gloved, / With table and tray' (CP 344), plunging her arm into a basin of cold water, careering off to town without saying goodbye, fleeing the approach of 'arrows of rain' (CP 341), lamp-lit in a moving car, silhouetted against the walls of a slate quarry, draped across a handpost, irked and bored in a hotel room in Bournemouth, wandering 'bare-browed' on a 'clammy lawn' (CP 432), haloed by a 'nebulous stream' of thistle seeds on a coastal walk (CP 811), singing and playing the piano in an old-fashioned gown.

'Poems 1912–13' ends with a final conjugation of the *veteris vestigia flammae* of its epigraph. In 1919 Hardy decided to add to the eighteen elegies that made up the sequence in the first edition of *Satires of Circumstance* the somewhat allegorical 'The Spell of the Rose', the muted 'St Launce's Revisited', which, like 'A Forgotten Miniature', is largely concerned with the passing of time, and 'Where the Picnic Was':

> Where we made the fire
> In the summer time
> Of branch and briar
> On the hill to the sea,
> I slowly climb
> Through winter mire,
> And scan and trace

The forsaken place
Quite readily.

Now a cold wind blows,
And the grass is gray,
But the spot still shows
As a burnt circle—aye,
And stick-ends, charred,
Still strew the sward
Whereon I stand,
Last relic of the band
Who came that day!

Yes, I am here
Just as last year,
And the sea breathes brine
From its strange straight line
Up hither, the same
As when we four came.
—But two have wandered far
From this grassy rise
Into urban roar
Where no picnics are,
And one—has shut her eyes
For evermore.   (CP 357–8)

This poem's ashy remains bleakly figure the widower's misery—but they might also be seen as emblematic of the fate of so many of the pages written by Hardy and Emma to each other and about each other: all her letters to him, swathes of his to her, most of their personal diaries, ended up reduced to a 'burnt circle' in the garden or in a fireplace at Max Gate. Much of the material that survived these purges was eventually consigned to the flames by Hardy's two executors, Sydney Cockerell and Florence. Our knowledge of the obliteration of what would have been a vast and revealing range of contexts for the poems that Hardy eventually composed and published about Emma after her death might be said to shadow these poems with a conceptual aura of violence, as if we had to pass through a 'burnt circle' to reach them. Emma's destruction of the letters exchanged during their courtship, 'much regretted at the time, & since' by Hardy (LEFH 312), must have been a particularly harrowing occasion.

In *A Defence of Poetry*, Shelley compared 'the mind in creation' to a 'fading coal which some invisible influence, like an inconstant wind, awakens to transitory brightness', a metaphor obliquely, if wistfully, evoked by this poem's charred stick ends and sea-breathed brine.[9] 'Where the Picnic Was' is one of many poems in which Hardy presents himself as the sole survivor of former joys, as the embittered equivalent of the embers that remain after the fire and 'strew the sward'. It has been suggested that the two visitors from London with whom he and Emma shared this picnic were Newbolt and Yeats, an alfresco meal on some 'grassy rise' possibly being part of the festivities laid on for their 'pleasant weekend visit' (L 385).[10] Whatever the identities of the guests who have since returned to the city, Hardy's reference to 'urban roar' mirrors the processes of dispersal and anonymity against which any elegy, even one as drained and 'fervourless' (CP 150) as 'Where the Picnic Was', must make its stand.

Initially the sequence concluded with the exhilarating image of Emma as 'ghost-girl-rider' haunting the 'shagged and shaly / Atlantic spot' where Hardy 'first eyed' her (CP 354). His decision, much lamented by such as Donald Davie, to make the sequence end not with the 'rose-bright' Emma singing 'to the swing of the tide', 'Warm, real, and keen', as recovered in 'The Phantom Horsewoman', but with the remnants of a long-extinguished fire in a 'forsaken place' can perhaps best be glossed by a couple of sentences from the penultimate paragraph of Sigmund Freud's 'Mourning and Melancholia', published in 1917:

> Just as mourning impels the ego to renounce the object by declaring its death, and offers the ego the reward of staying alive, each individual battle of ambivalence loosens the fixation of the libido upon the object by devaluing, disparaging and, so to speak, even killing it. There is a possibility of the process in the unconscious coming to an end, either once the fury has played itself out or after the object has been abandoned as worthless.[11]

[9] *Shelley's Poetry and Prose*, eds. Donald H. Reiman and Sharon B. Powers (New York: Norton, 1977), 503–4.

[10] See J. O. Baily, *The Poetry of Thomas Hardy* (Chapel Hill: The University of North Carolina Press, 1970), 307–8, and *Thomas Hardy: Selected Poems*, ed. Tim Armstrong (Harlow: Longman, 1993), 182.

[11] *The Penguin Freud Reader*, ed. Adam Phillips (London: Penguin, 2006), 324. Davie accuses Hardy of betraying the visionary or metaphysical elements in the sequence out of 'defensive small-mindedness' ('Hardy's Virgilian Purples', *Agenda: Thomas Hardy Special Issue* (1972), 156, rpt. in *The Poet in the Imaginary Museum* (Manchester: Carcanet, 1977), 235).

Fixated is exactly how Hardy portrays himself in 'The Phantom Horsewoman', lost in 'a careworn craze', with 'moveless hands / And face and gaze' (CP 353). The realist strand in the remarried widower clearly forced him to acknowledge that mourning must end up winning some of the ambivalent battles it fights, to use Freud's terms, and the enchantments of melancholy give way, at least on occasion, to the 'devaluing, disparaging' reduction to ashes of the lost beloved.

The poet pilgrim makes his way to the sequence's desolate final site through 'winter mire' while 'a cold wind blows'. Inclement, 'sullen' conditions prevail also in the only poem Hardy wrote that is set on the day of Emma's funeral, which took place on 30 November 1912, by which time her successor had already been summoned to Max Gate. The two linked stanzas of 'A Leaving', published in *Human Shows* of 1925, use the same rhymes in reverse order to recreate the moment at which the hearse carrying Emma's coffin set off for Stinsford churchyard. There, as predicted, she would eventually be joined by Florence and, between them, a casket containing just the heart of the man to whom these 'bright-souled women clave', for the rest of his body, in accordance with 'the nation's desire in the matter', as Sydney Cockerell phrased it in a statement to the press released two days after Hardy's death, would be cremated in Woking and his ashes placed, after what verged on a state funeral, beneath a gravestone in Poets' Corner in Westminster Abbey:[12]

> Knowing what it bore
> I watched the rain-smitten back of the car—
> (Brown-curtained, such as the old ones were)—
> When it started forth for a journey afar
> Into the sullen November air,
> And passed the glistening laurels and round the bend.
>
> I have seen many gayer vehicles turn that bend
> In autumn, winter, and summer air,
> Bearing for journeys near or afar
> Many who now are not, but were,
> But I don't forget that rain-smitten car,
> Knowing what it bore!   (CP 829–30)

---

[12] *Daily Mail*, 13 January 1928, 9.

Acknowledgements

I would like to thank the Leverhulme Trust for a Major Research Fellowship that greatly assisted work on this project. I am also grateful to Juliette Atkinson, Tony Fincham, Mercy Ford, Chris Stamatakis, and Clair Wills for their extremely useful suggestions and comments.

All illustrations are reproduced by permission of the Thomas Hardy Archive and Collection, Dorset Museum.

Quotations from *The Poems of T. S. Eliot* and *Collected Poems* of Philip Larkin are reproduced by permission of Faber & Faber Ltd.

Selected Bibliography

Poetry by Thomas Hardy

Thomas Hardy: The Complete Poems, ed. James Gibson (London: Palgrave Macmillan, 2001)

Thomas Hardy: The Complete Poems, Variorum Edition, ed. James Gibson (London: Macmillan, 1979)

The Famous Tragedy of the Queen of Cornwall (London: Macmillan, 1923)

Fiction by Thomas Hardy

Desperate Remedies, ed. Patricia Ingham (Oxford: Oxford University Press, 2003) [1871]

A Pair of Blue Eyes, ed. Alan Manford (Oxford: Oxford University Press, 2005) [1873]

The Hand of Ethelberta, ed. Tim Dolin (London: Penguin, 1996) [1876]

The Return of the Native, ed. Simon Gatrell (Oxford: Oxford University Press, 2005) [1878]

A Laodicean, ed. John Schad (London: Penguin, 1997) [1881]

The Mayor of Casterbridge, ed. Dale Kramer (Oxford: Oxford University Press, 2004) [1886]

Tess of the d'Urbervilles, eds. Juliet Grindle and Simon Gatrell (Oxford: Oxford University Press, 2005) [1891]

Life's Little Ironies, ed. Alan Manford (Oxford: Oxford University Press, 1996) [1894]

Jude the Obscure, ed. Patricia Ingham (Oxford: Oxford University Press, 2002) [1895]

The Pursuit of the Well-Beloved and The Well-Beloved, ed. Patricia Ingham (London: Penguin, 1997) [1892 and 1897]

An Indiscretion in the Life of an Heiress and Other Stories, ed. Pamela Dalziel (Oxford: Oxford University Press, 1994)

Poetry and Fiction by Emma Hardy

The Maid on the Shore (Dorchester: Dorset, The Thomas Hardy Society, 2018)

Poems and Religious Effusions (St Peter Port, Guernsey: The Toucan Press, 1966)

Life, Letters, Notebooks, and Miscellaneous Prose by Emma Hardy, Florence Hardy, and Thomas Hardy

Hardy, Emma, *Some Recollections*, eds. Evelyn Hardy and Robert Gittings (London: Oxford University Press, 1961)

Hardy, Emma, *Emma Hardy Diaries*, ed. Richard H. Taylor (Ashington and Manchester: Mid Northumberland Arts Group and Carcanet New Press, 1985)

Hardy, Emma, and Florence Hardy, *Letters of Emma & Florence Hardy*, ed. Michael Millgate (Oxford: Oxford University Press, 1996)

Hardy, Florence, *The Life of Thomas Hardy* (London: Studio Editions, 1994)

Hardy, Thomas, *Thomas Hardy's Personal Writings*, ed. Harold Orel (London: Macmillan, 1967)

Hardy, Thomas, *The Personal Notebooks of Thomas Hardy*, ed. Richard H. Taylor (London: Macmillan, 1978)

Hardy, Thomas, *The Collected Letters of Thomas Hardy*, 8 volumes, eds. Richard Little Purdy, Michael Millgate, and Keith Wilson (Oxford: Oxford University Press, 1978–2012)

Hardy, Thomas, *The Life and Work of Thomas Hardy*, ed. Michael Millgate (London: Macmillan, 1984)

Hardy, Thomas, *The Literary Notebooks of Thomas Hardy*, 2 volumes, ed. Lennart A. Björk (New York: New York University Press, 1985)

Hardy, Thomas, *Thomas Hardy's 'Studies, Specimens &c.' Notebook*, eds. Pamela Dalziel and Michael Millgate (Oxford: Oxford University Press, 1994)

Hardy, Thomas, *Thomas Hardy: Interviews and Recollections*, ed. James Gibson (London: Macmillan, 1999)

Hardy, Thomas, *Thomas Hardy's Public Voice: The Essays, Speeches, and Miscellaneous Prose*, ed. Michael Millgate (Oxford: Clarendon Press, 2001)

Hardy, Thomas, *Thomas Hardy Remembered*, ed. Martin Ray (Aldershot: Ashgate, 2007)

Hardy, Thomas, *Thomas Hardy's 'Poetical Matter' Notebook*, eds. Pamela Dalziel and Michael Millgate (Oxford: Oxford University Press, 2009)

Biographies of Emma Hardy, Florence Hardy, and Thomas Hardy

Gibson, James, *Thomas Hardy: A Literary Life* (London: Palgrave Macmillan, 1996)

Gittings, Robert, *Young Thomas Hardy* (Harmondsworth: Penguin, 1975)

Gittings, Robert, *The Older Hardy* (Harmondsworth: Penguin, 1978)

Gittings, Robert and Jo Manton, *The Second Mrs Hardy* (London: Heinemann, 1979)

Kay-Robinson, Denys, *The First Mrs Thomas Hardy* (London: Macmillan, 1979)

Millgate, Michael, *Thomas Hardy: A Biography Revisited* (Oxford: Oxford University Press, 2004)

Norman, Andrew, *Thomas Hardy: Behind the Mask* (Stroud: The History Press, 2011)

Pite, Ralph, *Thomas Hardy: A Guarded Life* (London: Picador, 2006)

Seymour-Smith, Martin, *Hardy* (London: Bloomsbury, 1994)

Tomalin, Claire, *Thomas Hardy: The Time-Torn Man* (London: Penguin, 2006)

Turner, Paul, *The Life of Thomas Hardy* (Oxford: Blackwell, 1998)

Books on Thomas Hardy's Poetry

Armstrong, Tim, *Haunted Hardy: Poetry, History, Memory* (London: Palgrave Macmillan, 2000)

Bailey, J. O., *The Poetry of Thomas Hardy: A Handbook and Commentary* (Chapel Hill: University of North Carolina Press, 1970)

Brooks, Jean R., *Thomas Hardy: The Poetic Structure* (Ithaca: Cornell University Press, 1971)

Clark, Indy, *Thomas Hardy's Pastoral: An Unkindly May* (London: Palgrave Macmillan, 2015)

Clements, Patricia and Juliet Grindle, eds., *The Poetry of Thomas Hardy* (London: Vision Press, 1980)

Davie, Donald, *Thomas Hardy and British Poetry* (London: Routledge, 1973)

Gibson, James and Trevor Johnson, eds., *Thomas Hardy: Poems* (Basingstoke: Macmillan, 1979)

Hynes, Samuel, *The Pattern of Hardy's Poetry* (Chapel Hill: University of North Carolina Press, 1961)

Paulin, Tom, *Thomas Hardy: The Poetry of Perception* (London: Macmillan, 1975)

Pinion, F. B., *A Commentary of the Poems of Thomas Hardy* (London: Macmillan, 1976)

Taylor, Dennis, *Hardy's Poetry, 1860–1928* (London: Macmillan, 1981)

Taylor, Dennis, *Hardy's Metres and Victorian Prosody* (Oxford: Clarendon Press, 1988)

Taylor, Dennis, *Hardy's Literary Language and Victorian Philology* (Oxford: Clarendon Press, 1993)

Zietlow, Paul, *Moments of Vision: The Poetry of Thomas Hardy* (Cambridge, MA: Harvard University Press, 1974)

Articles and Chapters on 'Poems of 1912–13'

Austin, Linda M., 'Reading Depression in Hardy's "Poems of 1912–13"', *Victorian Poetry*, Vol. 36, 1 (1998), 1–15

Buckler, William E., 'The Dark Space Illumined: A Reading of Hardy's "Poems of 1912–13"', *Victorian Poetry*, Vol. 17, 1 (1979), 98–107

Davie, Donald, 'Hardy's Virgilian Purples', *Agenda: Thomas Hardy Special Issue* (1972), 138–56, rpt. in *The Poet in the Imaginary Museum* (Manchester: Carcanet, 1977), 221–35

Dolin, Tim, 'Life-Lyrics: Autobiography, Poetic Form, and Poetic Loss in Hardy's *Moments of Vision*', *Victorian Poetry*, Vol. 50, 1 (2012), 1–19

Edmond, Rod, 'Death Sequences: Patmore, Hardy, and the New Domestic Elegy', *Victorian Poetry*, Vol. 19, 2 (1981), 151–65

François, Anne-Lise, '"Not Thinking of You as Left Behind"': Virgil and the Missing of Love in Hardy's *Poems of 1912–13*', *ELH*, 75 (2008), 63–88

François, Anne-Lise, '"Without Ceremony": The Inconsequential Address' in *Open Secrets: The Literature of Uncounted Experience* (Stanford: Stanford University Press, 2008), 180–7

Gewanter, David, '"Undervoicings of Loss" in Hardy's Elegies to His Wife', *Victorian Poetry*, Vol. 29, 3 (1991), 193–208

Hall, Louisa, 'An Alternative to the Architectural Elegy: Hardy's Unhoused Poems of 1912–13', *Victorian Poetry*, Vol. 55, 2 (2012), 207–25

Hughes, John, '"Metre and Mourning": "The Going" and *Poems of 1912–13*', *The Hardy Review*, Vol. 17, 1 (2015) 28–44, rpt. in *The Expression of Things: Themes in Thomas Hardy's Fiction and Poetry* (Brighton: Sussex Academic Press, 2018), 143–66

Mallett, Phillip, '"You Were She": Hardy, Emma, and the "Poems of 1912–13"', *The Thomas Hardy Journal*, Vol. 20, 3 (2004), 54–75

McSweeney, Kerry, 'Hardy's *Poems of 1912–13*: A Presence More Than Actual', *Victorian Poetry*, Vol. 33, 2 (1995), 191–220

Morgan, William W.,'Tradition and Consolation in Hardy's "Poems of 1912–13"', *PMLA*, Vol. 89 (1974), 496–505

Murfin, Ross C., 'Moments of Vision: Hardy's *Poems of 1912–13*', *Victorian Poetry*, Vol. 20, 1 (1982), 73–84

Ramazani, Jahan, '*Poems of 1912–13* and Other Elegies for Emma' in *Poetry of Mourning: The Modern Elegy from Hardy to Heaney* (Chicago: University of Chicago Press, 1994), 47–68

Richards, I. A., 'Some Notes on Hardy's Verse Forms', *Victorian Poetry*, Vol. 17, 1–2 (1979) 1–8

Sacks, Peter M., 'Hardy: "A Singer Asleep" and *Poems 1912–13*' in *The English Elegy: Studies in the Genre from Spenser to Yeats* (Baltimore: The Johns Hopkins University Press, 1985), 227–59

Sexton, Melanie, 'Phantoms of His Own Figuring: The Movement toward Recovery in Hardy's "Poems of 1912–13"', *Victorian Poetry*, Vol. 29, 3 (1991), 209–26

Shires, Linda M., '"Saying that now you are not as you were": Hardy's "Poems of 1912–13"' in *Thomas Hardy and Contemporary Literary Studies*, eds. Tim Dolin and Peter Widdowson (Basingstoke: Palgrave, 2004), 138–52

Spargo, R. Clifton, 'Wishful Reciprocity in Thomas Hardy's *Poems of 1912–13*' in *The Ethics of Mourning: Grief and Responsibility in Elegiac Literature* (Baltimore: The Johns Hopkins University Press, 2004), 165–208

Stewart, Susan, 'Hardy' in *Poetry and the Fate of the Senses* (Chicago: University of Chicago Press, 2002), 132–8

Thomas, Jane, '"Scanned across the Dark Space": Poetry, Desire and Aesthetic Fulfilment' in *Thomas Hardy and Desire: Conceptions of the Self* (London: Palgrave Macmillan, 2013), 164–91

Witek, Terri, 'Repetition in a Land of Unlikeness: What "Life Will Not Be Balked Of" in Thomas Hardy's Poetry', *Victorian Poetry*, Vol. 28, 2 (1990), 119–28

Zeiger, Melissa F., '"Woman Much Missed": Writing Eurydice in Hardy's *Poems of 1912–13*' in *Beyond Consolation: Death, Sexuality, and the Changing Shapes of Elegy* (Ithaca: Cornell University Press, 1997), 43–61

Other Sources

Armstrong, Tim, ed., *Thomas Hardy: Selected Poems* (Harlow: Longman, 1993)

Armstrong, Tim, 'Sequence and Series in Hardy's Poetry' in *A Companion to Thomas Hardy*, ed. Keith Wilson (Oxford: Wiley-Blackwell, 2013), 378–94

Barthes, Roland, *A Lover's Discourse*, trans. Richard Howard (New York: Hill and Wang, 1978)

Bayley, John, *An Essay on Hardy* (Cambridge: Cambridge University Press, 1978)

Benziman, Galia, *Thomas Hardy's Elegiac Prose and Poetry: Codes of Bereavement* (London: Palgrave Macmillan, 2018)

Blunden, Edmund, *Thomas Hardy* (London: Macmillan, 1954 (first pub. 1942))

Campbell, Matthew, 'Tennyson and Hardy's Ghostly Metres', *Essays in Criticism*, Vol. 42 (1992), 279–98

Carlyle, Thomas, *Critical and Miscellaneous Essays*, Vol. 1 (London: Chapman and Hall, 1888)

Clarke, Graham, ed., *Thomas Hardy: Critical Assessments*, 3 vols. (Mountfield: Helm, 1993)

Collins, Vere H., *Talks with Thomas Hardy at Max Gate, 1920–1922* (London: Duckworth, 1928)

Cox, R. G., ed., *Thomas Hardy: The Critical Heritage* (London: Routledge, 1970)

Dante, *Purgatorio*, trans. and ed. Robin Kirkpatrick (London: Penguin, 2007)

Davie, Donald, ed., *Agenda: Thomas Hardy Special Issue*, Vol. 10, 2–3 (1972)

Dema, Eva, 'Moments of (Re)Vision: Thomas Hardy Making Amends', *English: Journal of the English Association*, Vol. 70, 270 (2021), 272–93

Donne, John, *The Complete English Poems*, ed. A. J. Smith (Harmondsworth: Penguin, 1986)

Drabble, Margaret, ed., *The Genius of Thomas Hardy* (London: Weidenfeld & Nicolson, 1976)

Dryden, John, *Virgil's Aeneid: Translated by John Dryden*, ed. Frederick M. Keener (London: Penguin Books, 1997)

Eliot, T. S., *Selected Prose of T. S. Eliot*, ed. Frank Kermode, (London: Faber & Faber, 1975)

Eliot, T. S., *The Poems of T. S. Eliot*, Vol. 1, eds. Christopher Ricks and Jim McCue (London: Faber & Faber, 2015)

Eliot, T. S., *The Complete Prose: The Critical Edition*, Vol. 5: *(1934–39)*, eds. Iman Javadi, Ron Schuchard, and Jayme Stayer (Baltimore: Johns Hopkins University Press, 2017)

Fincham, Tony, *Hardy the Physician: Medical Aspects of the Wessex Tradition* (Basingstoke: Palgrave Macmillan, 2008)

Flower, Newman, *Just as It Happened* (London: Cassell, 1950)

Ford, Mark, *Thomas Hardy: Half a Londoner* (Cambridge, MA: Harvard University Press, 2016)

Freud, Sigmund, *The Penguin Freud Reader*, ed. Adam Phillips (London: Penguin, 2006)

Gowrie, Grey, *The Italian Visitor* (Manchester: Carcanet, 2013)

Griffiths, Eric, 'Remaining Faithful: Hardy' in *The Printed Voice of Victorian Poetry* (Oxford: Oxford University Press, 1989), 204–24

Howarth, Peter, 'Hardy's Indifference' in *British Poetry in the Age of Modernism* (Oxford: Oxford University Press, 2005), 147–81

Keats, John, *The Poems of John Keats*, ed. Miriam Allott (London: Longman, 1970)

Larkin, Philip, *Required Writing* (London: Faber & Faber, 1984)

Larkin, Philip, *Collected Poems*, ed. Anthony Thwaite (London: Faber & Faber, 1988)

Leavis, F. R., *New Bearings in English Poetry* (Harmondsworth: Penguin, 1979 (first pub. 1932))

Levinson, Marjorie, 'Object-Loss and Object-Bondage: Economies of Representation in Hardy's Poetry', *ELH*, 73 (2006), 549–80

Lucas, John, 'Thomas Hardy: Voices and Visions' in *Modern English Poetry: From Hardy to Hughes* (London: Batsford, 1986), 22–49

Mill, John Stuart, *Utilitarianism*, ed. Mary Warnock (Glasgow: Collins, 1979)

Miller, J. Hillis, *Thomas Hardy: Distance and Desire* (Cambridge, MA: Harvard University Press, 1970)

Miller, Susan M., 'Thomas Hardy and the Impersonal Lyric', *Journal of Modern Literature*, Vol. 30, 3 (2007), 95–115

Morgan, Charles, *The House of Macmillan (1843–1943)* (London: Macmillan, 1943)

Mottram, Stephen, 'Hardy, Emma and the Giffords: A Re-Appraisal', *The Hardy Society Journal*, Vol. 8, 1 (2012), 24–46

Ovid, *Metamorphoses X*, ed. Lee Fratantuono (London: Bloomsbury, 2014)

Page, Norman, ed., *Oxford Reader's Companion to Hardy* (Oxford: Oxford University Press, 2000)

Palgrave, Francis Turner, ed., *The Golden Treasury of the Best Songs and Lyrical Poems in the English Language, Selected and Arranged with Notes*, ed. Christopher Ricks (London: Penguin, 1991)

Pettit, Charles P. C., *St Juliot Church and Thomas Hardy* (Dorchester: The Thomas Hardy Society, 2010)

Phelps, Kenneth, *The Wormwood Cup: Thomas Hardy in Cornwall* (Padstow: Lodenek Press, 1975)

Pinion, F. B., 'Hardy's Visits to Cornwall' in *New Perspectives on Thomas Hardy*, ed. Charles P. C. Pettit (Basingstoke: Palgrave Macmillan, 1994)

Pite, Ralph, ed., *Thomas Hardy: 21st-Century Oxford Authors* (Oxford: Oxford University Press, 2021)

Pound, Ezra, *The Letters of Ezra Pound 1907–1941*, ed. D. D. Paige (London: Faber & Faber, 1950)

Purdy, Richard Little, *Thomas Hardy: A Bibliographical Study*, ed. Charles Pettit (London: British Library, 2002)

Richards, Jill, ' "The History of Error": Hardy's Critics and the Self Unseen', *Victorian Poetry*, Vol. 45, 2 (2007), 117–33

Rossetti, Dante Gabriel, *Collected Poetry and Prose*, ed. Jerome McGann (New Haven: Yale University Press, 2003)

Shakespeare, William, *The Riverside Shakespeare*, ed. G. Blakemore Evans (Boston: Houghton Mifflin, 1997)

Shelley, Percy Bysshe, *Shelley's Poetry and Prose*, eds. Donald H. Reiman and Sharon B. Powers (New York: Norton, 1977)

Small, Helen, 'Hardy's Tennyson' in *Tennyson among the Poets*, eds. Robert Douglas-Fairhurst and Seamus Perry (Oxford: Oxford University Press, 2009), 356–74

The Southern Review: Thomas Hardy Centennial Issue, Vol. 6, 1 (1940)

Taylor, Dennis, 'Hardy as a Nineteenth-Century Poet' in *The Cambridge Companion to Thomas Hardy*, ed. Dale Kramer (Cambridge: Cambridge University Press, 1999), 183–203

Tennyson, Alfred Lord, *A Selected Edition*, ed. Christopher Ricks (Harlow: Longman, 1989)

Thain, Marion, 'Thomas Hardy's Poetics of Touch', *Victorian Poetry*, Vol. 51, 2 (2013), 129–45

Tomalin, Claire, ed., *Unexpected Elegies: 'Poems of 1912–13' and Other Poems about Emma*, (New York: Persea Books, 2010)

Virgil, *The Aeneid of Virgil: Books 1–6*, ed. R. D. Williams (London: Macmillan, 1972)

Weber, Carl J. ed., *Hardy's Love Poems* (London: Macmillan, 1963)

Weismann, August, *Essays on Heredity and Kindred Biological Problems*, Vol. 1 (Oxford: Clarendon Press, 1891)

Widdowson, Peter, *Hardy in History: A Study in Literary Sociology* (London: Routledge, 1989)

Williams, William Carlos, *Selected Poems*, ed. Charles Tomlinson (Harmondsworth: Penguin, 1976)

Wordsworth, William, *William Wordsworth: The Poems*, Vol. 2, ed. John O. Hayden (Harmondsworth: Penguin, 1977)

Wordsworth, William, *Selected Poems*, ed. John O. Hayden (London: Penguin, 1994)

Index

For the benefit of digital users, indexed terms that span two pages (e.g., 52–53) may, on occasion, appear on only one of those pages.

Academy, The 211
Ainsworth, Harrison 43–4
Armstrong, Tim 180n.7
Arnold, Matthew 2
Atherton, Gertrude 149
Auden, W.H. 32
Austen, Jane 203–4

Barnes, William 23
Barthes, Roland 104–5
Bastow, Henry 177
Baudelaire, Charles 142–3
Bayley, John 11–12
Benson, A.C. 130–1, 160
Bergson, Henri 59, 185–6
Bernandin de Saint-Pierre,
 Jacques-Henri 177
Bliss, Harold 94
Blomfield, Arthur 156
Browne, Lizbie 152–3
Browning, Elizabeth Barrett 94
Browning, Robert 94, 189–90
Bugler, Gertrude 222n.8
Bunting, Basil 177
Burns, Robert 100
Byron, George Gordon, Lord 100

Carlyle, Thomas 55–6, 109
Carroll, Lewis 57–8
Chambers Journal 156
Chappel, Anne Tresider 67–8
Child, Harold 116, 188n.15
Clodd, Edward 67, 127, 155, 197, 205, 213, 215–16
Cockerell, Sydney 45, 71n.4, 203–4, 213, 216n.7, 218–19, 225, 227
Coleridge, Samuel Taylor 142–3, 166
Collins, Vere 98, 114
Collins, Wilkie 45–6

Cornhill, The 95
Cosmopolis 151
Crickmay, George 1
Crippen, Dr 128–9, 213

Daily Mail 206, 227n.12
Dante 117–18, 181–2
Davie, Donald xiii–xiv, 97n.1, 181, 226
De la Mare, Walter xviii–xix
Donne, John 108–9, 152
Dorset County Chronicle 125–6, 211
Douglas, Sir George 102n.3
Dryden, John 179, 196

Edmond, Rod 183n.11
Eliot, T.S. 61–3, 134–5, 177
Eliot, Vivien 61–2
Evening Standard 206

Fawcett, Millicent 210
Fitzgerald, Edward 206
Flower, Newman 67
Ford, Ford Madox 128
François, Anne-Lise 171n.13, 180n.7
Freud, Sigmund 196, 226–7

Gale, Dolly 183–4
Garnett, Richard 128
Gentleman's Magazine 28–9
Gibbon, Edward xiii
Gibson, James 21
Gifford, Charles 169
Gifford, Edwin Hamilton 129–30
Gifford, Gordon 127
Gifford, John Attersoll 73, 77n.5, 112–14, 125–6, 168–9
Gifford, Kate 68–9
Gifford, Lilian 127, 168–9
Gifford, Walter 119, 127, 146

Gifford, Willie 146
Gissing, George 130, 206
Gittings, Robert 137
Godley, A.D. 178–9
Gosse, Edmund 130, 151
Gosse, Eva 169
Gowrie, Grey 62–3
Grahame, Elspeth xix–xx, 127–9, 152–3,
    206–7
Grahame, Kenneth 127
Gray, Thomas 97–8, 100
Griffiths, Eric 56, 183n.11, 189–90
Grove, Agnes 152–3, 203

Hallam, Arthur 15
Hand, Betty 14–15
Harding, Louisa 43–4
Hardy, Emma
    Poems
        'Ballad of a Boy, A' 211–12
        'Churchyard, The' 211
        'God Save Our Emperor King' 211
        'Ripe Summer' 211
        'Spring Song' 132
    Prose:
        'Acceptors, The' 212
        Alleys 210–11
        Diaries 133, 136–9
        'Inspirer, The' 132
        Maid on the Shore, The 210–13
        Some Recollections 2–3, 5, 13, 67–9, 72,
            76–82, 85–6, 92, 97–9, 102, 106,
            119–20, 171–3
        Spaces 173, 210–11
        'High Delights of Heaven, The' 173
Hardy, Florence 45, 67, 71, 71n.4, 94, 127–8,
    203–8, 210–27
Hardy, Henry 96, 125, 127, 155–6, 197
Hardy, Jemima 14–15, 49, 125–7
Hardy, Kate 125–7, 142–3
Hardy, Mary xx, 123–7, 142–3
Hardy, Thomas (father) 125–7
Hardy, Thomas
    Poems:
        '"According to the Mighty Working"' 51
        'After a Journey' xx, 5, 40–1, 81–2, 89,
            180, 182, 192–7, 201
        'After Reading Psalms XXXIX, XL,
            etc.' 30
        'After the Last Breath' 183–4

'After the Visit' 206–7, 215–16
'Afternoon Service at Mellstock' 38
'Afterwards' 215–16
'Amabel' 30
'Ancient to Ancients, An' 100
'Any Little Old Song' 33–4
'As 'Twere Tonight' 93–4
'At a Bridal' 30
'At a Fashionable Dinner' 98, 154
'At an Inn' 93
'At Castle Boterel' xx, 6, 40–1, 92, 101,
    116, 179, 200–2
'At the Piano' 98, 154, 168–9
'At the Word "Farewell"' ' 15–17
'Beeny Cliff' 5, 14, 96–8, 101, 116
'Blow, The' 98
'Bride-Night Fire, The' 28–9
'By the Runic Stone' 107–8
'Change, The' 119–20, 207–8
'Channel Firing' 184–5
'Childhood among the Ferns' 47–8, 184
'Circular, A' 187
'Clock of the Years, The' 70
'Coming Up Oxford Street: Evening'
    5–6, 97–8
'Convergence of the Twain, The' 82
'Darkling Thrush, The' 134
'Days to Recollect' 143–4
'Dead Man Walking, The' 62–3
'Dead Quire, The' 183–4
'Death-Day Recalled, A' 192
'Discouragement' 30
'Discovery, A' 87
'Ditty' xvi–xvii, 93
'Domicilium' 21–3, 47–8
'Dream or No, A' xvi–xvii, 86–7, 191
'Duettist to Her Pianoforte, A' 7–8, 16
'During Wind and Rain' xix, 75–9, 100,
    149, 212
Dynasts, The 116, 136–7, 206–7
'Experience, An' 93
'Face at the Casement, The' 106
'Fetching Her' 91–2, 97–8, 120
'Figure in the Scene, The' 105–6
'Fire at Tranter Sweatley's, The' 28–9
'Forgotten Miniature, A' 223–4
'From Her in the Country' 23–4
'Frozen Greenhouse, The' 83–6
'Garden Seat, The' 184–5
'Ghost of the Past, The' 60–1

'Going, The' 4, 89, 162–3, 171–2, 179, 182–4, 197

'Green Slates' 11–12, 84–6

'Had You Wept' xvii–xviii, 140n.5

'Haunter, The' 68–9, 173–4, 185–7, 190–1, 193

'He Never Expected Much' 128

'Her Definition' 30

'Her Dilemma' 30–1

'Her Haunting-Ground' 12, 91–2, 218–19

'His Heart' 204–5, 215–16

'His Visitor' 173–4, 184–5, 187, 218

'Honeymoon Time at an Inn' xix–xx, 133–6, 159–60

'I Look Into My Glass' 93

'I Found Her Out There' 70, 84–6, 185–6

'I Rose and Went to Rou'tor Town' 113–14

'In a Eweleaze Near Weatherbury' 93

'In a Whispering Gallery' 40–1

'In a Wood' 22–3

'In Tenebris I' 151–3

'In the British Museum' 36, 40–1

'In the Seventies' 35

'In Time of "The Breaking of Nations"' 101

'In Vision I Roamed' 204

'Interloper, The' 98, 154, 167–9

'Ivy-Wife, The' 93, 160

'January Night, A' 153–4, 167–8

'Lament' 187, 224

'Lament of the Looking-Glass, The' 199

'Last Performance, The' 167

'Leaving, A' 227

'Lonely Days' 148–50

'Lost Love' 8–9, 16, 68–9, 165, 167, 198

'Louie' 43–4

'Love the Monopolist' 108

'Man Was Drawing Near to Me, A' 81–3, 141–2

'Man with a Past, The' 167–8

'Marble Tablet, The' 220

'Marble-Streeted Town, The' 70–1

'Midnight on Beechen, 187–' 118–19

'Minute Before Meeting, The' 107–8

'Moments of Vision' 39–41

'Monument-Maker, The' 220

'Musical Box, The' 144–6, 148, 218–19

'Musing Maiden, The' 30

'My Spirit Will Not Haunt the Mound' 91–2

'Near Lanivet, 1872' 115–17, 135, 202

'Neutral Tones' 6–7, 30, 139–40, 204

'Night in November, A' 174

'Obliterate Tomb, The' xix, 73–5, 78

'Old Furniture' 199

'Old Gown, The' 9–10, 167

'On the Departure Platform' 206–7

'On the Doorstep' 198–9

'On Sturminster Footbridge' 144–6, 218–19

'Once at Swanage' 141–3

'Overlooking the River Stour' 144–6, 148, 164, 218–19

'Oxen, The' 38

'Passer-by, The' 43–4

'Peace-Offering, The' 165

'Penance' 165–7

'Phantom Horsewoman, The' 13, 92, 179, 226–7

'Places' 70

'Poet, A' 215–16

'Prophetess, The' 107–8

'Proud Songsters' 42–3

'Quid Hic Agis?' 36–8, 132

'Rain on a Grave' 69–70, 182

'Riddle, The' 90

'Rift, The' 141

'Ruined Maid, The' 23–4

'St Launce's Revisited' 183–4, 224

'Selfsame Song, The' 42n.18

'Self-Unconscious' 116, 154

'Self-Unseeing, The' 144

'Seven Times, The' 95–6, 118–19

'Shadow on the Stone, The' 163–4, 201

'She at His Funeral' 183–4

'She Opened the Door' xvii–xviii, 4–7, 16–17

'She Revisits Alone the Church of Her Marriage' 126–7, 198

'She, to Him' (sequence) 6–7, 94, 204

'She, to Him I' 202

'She, to Him II' 45–6, 53–4

'Shelley's Skylark' 41–3

'Shiver, The' 89

'Shut Out That Moon' 160–1, 163

'Slow Nature, The' 56–8, 183

'Souls of the Slain, The' 142–3, 183–4

'Sound of Her, The' 72, 173–4

Hardy, Thomas (*cont.*)

'Spell of the Rose, The' 156–60, 173–4, 224

'Strange House, The' 199–200

'Sundial on a Wet Day, The' 83

'Temporary the All, The' 46–7

'They Would Not Come' 40–1

'Thoughts of Phena' 93

'To a Lady Playing and Singing in the Morning' 8, 167

'To Lizbie Browne' 43–4

'To Louisa in the Lane' 43–4

'Tree and the Lady, The' 160, 167, 199

'Two-Year's Idyll, A' 144, 147

'Under the Waterfall' 102–6, 118

'Upbraiding, The' 167

'Vatican: Sala delle Muse' 43–4

'Voice, The' xiv–xv, xx, 187–92, 218

'Voices from Things Growing in a Churchyard' 42–3, 184–6

'Walk, The' 170–2

'We Are Getting to the End' 41

'We Sat at the Window' xix–xx, 139–41

'Wessex Heights' 35–6, 38–9

'West-of-Wessex Girl, The' 70–1

'When Dead' 203–4, 215–16

'When I Set Out for Lyonnesse' 2, 88, 93, 113–14

'Where the Picnic Was' 224–7

'Where Three Roads Joined' 116–18, 132

'Why Did I Sketch' 105

'Wind's Prophecy, The' 87–9, 141–2

'Wistful Lady, The' 217–18

'Without Ceremony' 131, 183

'Without, Not Within Her' 132

'Woman Driving, A' 89–90

'Woman I Met, The' 184–5

'Woman Who Went East, The' 90–1

'Woman's Trust, A' 110, 112

'You Were the Sort that Men Forget' 131

'Young Churchwarden, The' 106–8

'Your Last Drive' xix–xx, 4, 172–4, 184

Novels and other prose:

Desperate Remedies 1, 45–6, 52–4, 107–10, 178–9, 181n.9, 206, 222

Far from the Madding Crowd xv, 95, 138–9, 206

'General Preface' to the Wessex Edition 33

Hand of Ethelberta, The 28–9, 126–7, 136–7, 141, 206

'How I Built Myself a House' 156

'Imaginative Woman, An' 24–9, 40–4, 46–7

'Indiscretion in the Life of an Heiress, An' 14–15, 184

Jude the Obscure 23, 32–3, 35, 52, 117, 128, 151–3, 178–9, 206, 210

Laodicean, A 28–9

Mayor of Casterbridge, The 143n.8, 202, 206

Pair of Blue Eyes, A 4–5, 9–10, 13, 15, 72, 95, 97–102, 112–13, 120, 178–9, 195

Poetical Matter notebook 49–53, 58, 134–5

Poor Man and the Lady, The xvi, 14–15, 45

Preface to *A Pair of Blue Eyes* (1895) 5, 72, 83

Preface to *Desperate Remedies* (1912) 45–6

Preface to *Poems of the Past and the Present* 32–3, 46–7

Preface to *Time's Laughingstocks* 32–3

Preface to *Wessex Poems* 61–2

Return of the Native, The 38, 146–7, 180n.8, 206

Studies, Specimens &c. notebook 29–30, 100

Tess of the d'Urbervilles xix–xx, 11–12, 23, 117, 128, 133, 135, 146–7, 149, 155–6, 165, 202

Two on a Tower 206

Under the Greenwood Tree 110–13

Well-Beloved, The 178–9, 206

Woodlanders, The 206

Plays:

The Famous Tragedy of the Queen of Cornwall xx, 79, 81, 221–3

Head, Mary 22–3

Henniker, Arthur 203

Henniker, Florence 68–9, 152–3, 169, 171–2, 213, 218–19

Hicks, John 3, 177

Hoare, Lady 206, 218–19

Holder, Revd Caddell 2–3, 37, 97–9

Holder, Helen 2–3, 80

Homer, Christine Wood 129–30

Horace 178–9, 189–90
Houghton, Lord 99
Hughes, John 162n.8

Jeune, Dorothy 149
Jeune, Lady 123–4
Johnson, Samuel 177
Jonson, Ben xviii
Jose, John 106

Keats, John xvi, 32–3, 40–3, 100, 104–5, 166, 189–90, 195–6

Lake's Parochial History of the County of Cornwall 10–11
Larkin, Philip xiv, xviin.9, 70, 78, 132, 142–3
Leavis, F.R. 188–9
Levinson, Marjorie xiv
Lock, Arthur Henry 125, 155–6
Lockhart, John Gibson xvi
Lowell, Robert 62–3

MacCarthy, Desmond 129
MacCarthy, Louise 129
Macmillan, Alexander 1–2, 45, 110–11
Marlowe, Christopher 100
Martin, Julia Augusta xiv–xv
Mill, John Stuart 55
Millgate, Michael 130, 155–6
Milton, John 100, 192
Moule, Horace 35, 154, 203

Nation, The 209–10, 220
Nation & the Athenaeum, The 6
Newbolt, Henry 164–5, 226
Nicholls, Eliza 7, 97–8, 204
Nicholls, Jane 7
Noyes, Alfred 177, 223

O'Connor, T.P. 149
Ovid xx, 84–7, 192, 200–2
Owen, Rebekah xix–xx, 67, 80, 93

Palgrave's *Golden Treasury* 97–8, 171–2
Pall Mall Magazine, The 24, 26
Paterson, Helen 152–3
Patmore, Coventry 100, 183n.11
Phillips, Jane 146
Phillpotts, Eden 111–12, 170
Pinion, F.B. 37, 97–8, 97n.1

Pitt-Rivers, General Augustus Lane Fox 99
Poe, Edgar Allan 167
Portsmouth, Lady 99, 155–6
Pound, Ezra 177, 201–2
Purdy, Richard 195
Putnam, George 198n.23

Richards, I.A. 189–90
Richter, Jean Paul Friedrich 55–6, 109
Robartes, Miss 13, 80
Rossetti, Dante Gabriel 24–5, 27n.2
Ruskin, John 87–8

Sacks, Peter 180n.7
Saleeby, Caleb 184–6
Scott, Sir Walter 100
Sergeant, Captain Charles 115
Sergeant, Jane 115
Shakespeare, William 100
    Hamlet 193–5
    King Lear 98
    Macbeth 110–11, 188–9
Shelley, Percy Bysshe 32–3, 36, 41, 45–7, 52–3, 189–90, 226
Shorter, Clement 132, 164–5
Smith, Roger T. 112–15
Sparks, Tryphena 97–8
Spectator 107–8, 206–7
Sphere 132, 206, 211
Stephen, Leslie 138–9
Stevens, Wallace 104–5
Stewart, J.I.M. 61–2
Stewart, Susan 189–90
Stoker, Sir Thornley 212
Sutro, Alfred 128
Swinburne, Algernon Charles xvi, xviii–xix, 156, 203, 205

Taylor, Dennis 196n.22
Tennyson, Alfred Lord xvi, 2, 14–15, 98, 100, 156, 163
Thain, Marion 109n.6
Theocritus 192
Thomson, James 152
Tinsley, William 109–10, 112–13
Tinsley's Magazine 112–13
Tomson, Rosamund 152–3, 203
Treves, Sir Frederick 203
Trollope, Anthony 112–13
Turner, J.M.W. 98

Victoria, Queen 203
Virgil xx, 177–84, 189–90, 192, 196–7

Weber, Carl J. xviin.9, 204n.1
Weissman, August 28n.3
Williams, William Carlos 91
Women at Home 209–10

Wordsworth, Dorothy 185–6
Wordsworth, William 21, 23, 40, 54–5, 58, 100, 118–19, 139n.4, 171–2, 185–7, 189–90
Wyatt, Sir Thomas 28–9, 100, 141

Yeats, W.B. 32, 164–5, 226